LISTENING FOR WELLNESS

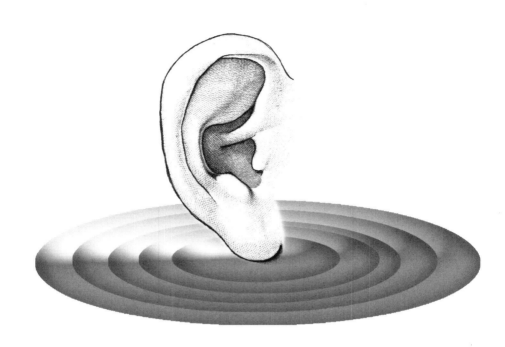

Pierre Sollier

LISTENING FOR WELLNESS
An Introduction to the Tomatis Method

The Mozart Center Press

Copyright © 2005, by Pierre Sollier, MFT

ISBN 0-9763639-0-9

All rights reserved. This book, or parts thereof, may not be reproduced in any form without written permission. No part of this book may be used or reproduced in any manner whatsoever without written permission, except in the case of brief quotations embodied in critical articles and reviews. For information address:
The Mozart Center Press
1399 Ygnacio Valley Road, Suite 21
Walnut Creek, CA, 94598, U. S. A

Designers: Diedro
Susana Wald & Mario Lugos
Macedonio Alcalá 305, Int. 3, Oaxaca, Oax., 68000, Mexico
Tel. 52-951-516-9862

Printers:
Everbest Printing C. Ltd.
7 Ko Fai Road, Unit 5, Block C, 10th floor,
Yau Tong, Kowloon, Hong Kong

Printed in China

Neither the publisher nor the author take any responsibility for possible consequences from any auditory stimulation program whether done in Tomatis Centers or otherwise.

To Alfred and Léna Tomatis
&
to Jan Gerritsen

Acknowledgements

It took eight years to write this book. From the start it confronted me with the challenge of not just repeating what is known about Tomatis, but also to present facets of his work that are almost ignored. When he died on Christmas day 2001, Tomatis left behind an enormous amount of writings: books, articles, texts of conferences, many of them difficult to find, and all in French. I have tried to present a synthesis of his ideas that reflects as faithfully as possible his thinking. His range of interests was wide and drew from many disciplines that seem at first unrelated, but his mind saw the connections and forged new concepts. Those often drew criticism and rejection from his peers, but he forged ahead, knowing that time would prove him right. He often said that it takes at least forty years for an idea to become accepted. More than forty years have passed since he started to research the power of listening, and now we might be able to finally understand his ideas and discoveries. If resistance to some of them still arises, it might indicate their degree of potency.

A book has many authors, hidden behind the one who does the writing. I want to express my debt to all of them for their contributions.

I am deeply grateful to Dr. Alfred Tomatis for opening for me the doors to a new world that I had never fathomed before meeting him. His influence on my life was profound, and his example continues to inspire me after his death. His wife Léna has been also a source of insights and knowledge.

My partner Jan Gerritsen was a tireless guide through the years it took to complete this book. Our many conversations and his thorough editing made this book much better than its original version. Apart from a very demanding job, Jan took the time to repair headphones and electronic ears, kept the books, filled tax forms, went shopping for equipment and supplies and did everything possible to make the life of the Mozart Center easier.

My friend Astrid Webster, a Tomatis practitioner living in Albuquerque, New Mexico, was also an excellent editor. Our many lively discussions and sometimes different points of view forced me to reconsider some of my ideas and to rewrite parts of the book. Without her, this book would not be as comprehensive as it now is.

Don Campbell, the author of the Mozart Effect, provided a vibrant example when so few people were aware of the power of sound and music on health.

My colleagues practicing the Tomatis Method have been a constant source of information and stimulation. Many thanks to Dr. Bob Roy, from Regina, for sharing his knowledge of the Listening Test; to Paul Madaule, from Toronto, who brought the Tomatis method to North America, and has contributed many practical applications; to Liliana Sacarin, from Seattle, who reads children's movements like a book and impacts deeply their lives through a combination of movement therapy and Tomatis; to Valerie Dejean, from Bethesda, who taught me a great deal about sensory integration; to Dr. Ron Minson, from Denver, who shared his medical training to explain some complex points; to Dr. Deborah Swain, from Santa Rosa, California, for enthusiastically doing research on autism and learning disabilities using the Tomatis Method; to Elizabeth Verrill, from Amherst, whose love for children and keen observation of their behavior has been a source of inspiration; to Emilia Florez, from Dallas, for teaching me how to run an outreach program; to Dr. Susan Andrews and Michelle Trump, from New Orleans, for the research they did on ADHD and the Tomatis method.

I am also grateful to Roberta Prada, with whom I co-translated Dr. Tomatis' book, *The Ear and the Voice*, published by Scarecrow Press. Thanks to her explanations, I was able to better understand vocal technique and better appreciate opera singing.

Many thanks to Susana Wald and Mario Lugos for designing beatifully this book and making a work of art as really true artists can do.

Also many thanks to Dr. Bernard Auriol, Victoria Brandon, Cynthia Chavez, Jim and Harl Assaf, Suzan Dallé, Dee Levan, Dr. Concetto Campo, Gloria Assmar, Helen Dazet, Joshua Leeds, Richard Lawrence, Joyce Carr, Marika and Ed Ray, Miguel Almiron, Phyllis Burt, Michael Prolman, Linda Ashley and John Durya.

Finally, I have to thank my clients, children and adults, who taught me more than anything else the value of observation and practice. I shared their tears and joys, their temper tantrums and their successes, throughout their difficult and exhilarating journey toward wellness. They provided some of the stories in this book, but, as it should be, I have disguised their names and sometimes their background history to keep their right to privacy intact. Many thanks to all of them for making me a better therapist and, I believe, a better human being.

Pierre Sollier

CONTENTS

FOREWORD BY LÉNA TOMATIS 13
PREFACE BY DON CAMPBELL 15

Part I • THE SOUNDS OF WELLNESS
    INTRODUCTION 19

Part II • A LITTLE COURSE ABOUT OUR EARS
    HEARING AND LISTENING 37
    THE ROLE OF OUR EARS 41
    THE EVOLUTION OF THE EAR 43
        Do Fish have Ears? 43
        The Long Road toward Verticality 44
    HOW DO WE HEAR? 46
        The External Ear 47
        The Middle Ear 47
        The Inner Ear 51
        Air and Bone Conduction 56
        Skin and Hearing 57
        The Human Antenna 58
    ENERGY THROUGH THE EARS? 61
        Charging Sounds, Wearing Sounds 64
        The Eardrum, the Vagus Nerve, and a Sense of Wellbeing 69
    TOWARD HUMAN LISTENING 74
        Raising the Antenna 75
        Listening Posture and Sound Analysis 80
        Selectivity 83
        Auditory Radar 86
        The Three Integrators: a Diagnostic Tool 91
        Conclusion 99
    THE EAR AND THE VOICE 100
        How the Ear and the Voice are Connected 102
        Lateralization 105
        The Leading Ear 106
        The Dominant Mouth 108
        We Speak with our Ears 111
        Shifting Sides 114
        The Body Image 116
    SUMMARY 123

Part III • THE LEARNING EAR

PRELIMINARIES 127
AUTISM 129
    Tuning up the Body 130
    First Results 133
    The mother's voice and the Desire to Communicate and to Speak 135
    The Course of Therapy 140
    Listening and the Therapeutic Process 142
A LOOK AT DYSLEXIA 145
LISTENING AND ATTENTION DEFICIT DISORDERS 155
    What is ADD / ADHD? 155
    Treatment Options 160
    Tom and Jeff: Two Case Studies 165
    Conclusion 168
THE GIFT OF LANGUAGES 170
    Ever heard of an "Ethnic Ear"? 171
    The Road to Success 177

Part IV • THE LISTENING TEST

PRELIMINARIES 183
THE IDEAL LISTENING CURVE 189
ADMINISTERING THE LISTENING TEST 193
THE MEANING OF THE AIR AND BONE CONDUCTION CURVES 195
THE THREE AUDITORY ZONES 197
    The Body Zone (Zone 1) 200
    The Communication Zone (Zone 2) 203
    The Creativity Zone (Zone 3) 207
    A Global View 209
SELECTIVITY 210
    Selectivity, Logic and Sense of Organization 210
    Selectivity and Psychological Development 212
SPACIALIZATION 220
    Spacialization Errors in the Body Zone 220
    Spacialization Errors in the Communication Zone 221
    The Chicken and the Egg 222
LATERALIZATION 224
    The Present, the Future and the Past 225
    Dominance in Disguise 227
    Shifting Dominance 229
    From Baby Talk to Language 231

PERSONALITY AND THE LISTENING TEST   236
    The Airborne Listening Profile   237
    The Controlling Listening Profile   243
    The Depressive Listening Profile   248
    The Flat-Line Listening Profile   253
LISTENING TO THE BODY   256
THE DIALOGUE BETWEEN THE EARS   258
SYMBOLIC EARS   265

Part V • THE PSYCHOLOGICAL EAR

MOTHER CARES FOR HER UNBORN CHILD   269
    Listening in Utero   269
    The Mother's Voice   272
    Hi-fi in Utero? What does the Fetus exactly Hear?   274
    The Sonic Birth   278
    Playing back their Mother's Voice to Adults   284
    Music for the Unborn Child   290
    A Child is Born   295
    The Child grows up   297
THE ROLE OF THE FATHER   304
    The Voice of the Father   304
    The Absent Father   316
    Listening to Father's Voice   324
REFUSING TO GROW UP   328
    Telltale Signs for Parents to Watch for   328
    Adults refusing to grow up   334
RECAPITULATING THE JOURNEY   337

Part VI • THE SPIRITUAL EAR

EVOLUTION AND CREATION   343
LISTENING TO "THE SOUND OF LIFE"   346
LETTING GO   349
THE LISTENING POSTURE   352
MAKING SOUNDS   356
SACRED MUSIC, SACRED CHANTS   360
"OUR HEART BREATHES THROUGH THE EAR"   364
THE DIVINE MOZART   366

CONCLUSION 371

APPENDIXES
　　Research Results 379
　　The Listening Posture 384
　　Humming Sounds 388

REFERENCES 391

FOREWORD

Listening was the central theme of the work of my late husband, Dr. Alfred Tomatis. As a graduate of the Paris School of Medicine and as an ear, nose and throat specialist, he was fascinated by all the various aspects of listening. He dedicated his life to the study of listening, and to developing therapeutic tools.

I am very pleased to see that listening, that very complex and subtle faculty, is the subject of this very well documented book that links listening and wellness.

Pierre Sollier, the author, knows his topic well: he followed the teachings of Tomatis during several decades, attended his seminars, shared his experiences as a practitioner of the Tomatis Method, and has written many papers about the results produced by the Electronic Ear.

First as a teacher, later as a licensed psychotherapist in California, Pierre Sollier launched himself into Audio-psycho-phonology with exemplary courage and dedication. Like many of his colleagues all over the world, he embraced Tomatis´ pioneering discoveries with passion and perseverance. Indeed, the discoveries of my husband about the functioning of the ear, its connections with the brain, the voice, the language, and the whole body represent a revolution in the field of auditory physiology.

Thus, this book is not a simple introduction, but a masterly presentation of the theoretical aspects of the neurophysiology of the ear as well as its many applications in the field of linguistics, especially in learning the mother tongue or foreign languages. Additionally, since psychological states condition the quality of listening, Pierre Sollier explores in detail the connection between both, first through an introduction to the Listening Test designed by my husband, and then through child development. No less important, synthesizing for the first time material scattered in many books, articles or lectures, he shows how deep listening is essential to spiritual progress.

My husband and I have followed Pierre Sollier's work with profound attention and admiration, and we very gratefully acknowledge his skill and know-how in the writings of this book.

Pierre Sollier demonstrates clearly that listening at its highest level allows the development of the most advanced potentialities in human beings, which can only lead to a true and well needed communication between them.

Léna Tomatis
January 7, 2005

PREFACE

For the past thirty-five years I have been fascinated with the multiple levels and complexities in the act of listening. As a music student, I was amazed when other students heard rhythms and harmonies that seemed to escape my attention. As a music teacher, I was fascinated when some students could hear melodies and intervals others missed. As a music critic, I often heard a full concert in a different way than my colleagues did while attending exactly the same performance.

Years later, as I learned about the brain, the ear, the voice and the ability to co-ordinate communication, I found listening was one of the major keys to understanding the world. Listening was more than hearing, but as a qualitative as well as quantitative science it has just recently started to be researched and explored.

In 1982 I heard a program on National Public Radio about a French physician who had explored the science of listening and how the ear was essential for many levels of health, expression and communication. Soon thereafter I found my way to Dr. Alfred Tomatis who was visiting The Listening Centre in Toronto.

At that time my work as a trained musician was completely changed with the talent and ability of Dr. Tomatis to define the perimeters of listening. I then realized that every student in my classes had an individual way of listening. Every ear hears frequencies a bit differently. Every person has a unique way of filtering out sounds, so an auditory ability to focus is possible. Every person has listening patterns that block out voices and sounds that are unliked. Some ears find certain sounds pleasant and empowering so they turn to them more often for pleasing, healing and joyous experiences.

By knowing that "Listening is a dynamic, not passive activity," we can change the way we work with our students, families and colleagues. The health of our listening abilities can change the way we know the world around us.

I am pleased to see Pierre Sollier's new book, Listening for Wellness. *Here is an accessible, interesting and firsthand approach to the wide world of potential that lies ahead of parents, students, teachers and musicians.*

Although many of these ideas are unorthodox, they serve to help us understand the remarkable integrative ability of the ears to process sound. The powers of filtered sounds, chanting, passive listening with emphasis on bone conduction and numerous other concepts can lead us into a new world of wellness and self understanding.

Dr. Alfred Tomatis was a pioneer. He opened the door to unlimited possibilities in the fields of language development, music therapy and learning disabilities. It is now our work to apply and transform his work into a more harmonic, understanding world.

Don Campbell
Musician, lecturer and author of *The Mozart Effect*

PART I

THE SOUNDS OF WELLNESS

INTRODUCTION

As I waited for the elevator, a woman and a little girl who walked with great difficulty entered the hall. I kept the door of the elevator open while the mother helped the child come inside. We were going to the same floor—the fourth—to the same address: The Tomatis Center. Again, I held the door open for the mother and the child. The mother thanked me and added with a smile: "At least, she walks now! When we came here the first time, she could not walk at all!" I followed them inside, eager to know how such a miracle could have happened.

I do not know what I had expected—probably the small office of a doctor or a psychologist. Instead, I found myself in a large hall, filled with people waiting patiently: mothers trying to keep their children on their best behavior, men and women leafing through popular magazines. Through a large door, I could see adults sitting in small cubicles, earphones on their heads. This was not the small medical office that I had envisioned, but a large operation. Indeed, I later learned that the Center treated over two thousand clients a year.

The difficulty that brought me to the Tomatis center was neither as visible nor as profound as a child's inability to walk, the outcome of my treatment not as dramatic. Yet, what I saw and learned in this amazing place was enough to alter the way I looked at things, to change my career and to become my life's work.

My difficulty was fairly minor: after two years in the United States, I still was unable to clearly speak English. My heavy French accent was a formidable obstacle for my American friends. They were nice enough to pretend that they understood me, but I could tell from their faces that they really had to strain their ears. I dreaded to hear one more time the usual question: "What did you say?" It made me feel ashamed and I preferred to keep silent as much as I could rather than to join the conversation.

Back in France in 1984, I once complained to a friend about my troubles. He understood my problem since he had lived in different countries and had faced the same difficulties. He had, however, a solution: "You should go and see Dr. Tomatis," he said. "He will tune your ears to the frequencies of the American language and you will be able to speak clearly." It sounded too good to be true. I could have laughed it off, but my friend was a very serious scientist. If he had thought that Dr. Tomatis was a joke, he would not have brought it up. I was intrigued: who was this Dr. Tomatis?

"Dr. Tomatis is a French Ear, Nose and Throat specialist," said my friend. "He has done extensive research on the functioning of the ear and has made some amazing discoveries. He has developed a "Listening Therapy." He uses an electronic device called the Electronic Ear to successfully treat a whole range of problems, for instance, dyslexia in children or lack of energy problems in adults."

It was certainly interesting, but how could such a therapy improve my accent?

"Tomatis" my friend continued to explain me patiently "has discovered that there is a clear link between the ear and the voice. If we don't hear a sound well, we cannot reproduce it accurately. That is to say that the quality of our voice depends on the quality of our hearing. Since our ears are mostly attuned to the frequencies of our native language, we have to hear and pronounce an entirely new set of sounds when we learn a foreign language. For many people that is difficult because they hear the foreign sounds through the filter of their native tongue. In your case, you try to pronounce the English sounds as if they were French."

It was intriguing. Not enough, though, to overcome my skepticism. My rational mind wanted to know more about it before making any commitment. In retrospect, this is not surprising. Many clients have the same attitude before embarking on the therapy developed by Tomatis. I believe it is a healthy reaction, since many so-called therapies promise too much and deliver too little.

Dr. Alfred A. Tomatis

I decided to read some of Dr. Tomatis' books to better understand the ideas that my friend had outlined during our conversation. I was then a teacher: it seemed appropriate to start with the books he had written on dyslexia and learning disabilities, since I daily confronted such problems in my classroom. It did not take much reading to realize that my training as a teacher had overlooked the obvious: the role of the ear in learning. Like many of my colleagues, I had assumed that dyslexia, for instance, was caused by some kind of visual impairment. Tomatis completely challenged that view. First, he pointed out that the ear controlled the muscles of the eyes. Yes, the eyes! He also noticed that hearing was not all: we could have excellent hearing, but it was of little use if we did not have the *desire to listen*. Listening was the key element leading to good learning. Poor students in my classroom were first of all poor listeners. They were so for many reasons: some because their brain could not smoothly integrate the sensory information they received from their environment; others because they had had traumatic histories and consequently had all kinds of emotional problems. As Tomatis made clear, not only neuro-physiological problems but also psychological problems could result in impaired listening.

Daily observations in the classroom gave support to Tomatis' ideas. In fact, they changed the way I looked at my students. Children that I had thought lazy or dumb were clearly suffering from some of the conditions described by Tomatis. The signs of their listening problem had been in front of my very own eyes all along but I had been unable to see them or to understand them. The good news was that those symptoms were not irremediable. Teaching children to listen efficiently, affirmed Tomatis, would make them good and eager students. If children could be treated successfully, I wondered, then what about my accent? It was after all a fairly mild problem compared to dyslexia or attention deficit. It was time to make an appointment and to put my skeptical mind to rest.

The Tomatis Center was then located in an affluent neighborhood in the northwestern part of Paris. Nineteenth century stone buildings with elegant carvings and high windows line the Boulevard de Courcelles. It had been one of those beautiful Parisian fall days when the sky is translucent blue and the trees have a golden glow often seen in impressionist paintings. Still in a reverie and wondering what to expect from my appointment, I was brought into the present as I saw the little girl struggle toward the elevator. I was still pondering her mother's words when my turn finally came.

I was led into a small room containing a testing booth. A young woman gave me some instructions and performed what I took for a hearing test. I was then asked to do a series of drawings that I easily recognized as projective tests. When I was through, a thin blond woman led me into another office to discuss my results. Her name was Ms. Forin.

"Your test shows very clearly why English is so difficult for you," she said in a quiet and well-timbered voice. "Your perception of high-frequency sounds is not very good. Unfortunately for you, English is very rich in these. Since you do not hear them well, it is almost impossible for you to reproduce them. That is why American people have trouble understanding you. The fact is that the voice contains only the sounds that the ears hear well. Your voice is flat and monotonous. It correlates with the flatness of your listening curve that you can see here on your test! That also makes you automatically sing out of tune."

"Another reason for your difficulty," continued Ms. Forin gently, is that you do not discriminate sounds well. Actually, the higher the pitch, the more difficult it is for you to distinguish a high pitch sound from a lower one, or the other way around. That makes English very difficult for you, because beyond a certain frequency level, your ears are very inaccurate. For instance, you said that 6,000 Hertz is higher than 8,000 Hertz. You repeated that mistake a few times. We call that a discrimination problem. Not only does it make it harder for you to speak English well but it also makes it impossible for you to become a musician. I read in your history that you have achieved a high level of education, but I suspect that you worked hard to get there. It didn't come easy, didn't it?"

How did she know that? I had not revealed anything and she certainly could not deduce this from the red and blue lines meandering on my chart in front of her! Or could she? And still it was true that, except for a few subject matters, I always felt that I had to try harder than my classmates did. No one would have suspected this from my class records: I was, after all, at the top of the class. By age six, I knew how to read, write and add. Learning at that age came so easily to me that it was like playing. I never felt that I was making a special effort.

But somehow, when I was nine or ten, things started to become harder and harder. Until the moment when Ms. Forin brought it up, no one had ever guessed how much it had cost me to achieve academic success. I looked at her wondering what was coming next.

"It seems that you get easily tired, she said after a brief glance at my chart. The fatigue may even border on depression at times." "How do you know?" I asked feeling suddenly on my guard. "Your curves are overall flat," she said pointing towards my chart. "They tend to drop in the high frequencies. For us, it means that your brain does not "recharge" enough. It does not get enough stimulation. That is why you get tired. If you are tired, you cannot remember things well, your concentration is weak, and paying attention is difficult. As I said, it seems that you may have bouts of depression when things get a little harder to handle."

I was no longer trying to fight the idea that she could read my chart as though she had opened the book of my life. By that time, I had forgotten the real reason of my visit. I was puzzled and eager to find out what she knew about me that was so mysteriously hidden in the red and blue lines crossing my chart. Later on, as the Director of the Lafayette Mozart Center in California, I would see the same puzzled look on my clients' faces. One of them, a shy young man, once told me that he didn't need to tell me how he was doing since I would know it just by testing him. Another time, the same young man tried to convince me that I should set up shop in Las Vegas or Reno. He assured me that I could make big bucks there just by doing "Listening Readings" as some do Tarot readings. He was, of course, grossly exaggerating the power of the Listening Test. But it is true that it quickly provides a wealth of information, as Ms. Forin was demonstrating during our first encounter.

It would be difficult to remember everything that we discussed that day. But I do remember my feelings of awe as we talked more about my periods of depression, my relationships with my family, my ambivalence about my teaching job. Ms. Forin was very tactful, never forcing me to admit or face something for which I was not prepared. I felt listened to and cared for in a genuine way. When the interview ended, we decided that the therapy should first address my need to improve my English but would also deal with some of the personal issues we had discussed. Since the Tomatis Method is about stimulating and improving perception, Ms. Forin felt that undertaking the English program would also benefit me in other areas of my life. I left the Center that day quite exhilarated, feeling that something new was just about to happen. Little did I know how right I was and how my life would change forever!

The "Listening Therapy" designed by Dr. Tomatis is sufficiently intensive to bring about a permanent and profound change. It takes on average about 60 hours, spread over a period of four to five months. I had to come to his office for 2 hours a day, 5 days per week, but fortunately there were several scheduled breaks of a few weeks each, to allow for integration of the sensory stimulation I received. I had to work around my schedule to come to the Tomatis Center day after day. This was not a simple matter: I lived on the other side of Paris and commuted fifty miles to go to work. I probably would not have been able to manage such a busy schedule if I had not experienced a surprising increase in energy almost immediately. It was astounding! I suddenly didn't need the eight hours of sleep I thought I needed and still felt fresh after sleeping barely six hours. I had no trouble getting up either. My mind was immediately alert as I looked toward each new day with anticipation.

On the way to work, early in the morning, driving through sleepy villages and forests shrouded in thick winter fog, I would pick up a tune played on the radio and it would stay with me for the rest of the day. Never had I been able to memorize a tune so quickly and without errors! I became known as the "singing teacher" among the kids at school. I could not stop: at recess, between classes, in the teacher's room or strolling the long dim corridors, I had to sing, hum or whistle. It got me a lot of attention: after all teachers are not known for singing, even less so at school where they are supposed to maintain an aura of authority and seriousness. But I was so full of lightness and joy that it would have been impossible to hide my feelings even if I had tried. This was my last year of teaching and probably my best. My enthusiasm was contagious and it motivated my students more than any kind of "teaching strategy." Looking back, I wish that my teaching had always been fuelled by the same enthusiasm, because there is nothing better for opening up the hearts and minds of students or unlocking abilities that, like Cinderella, lay dormant in some dark recess. Not that I want to give myself all the credit — the warm and often enthusiastic response of my students made me a better teacher too. Although difficult for me on a personal level, it was still a wonderful year! And throughout the year, I kept singing!

One morning, as we were crossing the snow covered schoolyard, one of my students asked me:

"Are you sick?"

"How's that, Mohammed?"

"You are not singing today, sir."

Obviously, I was now condemned to sing to make my students happy! Should my students remember me, I prefer to be remembered as the "singing teacher" rather than the teacher who bored generations of students. Boredom never leads to learning anyway!

Late one night, while driving back home on the freeway, I made another discovery. I had turned on the radio to keep me awake when I realized that the music and the voice of the soprano had an unusual quality. Neither the music nor the voice was extraordinary in any way but the quality of my perception of them was completely new and fresh. It was as if I had gotten a new pair of ears! Suddenly, the music had a depth, a richness that I had never heard nor felt before.

It was as if I had been deaf to a world of sounds and perceptions that waited for me just beyond the threshold of my awareness. A curtain had lifted and I could now delight in the brightness of the new world around me.

These new perceptions led to a clarity of mind that I had rarely experienced with such intensity. My mind didn't seem to be as clogged with irrelevant or distracting thoughts. Instead it attended to the task at hand without being derailed by internal or external stimuli. I don't think that I got smarter but rather that I learned to manage my intelligence with greater control and efficiency. This was even easier since I felt that I was controlling my emotions better. It wasn't that I didn't feel them anymore but I was not overwhelmed by them as much. Confronted with a difficult situation, I could more easily observe, looking at the facts from a distance, making appropriate decisions without feeling carried away or out of control. Certainly, clarity of mind and the sorting out of emotions can be achieved by psychotherapy, meditation and other techniques, but after using some of them, I still think that the Tomatis Method can be one of the fastest jump-starts towards this goal and may deepen those practices. My clients who practiced daily meditation often reported that they achieved deeper states and were able to listen more attentively to the voice within and without.

All of this was even more remarkable as it happened at a time when I experienced a lot of stress: I had to make an important decision for the future: whether to permanently relocate to the United States or not. Throughout the decision process, I stayed clear headed, weighing the pros and cons, without being excessively burdened by anxiety or fear. Later on, as a Tomatis practitioner, I saw some of my clients make decisions concerning the direction of their lives with the same clarity of mind. As a result, a move into a new career or to a new country was successful because it was not tainted by false and romantic expectations, or by an inflated sense of their self.

I was perhaps two months into the program when I started to experience a lot of tension in my shoulders. It felt like I was carrying around a fifty-pound weight. It was quite uncomfortable and I complained about it to Ms. Forin. She was not surprised. "Of course," she said, "the sounds are stretching your spine. What is happening right now is that your shoulders are releasing tension that was blocked for a long time and kept you slightly hunched. Quite often we see children that seem to grow a few inches in a very short time during the program. Their posture stretches out and they are able to stand erect. This is the result of improving their vestibular function. I don't know if you know this but the vestibule, which is the oldest part of the inner ear, controls balance, coordination and muscle tone. There is not a single muscle in the body that is not controlled by it. When we stimulate the ear, we also regulate the vestibule. Look at your students. You will quickly see how poor posture often correlates with learning difficulties. Even the quality of their voice is affected by it. Change their posture and they will quickly start to improve in school!"

My teacher training had certainly not prepared me to look at my students from this angle. If it was mentioned at all, the body was merely given lip service. Yet what Ms. Forin said made a lot of sense. The more I read Tomatis, the more I realized that his work offered a new approach for understanding human behavior. Not that Tomatis himself claimed to be original: many of the facts that he put together were already firmly established and documented in their respective field. In his autobiography, *The Conscious Ear,*[1] Tomatis tells how he had to progressively expand his own knowledge and incorporate seemingly unrelated elements to explain some of his clinical results. I even heard him remark once that many of his observations had been made before by the Greek philosophers or in the context of spiritual traditions. What was new, he believed, was the fact that he had been able to use electronics to bring about changes that would otherwise take years to achieve.

While feeling wonderful, I had not lost sight of my original goal: improve my English. I was four months into the program when I took a short trip to California. My friends were amazed. "What did you do? Now we understand you." It was a great relief: I no longer feared seeing a puzzled expression or hearing the usual question: "What did you say?" Words now flowed much more easily. I started to use idioms that made my neighbors and friends say: "You are becoming American." It felt like going under the surface of the words, to that indescribable place where words become charged with feelings, concepts, memories and the collective unconscious of centuries of culture. Long ago, I read *Civilization and its Discontents*[2], a book by Sigmund Freud in which he compared the unconscious to the different layers of ancient Rome excavated by archaeologists who revealed how buildings were piled up on top of each other over the centuries. Words are somewhat like the ruins of ancient Rome. They have layers upon layers of meaning, memories, and feelings that alter and shape our understanding of the world and ourselves. As long as we work with the basics, studying grammar, trying to memorize words, we stay at the surface. We have neither a feeling for the language nor a real love for it. What I was now starting to discover from the inside out was precisely a love, a resonance with the American English language and through it, with the culture of the United States. I could now tune in and listen to the resonance that eluded me when I was still trying to master the mechanics of the language. It was like being born into a different culture, to a different language. I sometimes jokingly say that American English is my second mother tongue. I feel this because when we begin living in a new language, we start to develop a new self, a new personality. If I describe the same experience in French, then in English, the feeling tone is different: it is not exactly the same experience, nor is it the same person who feels it. I credit the Tomatis Method with having provided me a short-cut toward experiencing the language and culture that would one day become mine from the inside out.

After my return from California, I decided to take things a little further. I had been intrigued and fascinated by Tomatis' idea that we start listening in the womb. The fetus, he believed, could hear not only the sounds from the mother's body but the mother's voice as well. Based on an exhaustive review of the scientific literature, Tomatis concluded in *La Nuit Uterine*[3] that the mother's voice was an emotional nutrient to the child and also prepared the child to acquire language after birth. The curriculum I had followed to improve my English incorporated those ideas. Part of my program consisted of listening to an American woman's voice that had been electronically filtered to amplify only the high frequencies. These frequencies, according to Tomatis, are the ones that a fetus perceives in the womb. It was no surprise then that I had felt English becoming my "mother" tongue since I had been provided with an "American mother!" But how would I experience the voice of my own mother? It took some convincing to have her come to Paris to record her voice.

A highly filtered voice doesn't sound much like the real thing. Actually, it sounds more like static or like a choir of crickets. I had gotten used to it progressively with my "American mom" and my "French mom" didn't sound much different. There was a difference though, a subtle one that owed its characteristics to the intonations and rhythmic patterns of the French language and to the timbre, articulation, and speed of my mother's voice. At times, as I listened to it, I felt overwhelmed by a brief but sharp emotion. I could not say what set it off or if some old memory had been triggered, but the overall sensation was one of release. These emotions had a very primitive quality, as if I had been re-experiencing what I had felt in

the womb. There were no words to describe them, no language. They seemed to disappear as quickly as they came.

I had been asked by Ms. Forin to draw during the sessions. The idea was that the music and the sounds might bring about mental images that could speed up the therapeutic process if they were projected onto paper. In fact, Tomatis asserts that clients who draw during the listening sessions have better results than the ones who do not. Of course, like many of my clients later on, I immediately claimed that I wasn't an artist and could not draw well. Ms. Forin reassured me: I didn't need to be a Leonardo da Vinci nor a Picasso. "Let your hand take the lead and see what happens." So I did and to my great enjoyment, gained some insight, here and there, into my behavior.

As I was listening to my mother's voice, however, my drawings abruptly changed. I suddenly could not stand the pastel shades I had used while coloring the broad outline of a landscape or a face. Only black and red pencils would suffice for coloring dark fragments of various dimensions, separated by streams of red. Imagine black ice drifting on a sea of blood or a volcano spitting out chunks of lava and red flames: those were the primitive images I couldn't stop drawing while experiencing sudden pangs of emotions that bubbled up to the surface of my consciousness. At that point I realized that my mother's voice was getting clearer and clearer. Soon I could follow the story of *The Little Prince*,[4] written by the French writer Saint-Exupéry word by word. At the same time, the images of the ice block and the volcano vanished as rapidly as they had appeared. I returned to using pastel tones and drawing landscapes of hills and meadows full of flowers. They didn't look very different from those I had drawn before, yet seemed brighter and more peaceful.

I learned from Ms. Forin that I had been through the "sonic birth." As dramatic as it may sound, for most people this is not really a very dramatic moment. The "sonic birth" is an attempt to recreate the transition from the liquid audition in the womb to air audition as our regular way of hearing after birth. The ear has to adjust to these new conditions. Sounds that were muffled in the womb suddenly become bright and crisp after birth. We are then confronted with the formidable challenge of making sense of the sonic world before we can begin to acquire an alphabet or grammar. The first years of life will be spent responding to this challenge and mastering, little by little, a world that is overbearingly loud and overwhelmingly present but still largely unknown.

Following the sonic birth, the program took a different turn. After the relative passivity of "being in the womb," a more active phase ensued during which I had to do a variety of vocal exercises. After all, once we are born, we need to learn to speak! Babies babble for practice, repeating sounds over and over until the mechanics of language are mastered. From the beginning of our development, our voices and ears are connected not only at a neuro-physiological level but at a psychological level as well. To "own one's voice" is to own oneself. In my practice, I have seen a few adults burst into tears because they suddenly "heard their voice for the first time."

As I sat in a booth, reading aloud or repeating words that had been filtered in order to force my ear to pay more attention, I heard my voice coming back to me through my right ear. This, I was told, is to train the right ear to become the leading ear. This would give me an advantage in processing information faster and more efficiently. The right ear, Tomatis believed, has an ability to focus that the left ear lacks. As I was shifting progressively from the left ear to the right, I noticed that my voice sounded fuller and flowed more easily without the usual little breaks that I had come to regard as natural. With this came a further mental clarity that stayed with me through the hustle and bustle of daily life. I seemed to be in charge of my emotions instead of being owned by them. "Coming home" may be a way to put how it felt, but it is a home that we rarely reach and then only for short periods. Only when we reach it can we feel whole.

The music of Mozart, the Gregorian Chant of the monks of Solesmes, my mother's voice and Tomatis' genius brought together various elements that built this magnificent house where I felt safe and wonderful. Regardless of the difficulties of my life, it is the house to which I strive to return, the place where the word "wellness" takes on all its shades of meaning.

I wrote this book for those who may be looking for such a place. The Tomatis Method is not a cure-all, but a wonderful tool for learning to listen. Listening is the skill that we desperately need if we want to cut through the noise of the surrounding world and reconnect with the vital parts of ourselves from which we too often feel alienated. It is when we stop listening that our lives start to get out of focus and we become estranged from ourselves and from the people around us. When we stop listening, life grows meaningless, boring, disconnected; we feel lost. Learning to listen is the way to recover the self, the key to wellness. I hope that this book will clearly demonstrate why this is so.

Part II

A little Course about our Ears

HEARING AND LISTENING

There is a great difference between hearing and listening, one that is not always understood. Many people use these terms interchangeably, adding to the confusion about their meaning. Much of today's music, especially background music, for instance, engages only our hearing. Indeed, one can hardly step into an elevator, store, airport, shopping mall or waiting room without being bathed by the barely conspicuous flow of a soft and bland music whose purpose is to relax us, boost our mood and create the ideal conditions for impulse buying. Many of us, whether we notice it or not, need this musical background, because silence makes us uneasy. You might wonder about being addicted to music if you reflexively turn on the radio whenever you get into your car.

Silence is a rare experience for many and some even seem to fear it, sensing that within it we may come face to face with our fears or ourselves. Background music creates a sonic cocoon-like environment that holds us, rocks us and wraps itself around us like a warm blanket. As long as the music goes on, we stay suspended in timeless space, reminiscent of our time in the womb. Forgotten are worries such as mortgage payments, threats of a lay-off, marital difficulties or an impending diagnosis. Sound pushes aside fears that silence lets in, subdues the pulsing beat of our hearts that ticks away the moments of our lives. Silence sets the stage for listening, but listening is hard, requires attention and is unpleasant at times. Hearing, on the other hand, requires no investment from us. It is passive. And so the beat goes on! Modern society tries to keep us happily wrapped up in a kind of sonic placenta that forms an increasingly invasive background standing between us and our ability to listen.

The stimulating effect of sound, our differing response to music, the difference between hearing and listening, and the role played by our ears were clearly demonstrated for me years ago, at a concert at the Verdi Theater, in Florence, Italy. After a long day spent admiring Renaissance masterworks at the Uffizi and walking around town, I felt tired but still had enough energy to go to a concert. The program was quite intriguing: a piece by the avant-garde Italian composer Luciano Berio was sandwiched between two classical pieces by Schumann and Brahms. The Schumann piece did not stir the faintest reaction in me. I felt unable to resonate with the music, as though I were listening to an orchestra playing behind a glass wall. The sounds were reaching me but were strangely muted and without brilliance. I could not fault the orchestra or the acoustics of the theater, though I first tried. No! It was I that was not in tune. My mind and body were dissociated from the performance for reasons I ignored. I was hearing the music but was not listening to it. I braced myself for a long evening of boredom and, since I had come with a friend, I could not leave the theater.

When the piece from Luciano Berio started, I closed my eyes hoping that I could concentrate better this time. The first measures woke me up pleasantly. Gone were the well-known rhythms, harmonies and movements characteristic of early romantic pieces. Instead, the new piece seemed to generate sounds at random. And what sounds they were! Shrill, percussive, thundering, unexpected and always amazing. Suddenly fully alert, I surprised myself by anticipating the next sound! The old lady sitting next to me didn't seem so entranced by this music; it was way out of the classical range that she probably preferred. She was not the only one: only half of the audience applauded at the end of the performance while the other half sat quietly, sulking.

During the intermission, I pondered my reaction: I am, after all, not a great fan of avant-garde music, yet I had felt swept away by that piece. Maybe exhaustion accounted for my being more receptive. I had relinquished what music "should be". My usual filters had obviously been bypassed. I suddenly understood better what contemporary music was all about: a way to shake musical habits from the mind, forcing it to listen differently, revealing the strength and beauty of a repertoire of sounds and feelings beyond the ordinary. Going back to my seat after intermission, I almost dreaded listening to the remaining program. I feared revisiting with Schubert the experience I had had with the Schumann piece and again feeling dead inside.

How wrong I was! For the next forty-two minutes, I was in a state of delight such as I had rarely experienced while listening to a piece of music. I flowed with the music, having lost sight of myself and of my surroundings. Each note resonated deeply in me with a brilliance and clarity that were a marvel. I realized that listening to the avant-garde piece had altered my perception drastically. I felt as though I had miraculously gotten a new pair of ears: each note was suddenly as crystal clear and alive as if some auditory curtain or filter had magically lifted. It was astounding! By engaging me differently, the contemporary piece had made me a better listener. This new perception had brought a freshness and delight to the music that charmed me completely. I felt one with the music, not separated from it. I had *heard* the Schumann piece; I had *listened* to the one by Schubert.

This distinction between hearing and listening is crucial. We constantly switch from one mode to the other, back and forth, many times a day. Though no change is apparent, we use our ears differently in either case. We are basically passive agents in hearing mode. Our ears pick up sounds at random, almost like two microphones at the sides of our heads. In our usual surroundings, at home or work for instance, we do not particularly focus on sounds around us. For example, I take for granted the regular tick-tock of the pendulum of the eighteenth-century French clock in my living room or the humming of the computer when I write at my desk. These sounds may even disappear just below the threshold of my awareness while I am engaged in an absorbing task. They are merely part of a familiar sonic background.

There are other moments when we feel we are in listening mode when we are, in fact, still in hearing mode. Remember the last time you were trying to get the attention of your youngest child. You knew all too well from the frown on her face and the impatient tone of her voice that you were wasting her precious time: "Yeah! I'm listening, mom!" Yet, you were certain that, whatever she said, she was not listening. She was physically present, but her mind was on something more urgent, more important than you. Her hearing mode was on; her listening mode off.

The listening mode operates quite differently. At the concert, I had switched to my listening mode only when my curiosity was aroused. I was not passive anymore, but instead an active participant. I clearly remember thinking: what's next? How is the composer going to surprise us now? The newness of the sonorities and the apparent chaotic aspect of the whole piece dazzled me. I wanted more. Suddenly, my mind was not wandering but fully alert, engaged, aroused. Actually, my body and mind felt as one and thus alive at that moment; this was not apparent a few minutes earlier. In fact, listening requires the participation of the body as much as it requires the engagement of the mind. In listening mode, they work together. The teenager answering distractedly: "Yeah, Mom! I'm listening!" does not listen precisely because her body and mind are dissociated at that moment.

These differences between hearing and listening may appear trivial at first but they have a profound influence on everyone's life. For that reason, we will explore the ideas developed by Tomatis: they offer the best map to understand why our listening — or lack of it — influences who we are, how we learn and how we feel about ourselves.

THE ROLE OF OUR EARS

In exploring how our ears work, Tomatis discovered that they have other functions than just hearing, a brand new idea for many of us. In fact:

- Our ears act as a dynamo, sending stimuli to our brain, keeping it alert and in good shape so it works optimally.
- Our ears control our balance and coordination as well as all the muscles of our bodies, including the muscles of our eyes.
- Our ears control the quality of our speech: indeed, we speak and sing with our ears.
- Even our skin and bones receive and transmit sound.

Tomatis often said that the human body is designed like an antenna for sending and receiving messages.

This information raises a few questions:

- Could we maintain our brain optimally stimulated, using sound stimulation?
- If so, how could it be done?
- Do some sounds stimulate the brain better than others?
- Could we improve our balance and coordination by stimulating our ears?
- How does our hearing affect our speech?
- Is it really possible to retrain the ear?

This list could go on and on.

To answer these questions, we'll have to look at the bones, cells and nerves that support hearing. Listening, though, belongs to a different dimension grafted onto those mechanisms. It involves desire, curiosity, focusing, and concentration. In short, it involves the workings of the mind, a mind that works better if the machinery of the ear functions to the best of its capacities. The mind reacts to the fluctuations in our environment, gets bored or passionate, depressed or clear-headed, attentive or careless. It becomes preoccupied with work, family concerns, a longing for love or recognition, taxes to pay, mortgage payments, and on an on. There are times when things are so overwhelming that the mind prefers to tune out. The ear adapts to that desire not to listen as well as it adjusts to the desire to listen. But what are the mechanisms that make those constant shifts possible?

Even as we look for answers, the list of questions keeps growing: What do I do to improve my listening skills? Does the perception of my ears deteriorate when I refuse to listen? What happens to my life when I turn a deaf ear to my problems? Still the list is not complete. We also need to factor in life circumstances, for we were not born in a vacuum. We have a family history, a social history, a health history, and a psychological history; all have bearings on the way we listen to ourselves and to others.

The question of listening is complex, and this book is an invitation to discover the many facets of listening so you can improve your sense of well-being. Fortunately, we have the discoveries of Tomatis to guide us through this exploration. And so, we will start where he started fifty years ago: by studying how the ear works.

THE EVOLUTION OF THE EAR

Do Fish have Ears?

Ears, like the nose, mouth or eyes, are clearly visible. While they may come in slightly different shapes or sizes, they are still easy to identify, whether they belong to an elephant or a cat. Birds are more puzzling, since feathers cover their ears. But what about a fish making his rounds of the fish tank, or the salmon swimming upstream? Do they also have ears?

If we look carefully, we may be able to observe a line running on either side of a fish. This line, called the *lateral line*, is what is visible of a long canal running beneath the skin. At the bottom of the canal you'll find sensory cells connected to the nerve fibers. Each cell is called a *hair cell* because a fine hair tops it. Although the lateral line has a perceptual function, we are still very far from a functioning ear as we know it. Can we then conclude that fish have ears?

Let's imagine that a prey is swimming around a fish. The movement of the prey creates pressure differences in the water. These differences register in the lateral line and alert the fish to the presence of the prey. As the little hairs sway in the water inside the canal, they excite the nerve in much the same way as the hair cells in our ears communicate sound to our auditory nerves. What fish and human beings have in common is that their ears are made from the same basic building blocks. Thus, the fish "hears" in a very primitive way, since it senses and responds to its environment. The human ear has far more complex functions but it still retains some of the functions that we can already observe in a trout or a goldfish.

The Long Road toward Verticality

For millions of years, life was restricted to water. When some species began moving to firmer ground, they had to adapt to very different life conditions, becoming far more complex in the process. They needed to learn to breathe air and to walk in their search for food and shelter. In order to stand, then walk, they had to resist the pull of gravity. Babies must do likewise when they take their first steps. As paradoxical as it may sound, achieving verticality was made possible by the evolution of the primitive ear.

At first, all the elements of the *lateral line* were centralized into a small bag, the *otic vesicle*. As it was very fragile, over time it became buried in a solid, bony structure. Later on the otic vesicle constricted in the middle and formed two little bags that remained connected by a small opening. One is called the *utricle*, the other, the *saccule*. This was a very significant development as the utricle allows us to move horizontally and the saccule enables vertical movement.

The addition of the saccule to the utricle freed the necks and heads of species which could only crawl up to that time. Now they could raise their heads. This was progress, but change often brings new problems. Up till now, their hearing was still limited to the vibrations picked up by the contact of their bodies with the ground. As the body moved away from the ground, the animals could no longer rely on "hearing" ground vibrations. The ear had to adapt further to perceive vibrations traveling through the air.

The addition of the *lagena* to the saccule marked another step in the achievement of an upright stance. That is why birds are able to raise their heads and necks even further from the ground than earlier species. To make the system more functional, the utricle has *three semicircular canals* that inform us about the speed of our movements in space.

This entire system, called the vestibule, controls balance, coordination and every single move we make since it controls each muscle of the body.

Humanity's long march toward erect posture took a step further with the addition of the *cochlea* to the vestibule. Now the whole body was able to rise, stand and walk. However, assuming this to be the final development may be a premature claim of triumph over gravity. We have only to look around to realize that many of us, if not most, are not fully vertical. Otherwise, we would not need the services of an army of chiropractors, occupational therapists, Yoga teachers, Feldenkrais or Alexander practitioners, etc. to "correct", "straighten up" or "align" our bodies.

In addition to its role in establishing verticality, the cochlea is very sophisticated at sound analysis. **For it to work best, the body should be perfectly vertical.** In that position, the cochlea is optimally oriented to perceive and analyze sounds accurately. In fact, the addition of the cochlea to the vestibule led to the development of speech. This evolutionary process is repeated by all of us during the first years of our lives: **babies start talking when they begin rising to their feet.** Thanks to the cochlea, our distant ancestors were able to verbalize what they saw and heard as they freely roamed the expanse of the earth. This impressive journey, which took millions of years, is worthy of close study.

HOW DO WE HEAR?

Answering this question could easily fill another book. While a complete study of the ear would be very interesting, we will only cover what is essential to an understanding of the following chapters. The study of the ear is traditionally organized in three parts, suggesting the existence of an external ear, a middle ear and an inner ear.

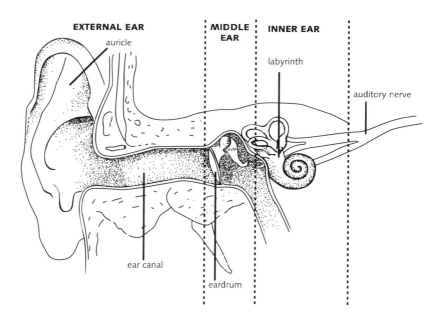

Figure 1: The human ear[5]

The External Ear

The external ear is made up of the *auricle*, the part of the ear that you see, and the *ear canal*, which is about one inch long and ends up when it meets the eardrum. Both the auricle and the ear canal direct the sounds to the eardrum. When children pretend they can't hear, they cup their hands behind their ears. The hand then becomes an extension of the auricle increasing perception by directing the sounds toward the ear canal.

The auricle and the auditory canal act also as filters, preferentially filtering out low frequencies. They selectively capture the sounds in a frequency band between 800 Hz and 4,000 Hz. This is certainly an advantage for understanding language since, as we will see later, most of the higher harmonics of many languages are located in this range. Individuals whose ears protrude are hampered by increased reception of low-frequencies sounds, making language more difficult to understand. Not so long ago, protruding ears were thought to signify retardation. However, in reality they are an indication of compromised sound reception.

Animals can prick up their ears and therefore easily locate the source of sound. We are less able to do so because humans have only three muscles for moving the auricle while the horse, for example, has seventeen to do the same job. Instead, we locate sounds in space by moving our heads toward their source.

The Middle Ear

The middle ear is a cavity filled with air and separated from the auditory canal by the eardrum. It contains three little bones: the hammer, the anvil and the stirrup. The middle ear is connected to the mouth by the *Eustachian tube*. This tube equalizes the air pressure on both sides of the eardrum. Many of us have experienced a sense of pressure in our ears when taking off or landing in a plane. Just swallowing or yawning is usually enough to take off that extra pressure because, when we do so, the *Eustachian tube* opens automatically. If it were not an automatic reflex, we would notice that we do indeed swallow every minute or so because the pressure decreases slowly inside the middle ear. This is due to the air being absorbed by the blood vessels in the walls of the cavity.

In his writings, Tomatis repeatedly emphasized the role of two tiny muscles located in the middle ear:
- The *muscle of the hammer*, which acts as a tensor muscle for the eardrum and increases pressure in the inner ear.
- The *muscle of the stirrup*, which decreases the tension of the eardrum and the pressure in the inner ear. This muscle is the tiniest muscle of the body and, in Tomatis' view, the most important.

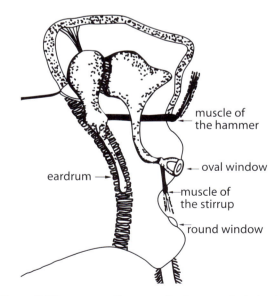

Figure 2: The two smallest muscles in our whole body[6]

Both muscles contract or flex, not only to move the bones of the middle ear but also act as mufflers for low frequencies. When a sound is too loud, its low frequencies tend to drown out its high frequencies. Hearing low frequencies at the expense of high ones would make it hard to make sense of what people are saying since speech contains many high frequency components. The two muscles are natural selectors of frequencies and act as filters. This is not only true when we hear people talk; it is also true when we speak. We do not always realize it, but when we talk, sing, cry or scream, it makes a lot of noise in our heads. This noise can be as deafening as the noise coming from our surroundings. Fortunately, nature has created the perfect protective mechanism: immediately before we vocalize a word, the muscles of the hammer and the stirrup move to reduce the anticipated pressure inside the inner ear. This is one of the ways in which the ear is actively involved in speech production.

The muscle of the stirrup seems to have the most important role in the mitigation of excessive noise. It dampens the low frequencies, making that they do not drown out the high frequencies. Because of it, we are able to discriminate between high and low frequencies. As long as this works well, we should, for example, have no difficulty understanding a conversation during a party with loud background noise. If this muscle doesn't work well, even the faintest sound, such the drop of a needle on the floor or shuffling of papers, would become deafening!

The muscle of the stirrup also improves our ability to hear when we speak. We can carry on a conversation and still hear the birds singing in a tree or the roar of a car coming up the hill. What our ears do not notice are "the intense low frequency vibrations that arise primarily from the enunciation of vowels ... Indeed, the muscles are what makes it possible to hear soft sounds while one speaks" [7]

Our bodies also make a lot of internal noise. We would go crazy if we had to constantly endure the sounds of our heartbeat, the gurgling of our stomach or the noise of the air filling up our lungs. Here again, the stirrup and its tiny muscle work at screening out the racket that goes on inside each of us.

Such is the role of the muscles of the stirrup and hammer that we can see them as the gatekeepers of the auditory system. They protect the inner ear, muffle the low frequencies, and improve hearing. To do this, the muscle of the stirrup must maintain a strong and almost constant tension. This can be a challenging task when the ear is subjected to exceedingly loud, sharp sounds like the bang of a gunshot. These muscles may not be able to perform quickly enough since they need some warning in order to build up tension. In that case, extremely loud noise enters the inner ear, which may result in hearing loss.

Learning disabilities are often rooted in a history of childhood ear infections. During the illness, the middle ear is filled with fluid and therefore the muscles of the middle ear are unable to do their job properly. They become flabby through lack of exercise. The result is analogous to any muscles that have not been exercised for a long time. But how can we retrain those two tiny muscles? We cannot give them a work out as one would do at the gym. And yet, this would be the best solution! The Electronic Ear built by Tomatis serves the same purpose as gym equipment: strengthening those muscles by presenting sounds and music in a way that forces them to react and exercise.

The Inner Ear

The inner ear consists of the *vestibule* and the *cochlea*. Together they form the *labyrinth*. The word itself conjures a world of inextricable mazes and it attests to the complexity of the ear. Through the vestibule, the ear controls the movements of the body, and through the cochlea allows us to hear and speak.

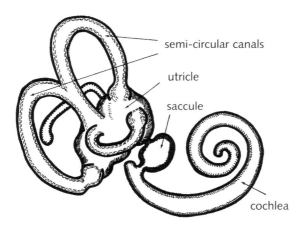

Figure 3: The inner ear[8]

The Vestibule

As we saw before, the vestibule includes the utricle topped by the saccule and the three semicircular canals. Each one has a specific role: the utricle organizes horizontal movements and the saccule vertical ones. Thanks to their cooperation, they control *static* equilibrium: that is why we can stand upright despite the pull of gravity. The *semicircular canals* are nearly at right angles to one another and monitor *dynamic* equilibrium, which is our ability to move around. They essentially work like gyroscopes in airplanes informing the pilots in which direction they are flying while constantly taking small changes of direction into account. Thanks to the vestibule, we can move against the pull of gravity and avoid getting lost or going about in circles.

The information obtained by the vestibule concerning balance and movement is dispatched to the central nervous system and brain, which in return send commands to the muscles to contract or relax to maintain balance. The vestibular nerve is also connected to the spinal column. This information system touches all the anterior roots of the *medulla oblongata,* thereby controlling the whole body through the action of the labyrinth.[9]

We may think of the vestibule as the main software which regulates movement so smoothly that it appears effortless. It is a "unifying system that forms the basic relationship of a person to gravity and the physical world" explains Jean Ayres,[10] adding that, "All other types of sensations are processed in reference to this basic vestibular information." The activity in the vestibular system provides a framework for the other aspects of our experience. Vestibular input seems to prime the entire nervous system to function effectively.

Any glitch in the vestibular program will result in symptoms such as poor muscle tone, motor planning, or bilateral coordination, gravitational insecurity, difficulties with auditory-language processing, visual-spatial processing, and of course problems with balance and movement. No wonder that children who are afflicted with some of these problems feel emotionally insecure: if they cannot trust their most basic senses, how can they trust themselves? They spend their time trying to compensate for their difficulties and, more often than not, suffer from low self-esteem since they think that they cannot do things, especially new things, and tend to feel stupid. Indeed, the influence of the vestibule reaches far and wide.

It is also interesting to note that there is a connection between the vestibular branch of the auditory nerve and the cochlear branch. Briefly, the side in charge of equilibrium (the vestibule) connects with the side in charge of hearing and speech (the cochlea). Children who do not speak often have trouble with erect posture. They may be stooped, have rounded shoulders, or walk on their heels or toes. When they are placed on a balance board, which challenges their sense of equilibrium, they may start to make sounds because of the activation of their vestibule. However, they'll immediately lose their balance and fall from the balance board. They cannot properly combine movement and speech.

The vestibule can already be seen in a two-month-old embryo.[11] That says much about how important it is for the development of that embryo. Movement in the womb primes the nervous system and stimulates the brain in the same way that it does after birth. Although the vestibule does not have a hearing function as the cochlea does, it is not totally deaf to sounds either. The saccule perceives low-frequency sounds (below 1,000 Hz) well and is highly attuned to rhythms. Listening to a drum (low frequencies) makes you immediately feel like dancing because your vestibule is activated.

The Cochlea

The cochlea is no less complex, but I'll limit its explanation to what is essential for understanding the rest of the book. The word cochlea means snail in Latin, which is an accurate description because it does resemble a snail's shell. Inside it, you'll find the *organ of Corti*. The inside of the organ of Corti is lined with hair cells (the Corti cells), and these are the ones that analyze the sounds and transmit their findings to the auditory nerve. There are about 24,600 Corti cells and each one is attuned to a certain frequency. This makes it possible to discriminate sounds, to analyze them, and to assign them an appropriate meaning. Damage to the cells results in poor discrimination, poor hearing and poor listening, and may possibly lead to deafness. As we will see later, there are many more cells for analyzing high frequencies, suggesting that high frequencies energize the brain more than low frequencies.

How sounds reach the cochlea is still open to question. Most text books cite the mechanism proposed by the Nobel prize winner Von Békésy. In his view, sound is transmitted through the three small bones in the middle ear (the hammer, stirrup and anvil). Tomatis has a different explanation but we will not go far into the thick of this scientific debate. Briefly, Tomatis argues that the Von Békésy theory is wrong as the gap between the anvil and the stirrup is so wide that sounds lose about 50 decibels in traversing it.[12] The traditional view is also challenged by the fact that sound transmission still takes place when the ossicles (little bones of the middle ear) are removed. In that case, the sound is somewhat dampened, but still sufficiently audible. Moreover, the ossicles do not easily transmit high frequency sounds.[13]

Tomatis, on the other hand, believes that sound reaches the cochlea through bone conduction, bypassing the middle ear. In his view, sounds channeled through the auditory canal induce vibration of the eardrum. The eardrum is solidly attached to a groove which runs along the bone of the skull. This bone is very dense and protects the inner ear. When the eardrum vibrates, its vibrations are transmitted directly through that bone to the inner ear. "Evidence for supporting this theory of audition comes from the well-known fact of physics that sounds travel with greater fidelity through a dense medium (such as bone) than through a less dense one (such as air, water, or cartilage)." [14]

When there is excessive pressure inside the cochlea, the cochlear fluid transmits the pressure to the membrane of the *oval window*, which pushes the ossicles towards the eardrum. This decreases the tension of the eardrum, which, in turn, lessens the vibrations traveling via bone conduction to the inner ear. The beauty of this system is that it acts as a safety valve.

To summarize the roles of the vestibule and the cochlea, I will quote Tomatis' book *The Ear and the Voice:*[15]

> "The function of the inner ear is to analyze movements, rhythms and sequences of frequencies or pitch. The various parts of the ear have different shapes to help them carry out their different tasks. The inner ear is the organ of listening, calling for a specific posture, a dynamic interaction with the environment and focused attention.
>
> The vestibule measures movements of great amplitude, namely the movement of the body. The cochlea measures infinitesimal movements, those of sounds. It is designed to work with the vestibule and is made from the same material but is organized differently to assume complementary functions. The adaptive mechanisms of the inner ear are complex, allowing it to analyze the extremely subtle movements caused by acoustic impulses on a molecular level as well as gross body movements occurring on a scale of far greater magnitude.
>
> The inner ear is a single entity. Any dysfunction of one of its parts leads to a more or less marked dysfunction of the entire system. Optimal efficiency of the cochlea, for instance, requires good positioning of the vestibule…. This is important, since the vestibule controls all the muscles of the body, those necessary to maintain verticality but also, in a more subtle way, the muscles involved in posture. When the posture is correct, the vestibule is well positioned and, consequently, the cochlea can work optimally. The result is good hearing, excellent listening and perfect body control, all elements which also promote good control of the voice."

AIR AND BONE CONDUCTION

You are probably familiar with the experience of listening to a recording of your voice only to find to your dismay that it does not really sound like you. This mystery is not such a great a mystery after all. When I talk to a friend, for example, she hears my voice being carried to her ears through the medium of air, that is, through air conduction. That's also what the tape recorder picks up. However, my voice makes my whole body resonate, especially the bones of my skull and spine. So, when I listen to my own voice, I also pick up those vibrations (through bone conduction). Neither my friend, nor the tape recorder, picks up these bone vibrations. That is why we too often feel as if someone else is talking when our voice is recorded, although we know very well that we are the ones doing the talking.

When we go to an audiologist to have ours ears checked, headphones are placed on our ears, a sound is produced and our response solicited. What is tested in this way is our response to sounds traveling through air. A vibrator placed on the mastoid bone right behind the ear tests our bone conduction response.

While everyone is aware of air conduction, many people are surprised to hear about the existence of bone conduction. Bone, it should be remembered, is not a dead thing, like a stone or a piece of driftwood, but rather a living organism, half solid, half liquid, in which sound travels faster than through air. In fact, the whole skeleton has the ability to transmit sounds. Perception through bone conduction is quite clear if the sounds delivered through a vibrator are amplified to compensate for the dampening effect of the skin and soft tissues between the vibrator and the bone. In fact, you could hear a symphony by Beethoven or Mozart perfectly through bone conduction alone. As we will see later on, Tomatis uses bone conduction to deliver sounds to help people with listening problems.

Testing bone conduction response provides a very important diagnostic tool. Audiologists obviously are able to pinpoint hearing problems based on the type of response they get. For Tomatis, responses on that test allowed him to detect listening problems as well. Autistic children, for instance, who do not seem to hear sounds delivered through headphones (air conduction), often react immediately and quite strongly to sounds delivered through bone. This is an indication of hypersensitivity to sound and also a sign, as we will see later, that they are unable to filter out irrelevant sounds. Thus, they feel bombarded by the stimuli in their environment and are unable to protect themselves against their onslaught. To a lesser degree, this is also true for children and adults with Attention Deficit Disorders, whether with or without hyperactivity.

Skin and Hearing

Finally, we need to consider another organ of hearing: the skin! Tomatis emphasized that the whole body is actually... an ear! He pointed out that the cells of the skin are made of the same type of cells as those found in the cochlea (they even have a little hair on the top!) In human beings, vertical posture has exposed the areas of the skin where most sensory receptors are located, such as the face and the chest. So, the whole body is a human antenna.

The skin has several types of cells that act as receptors. The Meissner cells, for instance, are sensitive to a frequency range of about 20 - 100 Hz with maximum reactivity at about 40 Hz. The Pacini cells are sensitive to higher frequencies with a range of about 100 - 1,000 Hz with a maximum sensitivity at 300 Hz. This explains why a deaf person can be trained to hear through the skin with the aid of special transducers. "It is not because the ear does not *hear* that it does not function," concluded Tomatis based on numerous experiments.[16] The vestibule is still working, processing all the sensory information captured by the skin and other senses. On the other hand, the fact that the skin "hears" might account for the tactile defensiveness often observed in autistic children or children with sensory integration issues. In that case, they "hear too much."

The role of the skin as a kind of primitive ear starts early. The unborn child perceives sounds through its skin in the first weeks after conception. Indeed, the skin is the primary sensory organ before the inner ear is fully operational at four and one half months.[17] Thus, even before the ear is fully functional, the sound receptors on the skin are already operational. The prenatal experience of the skin as a sensory organ probably lays the foundation for starting to perceive our body and gradually develop a body image out of which our sense of self will emerge. Later we will see how recreating the experience of perceiving sound in utero has important clinical benefits.

THE HUMAN ANTENNA

At this point, we will start focusing on how we receive auditory input. Tomatis often used an image that can help clarify this. People, he said, are like antennas. The "human antenna" receives the audio signals (all the sounds around them) which are then forwarded to a receiver, much as we see in TVs or radios.

The position of the antenna is critical. We know, for instance, that for the best reception, the antenna must be up as high as possible (on the roof, for example) and oriented toward the transmitter. The same is true for the human antenna. For best reception, we should be vertical, our posture straight and oriented toward the source of sound. In short, our whole body, under the direction of the vestibule, is like a big information receiver. Our posture is thus essential in getting good reception.

The receiver on our TV makes it possible to select different channels, depending on whether we want to watch the news or tune in one of the sports channels. In the same way, we can decide whether to tune in to information that we want to receive from our environment. By tuning in, we automatically tune out all the other information. For instance, by tuning in the news, we automatically tune out entertainment channels. This ability to *tune out* is critical: without it, we would be deluged with sounds that wash out information that requires our concentration. Children or adults who cannot tune out that flood of information suffer greatly from it. That's when we say that someone is hypersensitive to sounds. Autistic individuals are a case in point.

The cochlea analyzes incoming information before transmitting it to the brain. This, of course, is a higher order operation than just receiving information. Especially when decoding language, the cochlea is key. In fact, without a cochlea, we would not be able to decode words because we would not be able to analyze the sounds that make them. And, as we will find out later, the right ear does a better job at this than the left ear.

When we use the word antenna, most people immediately think about the antennas or satellite dishes we have on our roofs to *receive* signals, but antennas are also used for *broadcasting*. Our ability to speak is the human equivalent of broadcasting, and the air the medium through which messages are sent and received. The ear, more specifically the cochlea, supervises all the parameters of the broadcast (that is, of language) before putting it on the air. In fact, we will find out later that we speak with our ears! Here again, the verticality of the antenna assures the quality of the emission. If you stand up straight, your voice will have a better quality. Indeed, verticality is a prerequisite for clarity in speech; a child who does not walk cannot readily talk. The whole human antenna is primed neurologically to first master an erect posture and then language.

We will explore this simplified outline of the ear's functions in more detail as we go. Clearly, as we proceed, we will discover higher and higher levels of complexity. This follows our gradual movement away from the purely receptive nature of the human antenna toward the active component of it. In short, we will be moving away from hearing toward listening.

One last important detail: as a result of Einstein's theories, we know that sound waves are energy. Our ears capture this energy and make good use of it. Likewise, transmitters require a lot of energy. A radio station broadcasting with a strong transmitter can be heard much better, over a longer distance, without too many distortions, than can a weak one. Likewise, the human transmitter needs lots of energy as well. It is the role of the ear to provide this energy.

Electronic Ear

ENERGY THROUGH THE EARS?

According to Tomatis, a little known function of the ear is transforming stimuli from our environment into energy. Thus, for him, the ear is a generator for the nervous system and brain. There are, of course, some other obvious sources of energy: food and oxygen, for example. But even well-nourished people can lack energy and fall into depression. Sensory deprivation can, in some cases, even result in suicide or madness. We may complain of having too much noise around us, but the truth is that we could not live in an environment deprived of sounds. This does not mean that we should crank up the volume on our stereo or turn our houses into discos. Too many sounds and too much noise can be as detrimental to our hearing and health as too little. In fact, we need the proper kind and amount of auditory stimulation to function well.

Both the vestibule and cochlea contribute their share in producing energy. The vestibule transforms body movements into energy.

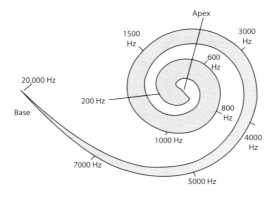

Figure 4: The cochlea[18]

Every time we move, bend or walk, when the muscles stretch or contract, even when the joints are compressed, we create sensations that are transmitted to the vestibule. These sensations are then transmitted to the brainstem and the cerebellum where they are processed and integrated. Tomatis believed that about 50% of the energy that the brain needs to function optimally comes from those body sensations which are channeled through the vestibule.

If we look back at the history of evolution, it becomes clear that it took a tremendous amount of cumulative energy for man to overcome the forces of gravity and stand upright. Yet, we need not go so far back in time, we need only observe babies as they try to sit, then stand and finally walk. The amount of energy it takes to make those movements is enormous. While movement obviously consumes energy, it also produces it.

Our own experience supports the idea that movement equates to energy. Think about how your mood is changed and how you feel energized after a good workout. Lifting weights, stretching, and running not only add bulk to your muscles and make you stronger; they also stimulate and challenge your brain. They make you feel more alert, even more alive. That is why depressed people should exercise, albeit they are often unwilling to do so because they "don't have the energy." But the more they sit, the more deeply depressed they become. A good amount of stimulation is necessary to our sense of wellness. The good news about it is that this energy is free and easily available, providing that we move.

The vestibule not only responds to movement but also to sounds. The *saccule*, that little bag that increased verticality, responds to sounds in the low frequency range. It is better at responding to rhythms, though, than it is at analyzing frequencies. Rock music, rap and drumming immediately activate a vestibular response. They make us feel like dancing, moving, following the rhythmic patterns of the music. Sound induces movement and, in doing so, contributes to our energy level.

When we consider the tiny size of the ear, the total amount of energy that it contributes to what is needed by the brain is quite extraordinary. On top of the 50% of the energy provided by the vestibule, the cochlea, according to Tomatis, adds another 30%. In short, about 80% of the energy needed by the brain to function optimally is supplied by the ear.

To understand how the cochlea transforms sound into energy, we need to take another brief look at it. As you remember, the cochlea is a snail-like structure which spirals up, making two and a half turns. The inside is filled with hair cells that analyze incoming sound. At the cochlea's base are hair cells that analyze high frequencies and at the top those that analyze the lower frequencies. But the distribution of the hair cells is not homogeneous: they are thinly spaced in the low frequency zone, becoming more numerous in the high frequency zone. Just the sheer number of cells receiving high frequency sounds already explains why they charge the brain more than low frequency sounds. In addition, high frequencies already carry more energy than low frequencies. For these two reasons, Tomatis often emphasized the charging effect of high frequencies.

There is, however, one big "but:" high frequencies can only stimulate the brain if the muscles of the hammer and the stirrup are tense enough to maintain a consistent pressure within the cochlea. When this is not the case, the cochlea does not analyze sounds as precisely. This particularly affects the reception of high frequencies; low frequencies are not affected as much since their sound waves are of greater amplitude. Lack of tension in the muscles of the middle ear also reduces the tautness of the eardrum, and thus the transmission of high frequency sounds. The charging effect of high frequencies thus depends on the proper tension of the muscles of the middle ear.

High frequencies are food for the brain. They energize it, stimulate it, make it alert, and enable it to focus and remember. This is what most people reading Tomatis for the first time remember best.

Some people will jump a little too quickly to the conclusion that they just need to buy some tapes of high frequency sounds, turn on their cassette player and ride the wave of an everlasting energy high. That is, unfortunately, too good to be true! Exposure to high frequency sounds should be gradual and, in some cases, may not be advisable. Only a professional trained in this field will be able to make proper recommendations. That is why it is now necessary to talk about the power of sound and how it can help or hurt us.

Charging Sounds, Wearing Sounds

We are constantly bombarded by sounds, yet we are so used to it that most of us pay little attention to them. Although we are usually good at screening out sounds, this doesn't mean that they have no effect on our health and wellbeing. Our houses are filled with the sounds of TVs, radios, heating systems, the hum of computers and the drone of dishwashers or dryers. Do those sounds affect us? What about the noises of the traffic on the freeway or those of a jack hammer in the street? What about the flow of music that we play in our cars or houses or through the headphones of a portable CD player as we jog in the park. Are we losing something by too much exposure to sound? Is our physical and mental health in jeopardy? Are there sounds that are good and others that are bad? Are there sounds that are food for our organism and sounds that are poison?

It is easier to answer those questions now, because we are starting to grasp how the ear works. We know that high frequency sounds stimulate the brain better than low frequency sounds. Tomatis called high-frequency sounds charging sounds, because they charge the brain in the same way that the battery charger replenishes the battery of our car. On the other hand, low frequency sounds tend to quickly wear us out. They make our bodies move by activating the semicircular canals of the vestibule. If these sounds are continuous and repetitive, our bodies are likely to move to the point of exhaustion.

Military marches are a mixture of both types of sound and for good reason. The low frequency sounds of the drums urge soldiers to move (vestibular activity) but also make them tired very soon. To keep the soldiers going, the trumpets add high frequency sounds that energize the brain (cochlear activity), enabling the soldiers to march longer.

Sounds are neither good nor bad, in themselves, but interact differently with our bodies and minds. No one would consider Mozart or Chopin more appropriate than rock music to make our bodies move during an aerobic class. I sometimes wonder how bodybuilders would react if they were subjected to a diet of Bach or Debussy during their hours of training. I frankly think it would be much harder for them to lift weights.

Sounds can be "bad" because they are used badly. It is certainly easier to manipulate a crowd by using drums or playing rock music than by playing Händel or Vivaldi. With rock, the liquid inside the semicircular canals of the vestibule starts to rotate, and we yield to its rhythms. If it keeps rotating as the music goes on, we may soon find ourselves in a state of trance. We become captives of our vestibule: we get in step, we stay in step, and we march in step. This is a desirable state for anyone who wants to manipulate or brainwash us with political convictions or racist slogans. I am told that all the major speeches of Adolf Hitler were preceded by a long sequence of drumming that would set the pace and sway listeners into a hypnotic trance. Some of the racist slogans heard at rap or rock concerts would not wash if they were not drummed into the mind with loud, low frequencies. "Music," in this case, is reduced to a pulsating beat, a great way to drum in whatever message one wants to deliver by appealing exclusively to that visceral, instinctive, reactive part of ourselves that Freud called the Id.

Low frequency sounds not only wear us out physically but they also loosen the grip of our conscious awareness. This is reason enough to be wary of how sounds can be manipulated to alter our moods, influence our beliefs or merely persuade us to buy a product advertised on television.

Low frequency sounds are more common than ever in our environment, exerting their increasingly tiring effects on us. They are the backdrop of our lives whether we like it or not. Most of the time, we do not even pay attention to them. Even when our ears are good, we are mostly not cognizant of the sonic landscape that surrounds us. I once moved into a house close to a railroad. At first, I could not sleep; each train (56 a day!) seemed to roar through the house. Soon after, the trains moved to the fringes of my awareness and most of them eventually disappeared beyond that point. Conversely, we are so used to the constant drone in our environment that we may become scared when silence sets in. Years ago, my neighbor, Jo-Ann, asked me to lodge two of her nieces who were visiting her from out of town. The next morning, the two young women told me they had been unable to sleep. "It is too quiet here," said one of them, "our house is right on Main Street in the town where we live. We are used to traffic and noise. It doesn't disturb us. We sleep very well there. Here it's too silent, we could not sleep."

We certainly are adaptable, and adaptation is, after all, the price we pay to survive. But nothing in history can compare to the onslaught of noise, the flood of low frequency sounds we are exposed to now. Controlled studies have shown that plants exposed to a regimen of rock music expire, while plants nourished with classical music thrive. If music can wither plants, what about its impact on humans? With no intent to malign rock music, one must ask what impact the constant background noise surrounding us has. And how can we learn to counter its effects?

Just as we watch for calories or fat in our food, we may have to monitor the level and quality of sounds that impact our lives. The time when modern medicine will prescribe a diet of specific sounds to support our wellness is still in the distant future. Meanwhile, we may decide to go on our own and experiment with sounds and music to find the right sonic diet for us. Tomatis' ideas regarding the role of low- and high frequencies provide us with some sound principles to guide us in that pursuit. In short, we should expose ourselves to those frequencies that fit with the needs of our physiology. There might be days when the beat of the drum is the best thing in the world to ground us in our body, while on other days Vivaldi or Mozart is what the doctor recommends to lift our flagging spirits. Baroque music will support long hours of studying better than the beat of rock'n roll roiling through our brains. In general, we will do better when there is a balanced mix of low- and high frequencies. To benefit from the charging effect of the highs, we may want to turn up the treble on our CD player slightly and decrease the basses accordingly. These are common sense solutions that are grounded in knowing how ears work and do not put our hearing at risk. And, as we know, there is not always an abundance of common sense and there will always be fools who crank up the volume enough to progressively destroy their ears.

One source of sonic stimulation that does not require any costly equipment is our own voice. We will study the ear-voice link later, but for now it is sufficient to point out that talking stimulates our ears and thus our brain. I have described how depressed people do not feel like moving, thereby depriving themselves of essential vestibular stimulation. Likewise, they often do not feel like talking (or listening to music for that matter), further depriving themselves of cochlear stimulation coming from the perception of the medium- and high frequency sounds. When we talk, we are our first listeners:

our ears analyze the sounds of our voices exactly as they do the sounds of the people talking to us. Talking is stimulating and produces energy. That self-produced energy is no more evident than after we have sung or given a speech. Opera singers are known to be unable to sleep right after a performance because they are so charged by their own voices that they feel alert and full of life. Speaking engagements leave me fully awake even when they end late at night.

I often wonder about families dining in restaurants who barely say a word to one another as they go through the meal. You would guess that food would energize them, but their energy seems to sink as they shovel the food mechanically into their mouths. They look so dispirited by the end of the meal that you cannot help but wonder why they even go through the motions of family gatherings. In my view, a good meal is one in which you certainly enjoy good food but also good conversation, sometimes even a good argument. Digestion might induce some lethargy, but conversation keeps you alert and engaged. By the end of the meal, you feel fully alive and have had a grand time. Such observations run counter to the idea that you have only to eat well and take your vitamins to feel well and maintain a good level of energy. While proper food is certainly important, sounds are also nutrients for the brain! The good news is that you do not have to buy those in a store: it is up to you to just open your mouth and talk, hum or sing.

The Eardrum, the Vagus Nerve, and a Sense of Wellbeing

Tomatis often reiterated that the ear is connected to the 10th pair of cranial nerves, also called the *vagus nerve*. There are twelve pairs of cranial nerves that transmit information to, and commands from the brain. For example, the first pair is the olfactory nerve which connects the nose to the central nervous system. The second cranial nerve connects the eyes to the central nervous system, and so forth. For the moment we'll concentrate on the 10th pair.

The *vagus nerve* is the longest of the cranial nerves. The Latin work *vagus* means "the wanderer." True to its name, the *vagus nerve* wanders from the brainstem to almost all organs of the body. For starters, this nerve is connected to the ear. One of the branches of the *vagus nerve*, called the sensory auricular branch, innervates both the lower part of the external ear canal as well as the eardrum. This is, in fact, the only external point of emergence of this nerve. The eardrum is thus like an antenna that receives messages from the external world and relays them to internal organs that are connected to the *vagus*. Time and again, Tomatis emphasized how important that connection is. In a speech he gave in 1972, he said, "I am asking you to write this down in golden letters because I believe that this is the key to understanding the whole system."[19]

Let's now explore why he put so much emphasis on this connection, beginning with a list of the organs the *vagus nerve* impacts. First of all, the *vagus nerve* stimulates the bronchi, the esophagus, the coronary arteries and the stomach. Further down, it reaches the small intestine, finally ending in the colon at the level of the sphincter. It also carries nerve fibers to the spleen, the pancreas, the kidneys, the suprarenal glands and ends in the gall bladder, sending on along the way, associative fibers to the pelvic plexus and the sacral plexus. No wonder Tomatis attributed such importance to the nerve that, in one way or another, links all these organs to the ear.

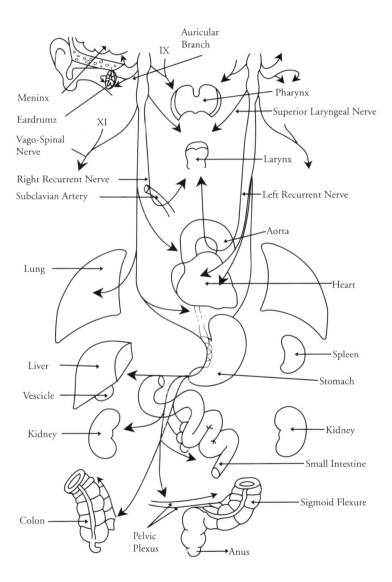

Figure 5: The path of the vagus nerve[20]

However, that is not all. The *vagus nerve* also controls several of the muscles in our neck and spine. When someone looks like a beaten dog, these muscles are not working properly. You can admonish such kids (or adults) to stand up straight a hundred times but they can't. However, by "exercising" the eardrum through sound stimulation properly applied, we automatically impact the *vagus nerve* and thus the muscles of the neck and back, allowing people to straighten.

Together with the 9th pair, the vagus nerve also plays an important role in speech. It enervates the Eustachian tube, the pharynx, and the larynx. We'll come back to the role of the vagus nerve in speech later, when discussing the connection between the ear and the voice in detail.

What may be most important of all is that the *vagus nerve* controls part of the autonomic nervous system, which keeps the vital rhythms of our body in balance (such as the cardiac, respiratory and circadian rhythms). Of the two parts of the autonomic nervous system, the *sympathetic* and the *parasympathetic* system, the 10th cranial pair controls the latter. That's why it is often called the *parasympathetic nerve* as well. Ideally, the *parasympathetic* system should be in perfect balance with the *sympathetic* system. For example, the *parasympathetic system* slows down the heart and dilates blood vessels. The *sympathetic system* does the opposite. Any imbalance between the two systems may ultimately result in respiratory problems or alteration of cardiac or other body rhythms.

Any stimulation of the eardrum may therefore echo throughout the whole *parasympathetic* system and thus affect the *sympathetic* system. It all depends on the tension of the eardrum. When the eardrum is not taut, incoming sounds will make it move extensively, causing the whole *vagus nerve* to reverberate, perhaps producing pressure at the level of the larynx, causing palpitations, digestive troubles, or other repercussions.

If, on the other hand the eardrum is taut, the incoming sound will not move it excessively and incoming sound will, therefore, have little impact on the nervous system. A taut eardrum vibrates minimally, preventing vagus nerve activity from dominating the parasympathetic nervous system. The ear then becomes an excellent tool for transmitting sounds accurately, particularly for perceiving high frequencies sounds well. It follows therefore, that increasing the tension of the eardrum is one of the objectives of any good sound therapy.

Tomatis achieved this tautness through the use of the Electronic Ear and filtered sounds. Usually, and often in a fairly short time, clients beset by anxieties become calmer, more relaxed and composed; their respiration expands, tight muscles relax bit by bit and they stand more erect. Their feelings often change as well, some become euphoric, more confident, with a greater desire to communicate. One of my clients, a young woman who had tried to kill herself several times, became so elated that she went around the office announcing that she had fallen in love during the Christmas holidays, retelling her story in great detail. I have also seen shy children become such chatterboxes that their parents were left begging for a break. Actors or singers experiencing lumps in their throats or butterflies in their stomachs every time they performed were delighted to discover that their stage fright had become quite manageable. Others who were suffering from asthma, gastric and intestinal troubles, or eating disorders such as anorexia and bulimia observed relief from their problems. The *vagus nerve* has such an extensive impact on the body that one observes a whole range of reactions, with each having a great impact on one's wellbeing.

Human nature is such, however, that it does not always look for the best. Some people, for instance, resist the benefits of therapy, seeing change as a leap into the unknown that is scarier than their familiar misery. They refuse to hear, they refuse to listen, and they refuse to communicate. They analyze sounds poorly and they do not hear high frequencies. When their eardrums are slack, they don't have to hear what they don't want to hear. Not listening is the psyche's way of creating distance between the self and suspected unpleasantness or harm. Most of the time, such directives originate below the level of our awareness, yet impact our lives through all kinds of physiological repercussions.

It is not uncommon to see patients resisting the treatment, albeit unconsciously, by suddenly falling sick. After only three days of auditory stimulation, a developmentally delayed and overweight seven-year old boy developed intense diarrhea that lasted for four days. It appeared to be a sure way to avoid coming to our Center. When his symptoms cleared up, he looked leaner, more alert than ever, somewhat more erect and was decidedly more cooperative. He also walked much better and for a longer time.

Other children who have trouble speaking or refuse to speak may develop a brief angina. This reaction is comparable to a fright-flight response resting temporarily in the upper chest. This is natural and a good sign that the treatment is actually working. Such a disruption on the way to a better balance has two parallel effects: vital rhythms become regulated and the perception of sound sharpens. It is, in fact, not possible to separate one response from the other, since they are complimentary.

These observations raise the perennial question of which came first. Is this a change at the physical level that brings about a change at the psychological level? Or, as the examples of resistance to listening suggest, is it the psyche that conditions our physiological response? It is here that it might be useful to remember that hearing is a passive act and that listening is an active one. If you tune up your ear, if you enter into the process of listening more deeply, you might actually give a tune-up to your psyche, increasing your sense of wellness. "The desire to listen," Tomatis writes, "has enormous power to induce change."

TOWARD HUMAN LISTENING

Borrowing the title of one of Tomatis' books indicates the direction in which the study of the ear will now lead us, which is from hearing to listening.

The shift from hearing to listening gives us a dynamic perspective of the ear. The ear is no longer just a piece of hardware, but rather comes with a software that enables the shift toward listening. The software is called "Desire to Listen." It is the interplay between the hardware and software that leads to excellent listening and, as is often the case, the total is more than the sum of its parts.

For Tomatis, listening is both the beginning and the end. It is the beginning, because the desire to listen makes us human and distinguishes us from animals. Listening is also the end result, because when we listen well we start to realize what it means to be fully human.

From this point of view, we are all engaged in an ongoing process of emotional, psychological and spiritual development, which truly progresses as we start to listen better. This requires that our body progressively becomes both a high quality transmitter and receiver. With each step forward, we increase our capacity to realize our potential. Observe a baby who gradually begins to walk, says his first words, moving, as he matures, from concrete to abstract thinking: this captures, in a nutshell, the evolutionary process that transforms us into listeners. It is this history of listening that we are about to explore. It is the reason why we need to look closely into the development of the human antenna. In doing so, we will not only get a better grasp of when the antenna works best, we will also be able to understand some of the difficulties that enter our lives when the pieces do not fit together perfectly.

Raising the Antenna

Tomatis affirmed that verticality is the first step toward human listening. That's because the body needs to be vertical for the cochlea to accurately analyze sounds and function optimally. We can quickly verify this by observing that the voices of people who stand fully upright have a better quality and are richer in harmonics than the voices of people who are hunched over. As you remember, this is because our voices reflect what we hear.

However, the mere fact of having a cochlea doesn't lead to speech. Rats also have a cochlea, but neither speak nor stand on their hind legs, except perhaps for a few moments. Human development shows that language starts to expand as young infants are increasingly able to stand upright for longer periods of time.

A vertical posture is, however, not natural: it takes a long apprenticeship and specific steps must be followed before reaching that final stage. Liliana Sacarin, an accomplished Tomatis practitioner and movement therapist from Seattle, remarks that an awareness of the position of our hips plays a central role in this process. The ultimate postural consequence of reaching verticality is that our center of gravity is well supported by our feet and that the trunk and head are in a vertical alignment that is unique to human beings. To achieve this, the hips should extend forward.

Looking back at the ascent of man, we can assume that the angle of the hips of Neanderthal man was different from ours because his head was projected forward with respect to the cervical vertebrae. Even though his vocal tract resembled that of a present-day human infant,[21] his ability to produce sounds was limited. Because of his hunched over position, his mouth organs were positioned in a way that would not allow speech. Thus, the Neanderthal was at a disadvantage in moving around as well as in trying to communicate. He moved slower and was primarily dependant on non-verbal communication, using gestures and facial expressions, requiring that interlocutors stand close together. This may explain his quick disappearance and his replacement by the Cro-Magnon man, a more advanced form of Homo sapiens who had a skeletal structure and a vocal tract practically identical to ours. These gave him a greater ability to produce sounds and therefore an increased capacity for verbal language, thinking and planning.

Finally reaching verticality required increased body tone to maintain equilibrium and resist the pull of gravity. While these evolutionary steps took thousands and thousands of years, babies retrace them in a matter of months. Each step upward requires greater muscle tone. Although the vestibule contributed an enormous influx of stimuli, it was not enough to maintain the body's upright position. The addition of the cochlea was needed to provide the remaining stimuli required to ultimately gain a vertical posture. Even the skin took part in this dynamic mobilization of verticality since it responds to sounds through sensory receptors located in different areas of the body, primarily, the face, the anterior part of the thorax, abdomen, the palms, the inside of the thighs and legs as well as the soles of the feet. The change in orientation of the body, from a horizontal plane to a vertical one, meant that those areas were now positioned to receive a greater amount of stimulation, thus increasing the body's dynamics and its verticality. The reception and processing of an ever-increasing amount of stimuli caused numerous adaptations of the body to accommodate and respond to this upsurge of information.

One of the first consequences of an upright posture is that it frees the diaphragm, the lungs and the larynx, priming the body to become an instrument of speech. This is not a small accomplishment considering the fact that neither lips, mouth, larynx, pharynx nor lungs were originally designed to produce speech. In fact, the vocal tract was fully reshaped to accommodate this new goal. This evolutionary process is mirrored in the development of each newborn.

You have only to think about a baby first crawling on all fours, then trying to stand against the pull of gravity, and finally taking his first cautious steps. Concurrent with his first attempts at verticality, his vocal tract reshapes to prepare for speech. At about three months, his larynx descends in his throat; by six months, he can no longer breathe and swallow simultaneously, as do all other mammals. Moreover, this greatly elongated pharynx now joins the oral cavity at a right angle, allowing greater variety in the production of sounds. In fact, Tomatis asserted that this innate language potential forces its way through the body, straightening it and assigning new functions to different body structures (mouth, larynx, and tongue) in order to realize that potential in a concrete form: speech.

The increased ability to speak reinforces the body's tone since the sounds we make stimulate our brain and charge it with energy. Sounds made by others work in the same way, especially if they are of good quality. From the standpoint of evolution, man's expanded ability to verbalize reinforced his verticality by increasing the tonicity of his body. This, in turn, expanded his ability to speak even more. Thus, each step toward verticality was matched by ensuing progress in speech, and vice-versa.

When engaged in a conversation, we face each other, orienting our bodies in such a way that all the skin receptors (present mainly on the front of our bodies) are optimally activated. In fact, a simple touch of those skin receptors, according to Tomatis, is enough to make the muscles of the hammer and stirrup react as if they were responding to a sound. We experience this quite physically when we listen to a beautiful voice: we may feel touched, caressed by this voice as if it were an actual touch. The whole body vibrates in this case. Opera lovers often report such experiences. For a moment, their physiology is in tune with the physiology of the singer. It is doubtful that they would react in this manner if either singer or listener turned his back to the other, because the frontal receptors of their skin would not be directly stimulated by the other's voice.

As anatomical parts continued to change, their relationship with the central nervous system became more elaborate. This contributed to the development of more sophisticated abilities, such as the emergence of consciousness and the expression of abstract ideas through speech and writing, all characteristic of human beings' current phase of evolution. This also accounts for a higher organization of the neural processes, such as the creation and expansion of the neo-cortex.

Rising from the ground and standing erect had an additional advantage: hands and arms were now free instead of being needed on the ground for balance and walking. Arms could now be extended to achieve complex tasks. Discoveries of prehistoric paintings, sculpture, pottery and a whole array of handicrafts bear witness to that evolutionary jump. Today, our hands do with ease things that our distant ancestors could not have dreamed of, such as driving a car, threading a needle or playing the piano. The more we use our hands in a variety of tasks, the more accomplished they become, performing both fine and gross motor skills like virtuosos.

Young children learning handwriting clearly demonstrate the lengthy process required to accomplish such a feat as writing their name. It may appear, at first glance, that only the hand and the eye are involved in the process, but that is far from true. In fact, the ear guides the hand, since the vestibule controls body movements and the cochlea analyzes the sounds that are represented by the letters of the alphabet. Although we will delve into this aspect in more detail later on, we can already say that good perception of high frequency sounds promotes fine motor skill development. The Listening Test developed by Tomatis corroborates this surprising assertion. Moreover, improved auditory perception, resulting from auditory stimulation, automatically leads to a more precise use of the hand in writing. The vestibule alone could not have fostered that level of mastery but was able to do so under the control of the cochlea.

It is obvious that the invention of writing expanded the limits of our world. As a result, people could communicate with one another without needing to be in one another's presence. Knowledge passed on through oral tradition could now be written down and safely stored in rapidly expanding libraries. In fact, the invention of writing led to recording history, resulting in an archive of human activity which in turn increased our conscious awareness of being human.

Listening Posture and Sound Analysis

Analyzing sounds correctly is a very complex task involving both the cochlea and the vestibule. The cochlea is the frequency analyzer, but for it to work well, the body needs to be absolutely vertical. Achieving that is the job of the vestibule. In fact, the cochlea is attached to the vestibule, more precisely to the *saccule,* to keep the cochlea in the best position to analyze sounds accurately. As was said before, a well functioning vestibule orients the body upward and as a result aligns the head with the spinal cord. This is the optimal working position of the cochlea, enabling us to truly listen. That's why Tomatis calls this the "Listening Posture."

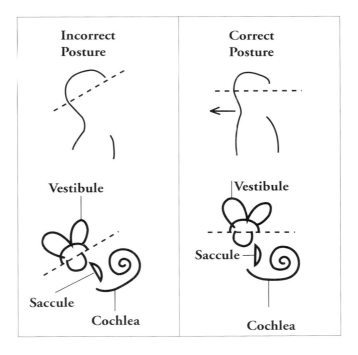

Figure 6: How posture impacts the position of the cochlea

Assuming the correct listening posture is quite difficult for some people, as their vestibules do not work optimally. You can tell them as often as you wish to sit (or stand) straight, but they can't. In that event, treatment will be directed at the vestibule first. Once the vestibule is working well, assuming the listening posture and standing straight will become possible. And as a result, the cochlea will be positioned for optimal sound analysis.

Yet, how is it possible that such a tiny organ can control such major effort as standing erect? As we already have seen, the vestibule activates the muscles of the entire body. It does so through a series of tracts which Tomatis grouped under the term *vestibular integrator*, which consists of the vestibulo-spinal tract, both homo and hetero lateral, and the vestibular-mesoencephalic tract, direct and opposite. It also comprises the sensory responses that follow the return tracts. When this integrator functions optimally, the body is on autopilot: movements flow effortless without wasted energy.

When we have attained the listening posture, the right and left vestibule will work synchronously and symmetrically. The lack of symmetry between the two vestibules may result in motor difficulties, poor posture of the spinal cord and possibly vertigo. It also induces troubles of rhythm when one speaks, constituting further evidence, should it be needed, that the vestibule and cochlea are linked.

With the body fully vertical and the cochlea working optimally, cells localized along the cochlear duct of the organ of Corti analyze sound accurately. As you remember, each of the 24,600 hair cells corresponds to a given frequency, thus sound is broken down into a frequency spectrum. This information is sent to the cerebral cortex, more specifically to the *left temporal lobe.*

This *left temporal lobe* is very important for memory and concentration. It is divided into three zones:

- The area of sound reception
- The underlying area where sounds are recognized
- And below, the area that stores the memory of sounds

The area that stores the memory of sounds plays an essential role in speech production, since it pieces together groups of syllables, leading to the formation and recognition of words and sentences. Groups of sounds need to be repeated over and again before the brain and the nervous system archive them and recognize them correctly. In the end we should be able to retrieve this information as efficiently as a computer retrieving a file from a hard disk. This apprenticeship is clearly demonstrated by children learning to speak or students acquiring a foreign language. Each goes through a long period of trial and error. It takes time and repetition to memorize sonic information that leads to the mastery of language.

After the *left temporal lobe* of the cortex recognizes certain sounds, the information is disseminated throughout the cerebrum, the most recent addition to the brain. The cerebrum in turn distributes them throughout the body. It would be a complex task to follow the route taken by sounds as they go from the cochlea to the brain before being diffused throughout the body. Tomatis carefully mapped out the different motor and sensory tracts that are involved in this task. He saw them as a unit that he called the *cochlear or linguistic integrator*. Thanks to the cochlear integrator, our innate language potential resulted in speech. Because the human antenna acquired the listening posture, it became ready to receive, decode and transmit messages.

Selectivity

Not everyone, though, is convinced that we need perfect perception of sounds—that is, an ability to discriminate correctly between sounds—to learn and manage our lives well. I still hear the dissenting voices of some children who came to my clinic, when they were told that they were not listening well. "But I DO hear!" they protested in outraged voices. Peter was one such nine-year old boy with reddish hair and freckles all over his face, who looked at me as if I were a madman. I had explained, or rather tried to explain, that his poor listening skills were responsible for his learning difficulties. He was not buying that! He did hear me, he heard his parents, and he heard his friends! Why would I need to fix his ears since they worked fine? Still, he constantly asked a resounding "WHAT?" every time his parents, his siblings or his teachers asked him a question. His ability to discriminate sounds was so poor that he could not comprehend what he heard. It was like trying to listen to a radio that has lots of statics and is constantly fading in and out. How could he know that there was a clearer way of hearing?

He probably thought that everyone heard as he did. It was only after the completion of his program that he realized that this was not true. He could suddenly hear a universe of new sounds. Voices now had a variety of tones, a depth and a richness he had never suspected. He was certainly not deaf before the treatment as he had vehemently insisted ("I can hear"), but his hearing was unfocused and lacked acuity. The difference is somewhat comparable to what gross motor skills are to fine motor skills. This is not an arbitrary comparison: indeed, after treatment, his movements were now flowing, his gestures were more precise and his handwriting finally rested on the line. He stood naturally erect when he proudly announced: "Now I can hear!" Repositioning his antenna clearly did wonders.

The experience is somewhat similar to sitting in a waiting room, hearing people talk behind the doors of a nearby office. We may also remember when we, as children, were in bed, trying to follow a conversation between our parents in the living room. Their voices were muffled, most words unclear: a generally frustrating experience that could lead a young child, and sometimes even an adult, to eavesdrop. The door, the walls, the ceiling and the distance act as a filter. If the filter is too thick, little sound will go through. This is exactly what had happened to Peter. He could hear a jumble of sounds but lacked the ability to differentiate them and make them clearly identifiable.

Here is a simple exercise to check your ability to discriminate between tones. It is not a foolproof exercise because the exercise uses complex sounds and not the pure sounds that you would hear if your ears were being tested by an audiologist. Nevertheless, the exercise can at least give you an inkling of potential difficulty in discriminating tones. First, find a piano and ask a friend to play, one after the other, pairs of notes separated by half an octave. Do not look at your friend or at the keyboard, but concentrate on the sounds and try to tell quickly whether the pitch you last heard is higher, lower, or the same as the preceding sound. Repeat the sequence several times, using the whole width of the keyboard. If your selectivity, that is your ability to discriminate, is good, you should be able to select the correct answers in a split second, without hesitation. In this case, your selectivity is open: there is no filter that prevents you from correctly identifying sounds. If you made mistakes, your selectivity is closed. Selectivity can be fully closed, meaning all your answers were false, which was true for Peter. Your hearing can also be partially closed: in this case, you perceive some comparisons correctly, usually in the lower frequency range, and other comparisons incorrectly, most commonly in the high frequency range.

The value of this ability to discriminate between sounds is nowhere more evident than when we learn to read. If the selectivity of the first grader learning to read is closed or partially closed, he can only make decisions based on incomplete information and, consequently, may fail miserably. It does not matter how many times the teacher patiently tries to explain the difference between an S and a Z, or a T and a D, or a P and a B: to the child, they sound exactly the same. Why would that be? How could an S sound like a Z? To understand this we need to take a close look at the differences and similarities between letters like S and Z. Like all sounds, the sound S or Z is a complex mixture of many frequencies. First of all, there is a fundamental tone, on which a series of higher frequencies rest.

When I make a sound, my vocal cords produce a fundamental tone that is modified and amplified by resonance in the cavities of my mouth and face, just as the vibrations of strings are amplified by the body of a violin. Sounds are bounced back and forth in the mouth cavities, amplifying the sound and creating higher frequencies. By changing the shape of those cavities, that is, for instance, by moving the tongue, a large array of sounds can be produced. Some of the new vibrations produced by resonance are called the *higher harmonics* because their frequency is a multiple of the fundamental tone. The difference between an S and a Z, is that while they have a very similar fundamental tone, they have essential differences in their higher frequencies. An open ear can discriminate between the subtle differences of the higher frequencies and can identify them correctly. A closed ear cannot. That is why good selectivity is important.

A young reader with closed or even partially closed selectivity makes decisions based on incomplete information. If, for instance, he cannot discriminate correctly beyond the range of 1,000 Hz, he has a hard time telling an S from a Z. That's because he does not perceive the subtle differences between harmonics above 1,000 Hz that differentiate an S from a Z. What he experiences is not different from what a child hears when eavesdropping on his parents behind a closed door. He perceives through the filter of closed selectivity and, thus, what he hears is distorted. His experience is similar to that of a color-blind person who is unable to distinguish green from red. If asked to go into the garden to pick some strawberries, he will bring back a mixture of red and green strawberries, because his eyes cannot discriminate the frequency of red from green. And so it is with distinguishing sounds, even if the child knows perfectly well that S and Z look different.

The analysis of sound that occurs when we read also takes place when we speak or sing. We are after all our first listener. Even before the words come out of our mouths, our ears have checked the sounds that make them up. Our voice precisely reflects the way we hear, as we will see later on. A well-timbered and bright, easily flowing voice indicates that the ear analyzes sound well. This also goes with a good listening posture. One cannot imagine, after all, that great music would come out of a flute that is bent or from violin that is poorly built. The little music that we make when we speak sounds brighter when we use our bodies as an instrument or like an antenna well positioned to benefit from optimal reception and emission.

Auditory Radar

Once our ancestors stood erect and walked on two legs, they were able to move around more freely. One drawback of being upright was that they lost part of their ability to localize sound through vibrations picked up from the ground. To compensate for this loss, they began using their ears to detect the location from which sounds came. It is likely that their ears had to adapt before they could localize sounds.

The ability to localize sounds was of paramount importance to the survival of our ancestors and it serves us well even today. The roar of a lion in the distance told prehistoric men that they had better flee in the opposite direction to escape possible death. Without the presence of this "auditory radar," they might have run towards the lion, rather than in a safer direction. While it is unlikely that we will encounter a lion these days, we too have to confront our share of dangers: just think of the perils of crossing a street at rush hour. Imagine that you want to cross a busy intersection. You are about to leave the safety of the sidewalk when your "second sense" orders you not to move. In this case, what we call a second sense or intuition is nothing more than our ears telling us that a car is rapidly approaching and that we will not reach the other side of the street without being run over. Thanks to the ability of our ears to localize sound and to estimate the distance between the source of sounds and our physical location, our world has expanded beyond our visual field. Thus, our ears protect us, even when we are not aware of it.

We use several techniques to localize sound. While some of them are well understood, other mechanisms are still under scientific scrutiny.[22, 23] The fact that we have two ears, one on either side of the head, is one of the more obvious ways we localize sounds. For example, when a sound comes from the right, our right ear will hear it before the left ear. Sound coming from a source in front of us reaches both ears at the same time. So, the difference in their time of arrival is a function of the direction from which the sound is coming, *on a horizontal level*, and will be interpreted by the brain as localizing the sound. This time difference is called the *interaural timing difference* or ITD in scientific literature. This mechanism, however, does not help us determine the source of sound on a *vertical* level. For example, regardless whether the sound is in front of us or above our head, the right and left ear receive the sonic information at the same time.

There is, however, another complication. Let's take the example of a sound coming from the right again. It hits the right ear undisturbed, but it has to bend around the head to reach our left ear. Low frequencies (below 1,000 Hz) have long wavelengths that bend around obstacles fairly easily. In this case, horizontal location of a sound source can be determined quite accurately by the *interaural timing difference*.

High frequencies, on the other hand, have short wavelengths that do not bend easily. The head thus becomes a sound barrier and the intensity of the sound reaching the left ear will therefore be lower. The ear can thus use the difference in intensity, *interaural level difference* or ILD, as a means of determining where the sound is coming from on a horizontal level. The two mechanisms are obviously complementary: one operates at very low range frequencies and the other at high frequencies. A result of this specialization, however, is that both mechanisms are fairly inaccurate at localizing midrange frequencies, with most errors occurring at about 1,500 Hz. Furthermore, while both mechanisms work well to localize sounds coming from the left and right on a horizontal plane, they can not localize in the vertical plane or distinguish between sounds coming from the front or the back.

One way to overcome some of these problems is to turn our head. When, for example, sound comes from a source in front of us, neither the ITD nor the ILD are much help in localizing the sound, because the sound reaches both ears at the same time and at the same intensity level. By turning our head, however, we introduce a time difference (ITD) as well as an intensity difference (ILD), and so we are able to localize the source of the sound more accurately. Likewise, we are unable to distinguish a sound coming from the front from one coming from the back. Again, by turning our head, we will be able to distinguish the sound sources.

The curious shape of our external ears (*pinna*) also helps us localize sounds, especially on a vertical level. We are so used to seeing them in the mirror that we have probably never wondered about the purpose of the cavities and folds that give our ears their distinctive look. Gardner and Gardner[24] did some tests that at first glance may seem quite funny. They progressively occluded the pinna cavities and found that the more they did so, the poorer the subjects were at localizing sounds, especially on the vertical plane. There are several theories to explain this phenomenon. Some scientists believe that the folds and cavities of the *pinna* produce numerous micro-second delays, which help localize sounds. Others have shown that the external ear is a direction dependent filter that causes spectral changes which can also be used as a cue to localize the source of sound.

Interestingly, Gardner and Gardner also found that high frequencies were especially useful in localizing sounds on the vertical plane, which may explain why improving our ability to perceive high frequencies improves our ability to localize sounds at the same time. Still there is much about sound localization that it is not understood so these investigations continue.

Spatialization errors (not knowing where the sound is coming from) continue to be a source of personal difficulty. In my clinical practice, I often noticed that children with a history of ear infections made many spatialization errors when the acuity of their air conduction response was tested. Some of them kept indicating the wrong ear even as the decibel level increased. It was often necessary to increase the decibel level by up to forty decibels before those children correctly localized the sound. A preponderance of errors was made in the high and midrange frequencies. Fortunately, it is fairly easy to correct this type of error using the Tomatis Method. After treatment, these children could again determine where things and sounds were located in space.

Some people also make spatialization mistakes when their bone conduction response is evaluated. In that test, one places a vibrator on the mastoid bone right behind the ear. Sometimes, they identify sounds coming from the left as if they were coming from the right or vice-versa. Sometimes, they are unable to decide: "I hear the sound on both sides of my head" or "I hear it in the middle." Mistakes are extremely frequent in people who have suffered whiplash during a car accident. It is possible to reduce the number of these spatialization errors but they tend to be more resistant than air conduction spatialization errors.

Errors of spatialization affect the way people experience themselves as they move in space. As sound moves through their bones, it seems to reach the wrong destination, perhaps even the opposite side. In the same way, when people are asked which their right hand is, they might raise their left one, or vice-versa. Such errors of orientation certainly undermine the perception that people have of themselves, though sometimes in very subtle ways. After all, if you cannot trust what you perceive, how can you trust yourself?

One of my friends, an elderly woman, made error after error every time I tested her bone conduction response. She had no idea whatsoever from where the sounds came. That strongly impaired her ability to move through her environment, since she often felt lost. As you can imagine, she had a terrible time finding her way around. I once saw her circling a neighboring building, in search of my office, even though she had been there several times before. Her excursions in the outside world were limited to the same places, stores, offices and friends' houses. Although she was intelligent, full of humor and a first-class storyteller, she had low self-esteem. She could not trust her perceptions sufficiently to allow her to move about freely; it kept her within limited boundaries where she felt safe. Most people with spatialization errors do not have such extreme symptoms. Still, sometimes, the knowledge that they have trouble locating the origin of a sound may explain behavior that might otherwise appear curious.

This reminds me of one of my students, Daniel, a fifteen-year old boy who was severely learning disabled and remarkably clumsy. He was always looking over his shoulder toward the back of the classroom. However hard I tried to understand his behavior, I found no explanation. Was it some kind of tic? I did not think so. Daniel clearly did not try to disturb the students sitting at the table just behind him. So why was he turning his head constantly as if he were looking for something invisible? I finally concluded, though it may seem strange, that he was trying to locate my voice somewhere in the back of the classroom, despite my facing the class from the front. To him, it was logical to turn his head constantly to try to hear me, since his ears were telling him that I was in the back of the class, even though his eyes said otherwise. It is hard to imagine what he really heard: the distortions in his perception were certainly important and added to his difficulty learning. His poor posture added to his difficulty analyzing sound correctly, both of which were confirmed by his low and monotone voice. It was obvious that his antenna was not positioned for optimal reception or transmission.

The Three Integrators: a Diagonistic Tool

In trying to explain the relationship between the ear, the brain and the nervous system, Tomatis identified three basic units that are the building blocks for physical, cognitive and emotional development. Tomatis called these three units integrators because each one of them integrates a series of nerves which share common purposes. These nerves control, among other things, the muscles in our body. Their joint efforts take us to the next level of neurological organization, increasing the human quality of our abilities. The concept of three integrators also provides a useful framework for helping parents and teachers understand what might have gone wrong when a child learns with difficulty or has other problems.

We have already mentioned two of these integrators: the vestibular integrator and the cochlear integrator. We need to now add a third one: the visual integrator. If one of the three integrators does not function optimally, a series of problems may occur.

The three integrators work as a team to integrate perceptions and create awareness and consciousness about ourselves, others and the surrounding world. When the link between two integrators does not function smoothly, additional problems may arise that can impair both our performance and our way of being.

Building on Tomatis' theory, Paul Madaule, one of the first students of Tomatis and Director of the Listening Center in Toronto, has classified the symptoms of dysfunctions of each of these integrators and its links. His classification has proved to be very useful in arriving at functional diagnoses. In the ensuing sections, we will describe some of the most common symptoms that occur when an integrator or a link between two integrators is faulty.

Cochlear Integrator

The cochlear integrator makes differentiating sounds possible so that we can develop speech and language. It is important to stress, at this time, the difference between speech and language. Speech is the result of neuro-anatomical conditions that make it possible to perceive and produce sounds. Language, on the other hand, is an aspect of human behavior that involves the use of sounds, motions and expressions in meaningful patterns to form, express, and communicate thoughts and feelings.

Individuals with cochlear problems are likely to have had several serious ear infections. This could have slowed down or delayed language development, usually without affecting motor development. Such a person may experience problems of sequencing and decoding, which makes reading difficult. When the cochlea is not working optimally, it does not analyze sounds properly, causing hardship with phonetics and consequently with schoolwork, but leaves the tendency to be fairly well organized in other aspects of life intact.

Vestibular Integrator

The vestibular integrator helps to control all the muscles of the body, maintaining either static or dynamic equilibrium. Because the vestibular integrator also controls the regulation of muscle tone at any given moment in time, it is instrumental in keeping the body vertical.

A child with a *vestibular problem* may have delayed motor development which in turn slows down his language development. He may show other signs of sensory integration difficulties, such as tactile defensiveness, and might be oversensitive to sounds. Often he is clumsy, accident prone, fidgety while talking and has a very short attention span. He may speak too loudly or with a high-pitched voice without being aware of it. His thoughts often shift from topic to topic, accompanied by dubious logic. He tends to procrastinate, which often puts him at odds with his family. This leads to much disorganization except in his favorite activities. When he reads, he can decode the letters fairly well but does not necessarily understand what he reads. His writing is slow, painstaking and usually highly irregular. Overall, he tends to be rigid, even intolerant, and does not adapt well to change. The older he gets, the more difficult it is to treat him. Madaule notes that adolescents in this diagnostic category represent the highest rate of treatment failure.

The Vestibule-Cochlea Link

Good teamwork between the vestibule and the cochlea results in good receptive listening and language skills. While the vestibule keeps the body upright and does the preliminary work leading to speech, i.e., parting the lips, positioning the larynx and tongue properly, etc., the cochlea analyzes sounds and sets the mechanisms that lead to the production of speech in motion. "When man speaks," wrote Tomatis, "he speaks with his entire body."

Problems arising from a faulty link between these two integrators account for the greatest number of children with learning difficulties. The symptoms are a mixture of obvious awkwardness and language processing difficulties. These children tend to be slow to process auditory information and slow when they talk. Their spelling is inconsistent, their sentences grammatically incorrect or incomplete, the rhythm and flow of their speech hesitant and broken. Such children are usually immature, slow learners and socially shy, but are often willing to get help. Change in body posture is always the first noticeable improvement when they are treated due to the repositioning of the human antenna. It is only after the vestibular problems have been resolved that academic skills start to improve. This obviously sometimes makes parents impatient, since in most cases the child is in treatment for learning difficulties. They would prefer that progress went the other way around—intellect first, body second—but that is not the way it works! One needs to build the foundation of a house before building the first floor, and so it is with people. There is a hierarchical progression from one level to the next, one that cannot be skipped or hurried.

Despite Tomatis' observation that "when we speak, we speak with out entire bodies," not everyone is able to do so. I saw that clearly the day we placed a mute, autistic 10 year-old boy on a balance board. He was a child who combined the poise and agility of a ballet dancer with the strength and endurance of a long distance runner. We had expected him to do well on the balance board since his vestibule worked extraordinarily well, yet, we were to be disappointed. As soon as he stood up on the balance board, he started to make sounds and fell almost immediately. Movement seemed to stimulate an attempt at speech, but he could not maintain it because his vestibule appeared suddenly out of sync. The vestibule-cochlea link was strained as soon as there was an attempt to exploit the connection. This sad example illustrates how much body and speech are intertwined.

A dysfunctional relationship between vestibule and cochlea may, according to Tomatis, also account for stuttering, which is similarly characterized by a lack of rhythm and flow. This may also explain why elderly people treated for balance problems often claim that they hear better and speak more easily as their balance improves.

Visual Integrator

The visual integrator allows the perception of our environment in terms of form, dimension and color. Muscles of the eye are controlled by the joint efforts of the visual and vestibular systems. In the context of this book, links between this integrator and the vestibular and cochlear integrators are of special importance.

The Vestibule-Vision link

To determine whether your vestibule and eye work well as a team, you might try the following exercise: take a pencil and draw a tree or a house, first with your eyes open, then with your eyes closed. If the second drawing is fairly similar to the first one, you can be assured that your vestibular and visual integrators are a good team. If, however, the roof of your second house is askew or seems to fly into the sky, it is a good bet that the two integrators do not work well together. The same is true, of course, if the crown, branches and leaves of your tree wander across the page independent of the trunk.

The relationship between eye and ear is not obvious for most of us because we identify our ears with hearing and our eyes with vision, and are unaware that the muscles of the eyes are under the control of the vestibule. We readily accept that, thanks to our ears, we can hear the whistle of a blue jay, enjoy the voices of children playing outside or be annoyed by the barking of a neighbor's dog. It is, however, hard to imagine that our ears also are instrumental in using a spoon to eat our soup, typing a letter on the computer or cooking a Thanksgiving turkey.

It is even harder to imagine that our eyes are partially responsible for maintaining our body's balance, regardless of whether we are moving or still. Our eyes, we are likely to think, exist only for vision, to thread a needle, watch a movie or voraciously read a mystery. The fact is, though, that about twenty percent of the eye's capacity is involved in simply maintaining our balance. When balance is poor, that percentage is even higher. In that case, the processing of visual information slows down since the eyes are even more engaged in maintaining balance. In the extreme, it may even become difficult to maintain eye contact.

Many years ago, I worked with a 10 year-old boy who, according to his mom, looked "like a little monkey." His gait was quite unsteady and his arms constantly flailed about in a vain effort to maintain his balance. He had severe developmental delays and no language apart from frequent screams of frustration. His eyes had never focused; instead they rolled at random, admitting only scattered images of the world around him. After a week of treatment, his mother and I observed something different about his eyes but we couldn't tell what exactly it was. On the twelfth day of the program, it suddenly dawned on us that his eyes were focusing on us! We also noticed a simultaneous and marked improvement in his balance and gait. Clearly, the vestibular integrator was finally starting to connect with the visual integrator.

When the boy returned to his Special Ed class, his teachers were able to sit him in front of a computer for twenty minutes at a time and teach him some basic communication skills, feats they had never dreamed of achieving. As soon as the ear-eye connection was established and his balance improved, he became more able to learn since his eyes were now tracking instead of shifting almost continuously.

A good ear-eye connection can work wonders. It gives us the ability to orient ourselves in space with a clear appreciation of proximity and distance. It adds dimension to our sense of space. Fluid eye movement allows us to decode words on a page, enabling us to read. When the ear-eye connection works well, it guarantees good hand-eye coordination, allowing us to form the letters of the alphabet clearly, write messages and, should we wish, we can refine our skills even further, learning calligraphy or drawing.

Conversely, children whose ears and eyes do not collaborate well often write block letters that meander up and down the page with obvious disdain for keeping to the line, their drawings are imprecise and they are clumsy when doing practical things. They are not superstars on the field either! The fact that they lack good depth perception enrages their teammates when they regularly fail to catch the ball. They act as though they cannot locate their bodies in space, often running all over the field with little understanding of the game. Both fine and gross motor skills are affected by the faulty linking between ear and eye. Poor or absent eye contact in autistic children may result from the same problem. Parents and teachers would do well to suspect a lack of eye-ear coordination when they observe the symptoms described above.

The Cochlea–Vision Link

Language sometimes has a way of accentuating connections that are not necessarily obvious at first glance. We sometimes talk about voices as though they were made of light rather than sound, referring them as being dark or bright. This may be because we instinctively sense that the spectrum of audio frequencies parallels the color spectrum. Therapists using the Tomatis Method frequently observe a gradual expansion of the range of colors used by clients who draw or paint during the listening sessions. This corresponds to the opening of the ear to a broader range of frequencies.

While we identify many shades of yellow and blue, most of us see only a few variations of green. Greens correspond to a frequency band where auditory acuity is often diminished, around 3,000 Hz. We have no problem, on the other hand, with yellow (around 2,000 Hz) and blue (around 6,000 Hz). Our eyes literally jump over the spaces between the greens. One of my friends, a talented young painter, began using greens for the first time after about fifteen hours of auditory stimulation. One of his paintings, a symphony of greens and blue-greens, totally stunned him. It was a beautiful painting, completed in a couple of hours, but he refused to claim it as his creation and for a long time resisted putting his signature on the canvas. His Listening Test easily explained what was such a mystery for him: his auditory acuity at around 3,000 Hz had improved significantly. This has been equally true of painters treated by Dr. Alfred Tomatis: their palette of colors increased as their "auditory diaphragm" expanded. In fact, careful observation of the colors used in the clients' drawings often indicates change and doing art may accelerate the pace of the treatment.

Other difficulties that may arise when the link between vision and the cochlea is not working properly will be explored in more detail when we look into the problem of dyslexia.

Conclusion

All of the examples of dysfunction cited above are primarily due to an incorrectly positioned and therefore poorly functioning antenna. Reception would be greatly increased if all of us could acquire the recommended posture for listening. This is certainly worth working on since it would assuredly enhance the quality of our lives by making us better listeners.

The posture that makes the human antenna a good receiver also makes it a good transmitter. Conditions that help us to communicate our thoughts and wishes clearly apply not only to the external world but also to ourselves. Communicating with the world and dialoguing with ourselves is, in reality, the same thing and requires desire, order and clarity.

THE EAR AND THE VOICE

Tomatis' interest in the voice started at an early age. His father, Humbert Tomatis, was an opera singer whose career spanned over 40 years. Often at his father's side, Alfred, was immersed in a world of music and song that was his father's passion. He got to know all the famous opera stars of the time and became well acquainted with the Bel Canto style of that era. Unlike his father and the other members of his large Italian family, he had no natural vocal ability. Instead, he became an Ear, Nose and Throat specialist.

The father helped his son, the doctor, build his practice by referring friends with voice problems to him. Tomatis soon became a fashionable voice specialist. With his background, he thought he knew everything about the voice and singing. He soon realized that neither his association with opera singers nor his medical training had fully prepared him to treat damaged voices. To become a more effective physician, he needed to take a fresh perspective. So, he embarked on a lifelong inquiry which led to a theory and a method that would ultimately benefit innumerable people with speech and voice problems. The singers he treated were the first beneficiaries of his studies.

While he was investigating ways to improve the voice, Tomatis was working for the French Air Force. His task was to evaluate factory workers who had been subjected to intense noise on the job. He needed to determine whether they should be entitled to worker's compensation. He noticed that the decline of the worker's hearing was accompanied by a parallel deterioration of the voice. Could it be, he wondered, that singers suffering vocal problems also had hearing difficulties? To his surprise, he found that the singers indeed had ear problems as well! More investigation led to a paper he presented in 1957 to the French Academy of Sciences in which he stated that **"the voice reproduces only what the ear hears."**

Briefly, this means that, if the ear does not hear a certain range of frequencies, the voice cannot produce them either. The reason is that the ear controls the voice through a feedback system, and feedback cannot take place in a frequency band that the ear cannot hear. In other words: a "gap" in audition brings about a parallel "hole" in the voice.[25] For Tomatis, most speech problems or singing difficulties were due to faulty control of the ear. This was, at the time, a revolutionary idea that represented a significant expansion of the traditional view of the ear as a mere sensory organ.

This observation became the subject of an intense controversy among professionals. Some of Tomatis' earlier clients were quite skeptical and some even more resistant to the idea that auditory training would improve their voices.

The following case, recounted in his book *The Ear and the Voice*,[26] is a good example of the resistance and incredulity he faced for years. Friends had referred to him a young Spanish singer who had a badly damaged larynx. A medical examination performed by Tomatis revealed that the singer had intercordal nodules. Few patients with such a clinical picture could expect to recover. Still, Tomatis was convinced that the main reason for the deterioration of the singer's voice was his inability to listen to himself, which the audiometric examination confirmed. Tomatis reasoned that if he could re-educate the young singer to listen correctly, specifically with his right ear, he might be able to re-educate his voice. Although the treatment appeared to be a gamble, medicine had nothing to offer under these circumstances.

The young singer was not pleased with the unorthodox treatment proposed by Tomatis. "He was suffering from his larynx, wrote Tomatis, and I was talking about his ear! Why not his toes? He smiled politely and went off to consult with others."

The singer then set out on a quest that reads like a horror story. He first consulted a voice expert who recommended a surgery that would take care of the problem. The surgery went as planned but the singer's voice got worse. Two other voice experts were consulted, additional surgery was recommended but it made things even worse. After the third surgery, not only was the singer's voice gone but also he could barely breathe. His career was over.

The friends who had referred him in the first place, convinced the now ex-singer to consult with Tomatis one more time. Tomatis taught him to breathe properly and again proposed the re-education of his ear. This time the singer was too desperate to refuse and was hooked to the Electronic Ear. Four weeks later, he had recovered his speaking voice and was even able to sing a little. Two additional months of therapy helped him to fully regain his voice. He was hired as the lead tenor in a major theater and again had a successful career. "He was," Tomatis wrote, "a living testimony of the power of the re-education of the ear."

How the Ear and the Voice are Connected

The links between the ear and the voice are complex, and start to develop soon after conception. Sometime between the fifteenth and the eighteenth day after conception, the fetus develops a series of *branchial arches* along the lateral sides of the neural tube that will one day become his head.[27] Over time, the *first branchial arch* will become the lower jaw and the two ossicles found in the middle ear, the anvil and the hammer. The *second branchial arch* develops into the stirrup (and its muscle) and a series of muscles involved in speech. These changes happen very early on in the development of the embryo. In fact, the stirrup is formed when the embryo measures only 7 mm (one quarter of an inch), and its muscle is attached when the embryo measures about 20 mm (three quarters of an inch).[28] The key point is that parts of the ear and some of the organs involved in the production of our voices have a common origin and that this connection began early on in the development of the embryo.

As we have seen before, the ear and the voice are also connected via the cranial nerves. As you may remember, the cranial nerves transmit information to, and commands from the brain. There are twelve pairs; three of them (the 5th, 7th and 10th pair) link the ear to the sound producing organs. We will now look at these connections in more detail.

The 5th pair (*trigeminal nerve*) is connected to the masseter muscles that allow us to chew, as well as to the temporal muscles that allow us to open and close our mouths. Interestingly, it is also connected to the *tensor tympani*, the muscle of the hammer in the middle ear. In fact, there is a constant link between the tension of the eardrum, regulated by the muscle of the hammer and the mobility of the lower jaw, regulating the movements of the mandible, and thus of the mouth as we speak.

The 7th pair (*facial nerve*) controls all the muscles of facial expression except those that control the eyelids. It also regulates the digastric muscle that controls the opening of the mouth. Interestingly, it also controls one of the muscles of the middle ear, namely the stirrup. What is the significance of this piece of information? Well, it provides a key to understanding some speech difficulties. For instance, if there is a lack of coordination between the different muscles, articulation problems develop. If the muscle of your stirrup is not properly regulated, the position of your lips and mouth is such that you constantly grimace as you talk. And if the muscle of your stirrup is too tense, your face will also be tense and you may risk being taken for rigid, too serious or contentious, because a stiff upper lip will mar your face. In that event, people will think that you are not listening, and they are probably right.

We already saw that the 10th pair (*vagus nerve*) is linked to the ear as well as the pharynx and larynx (which animate the vocal cords). The sensory component of the *vagus nerve* is connected to the external ear. "The basis for this curious fact lies in the embryologic development of the first and second branchial arches, from which the external ear is derived."[29] The motor component of the *vagus nerve* controls the muscles of the *larynx* and is connected to the ear via the *recurrent laryngeal nerve*.

This information from embryology and neuro-physiology clearly establishes the link between the ear and the voice. Three cranial nerve pairs (the trigeminal, facial and vagus nerves) control the ear as well as the organs that produce sounds and are thus clearly connected and interdependent. That is to say, **we speak with our ears**.

Improving our voice through speech therapy or voice lessons is often a very lengthy process. The reason is quite clear: if you can't hear a sound correctly, you can't reproduce it correctly either. A poor voice also indicates that we have poor control over the muscles which control the emission of sounds. Both problems can be addressed by auditory stimulation. When the ear improves, speech automatically improves because the muscles involved in speech work in synergy with the ear. Speech therapists have often told me how much faster and how much more efficiently they could work with a child whose ears had been retrained. The typical feedback was that the client was finally "getting it." That was especially true of the cases that were the least responsive to treatment.

The link between ear and voice is also clearly visible when one compares the way someone speaks or sings with his Listening Test. As we will see later, the Listening Test is a type of audiogram, measuring how well we hear in certain frequency ranges. If, for example, the Listening Test shows an increased acuity for higher frequencies (2,000 Hz and above), the lips will extend forward and all the muscles controlling speech work optimally. The voice, then, will be rich and melodious. If, on the other hand, the acuity in that frequency range is flat or descending, the muscles do not open the mouth sufficiently to produce high frequency sounds. Hence, the voice lacks timbre and tends to be monotonous. Tomatis' theory of speaking and singing with one's ear may sound paradoxical but has a sound neuro-physiological basis.

This neuro-physiological system works in a way that merits closer examination. When Tomatis says that we speak or sing with the ear, he immediately adds that we do so with the right ear. The right ear is the one that controls the quality of the sound produced; the left ear does not normally have that capacity. The fact that the right ear is differently specialized than the left ear raises the issue of lateralization.

LATERALIZATION

At first glance, our body appears to be built symmetrically. If we draw a vertical line down the center of the body, each side seems a mirror image of the other. This apparent symmetry is deceptive. For example, our heart is not in the middle, but on the left side. Even though our brain has two hemispheres, they are usually slightly different in size and each one is very specialized. Following this tendency to specialize, most of us lean toward using the right or the left hand. This specialization is the result of a maturation process, starting at age two or three and continuing until age eleven. By age six, at most seven, a clear tendency to prefer one hand over the other has usually occurred. Although some of us never reach that stage and turn out to be ambidextrous, lateralization is established when one side is clearly used in preference to the other.

When we talk about lateralization, most of us think about hand preference. In *The Left-hander Syndrome*,[30] Stanley Coren reports that a careful review of 66 studies on handedness found that an average of 91.1 percent of the people are right-handed, regardless of race or country.[31] Most lateralization studies are about handedness because it is critical to the way we are living and it is also the most obvious sidedness. This masks the fact that we also have a dominant foot, a dominant eye and a dominant ear. In most cases, the right side is strongly favored. Coren summarizes "the basic pattern of human sidedness" with the following statistics:

- 9 out of 10 people are right-handed
- 8 out of 10 people are right-footed
- 7 out of 10 people are right-eyed
- 6 out of 10 people are right-eared

Coren also notes that "only 63 percent of the population have their dominant hand and their dominant ear on the same side," an even weaker correlation than the ones found relating to hand, foot or eye dominance. Striking too is the observation that, when sidedness is firmly established, it is difficult to shift to the other side. If you are right-eyed and suffer some visual loss on that eye, you will generally still use the right-eye as your dominant eye. The same is true for your ears: if you suffer a hearing loss in your dominant ear, it will still persist as your dominant ear, which might not be to your advantage.

THE LEADING EAR

The concept of a leading ear is, at first, somewhat puzzling. It certainly does not mean that one ear is more worthy than the other. Both have to work in harmony, with one being the leader and the other one the supporter. Tomatis discovered that to process language optimally, the right ear should play the role of the conductor and the left should play a supporting role. To understand this, we need to look more closely at the way the brain works.

Each hemisphere is specialized. The *left brain* operates in a kind of digital mode, breaking down input into small bits so it can analyze and classify the information it receives. The *right brain*, on the other hand, works in a more analog fashion, looking at input as a whole, reacting to feelings, and leading us into flights of imagination. For example, the left-brain will dissect the details of a painting, looking carefully at the composition, the colors, the rendering of a body or a landscape. The right brain will embrace the picture as a whole and react with feelings, memories and images. Our appreciation of the painting emerges from this teamwork.

The left-brain, then, specializes in processing language. This has to do with the fact that words are bits of sounds that the left-brain knows how to analyze, identify and classify. When these operations are done, a meaning is assigned to the sounds that constitute a word. The same operation of breaking down sentences into smaller units is repeated until meaning is extracted from the mass of acoustic information that first strikes our ears.

The seeming symmetry of the body is further complicated by the knowledge that organs on one side of the body are mainly controlled by hemispheric centers on the opposite side of the brain. Thus, the left hemisphere controls the right hand and the right hemisphere the left. Likewise, the right ear is directly connected with the left brain, the seat of the major centers for processing language and for producing speech. So, if someone is right ear dominant, acoustic information goes to the left brain where it can be analyzed right away. However, if someone is left ear dominant, the acoustic information is first routed to the right hemisphere and then has to be transferred to the left hemisphere (via the *corpus callosum*) in order to be processed. This obviously constitutes a handicap, since the information takes a longer route before reaching its destination in the left brain.

All of us are well aware that any detour means more time spent on the road, not to mention the possibility of getting lost. That is unfortunately what happens when the left ear is the dominant one. The auditory information takes additional time to reach its goal and along the road some of the information is lost. Even more seriously, high pitch frequencies are the most likely to get lost along the detour. As you remember, high pitch frequencies are essential to discriminate closely related sounds like "P" or "B." Also, a left ear dominant person may never be completely able to make his point of view known as his right ear dominant counterpart is always a little faster in expressing his! Unfortunately, people may draw the erroneous conclusion that the left ear dominant person had nothing to contribute to the discussion, and may consequently not invite him another time, which is certainly unfair.

Timing differences may be a question of milliseconds but they still put the left-ear dominant person at a disadvantage. Computers have made us very aware of the importance of processing speed; that's why people always want to get the fastest computer. We cannot help contrasting the supposed slowness of our home computer, which we bought just a few years ago, with the speed of the brand new one we have at the office. The right ear dominant person is like the office computer: fast, "getting it," responding in a split second to any command. The left-ear dominant person is more like the slower home computer. While we can replace an old computer, children and adults are irreplaceable. But we can upgrade them by making the right ear the dominant one, so that they can start to process input faster and better.

The Dominant Mouth

How is it possible to determine which ear is the leading one? The answer is paradoxical: look at whether the person is right or left mouthed. "How can someone have a right mouth?" one might protest. We all have two ears, two eyes, two arms, and two legs, but only one mouth." Of course, the mouth we do have has a right side and left side. When we talk, the corners of the mouth go slightly upward and toward the right or the left depending which ear is the lead ear. Using the terms, right or left mouth, describes the orientation of the mouth and indicates which ear controls it. Carefully observing people as they talk thus reveals their auditory laterality.

It takes some training to see which side of the mouth people use. While it is impolite and embarrassing to stare at someone continuously to figure this out, you could train yourself indirectly. Observe people talking in a group or on TV. Observe whether they usually tilt their head toward the right or the left side. Is the right or left hand corner of their mouth more likely to move upward? Do they prefer looking toward one side as they talk? Are ear and mouth likely to move preferentially toward one side? Look carefully at the two pictures below. The first one shows a person who is right ear dominant; the second shows another who is left ear dominant.

Figure 7: Right and left ear dominant person

When you observe people, do not jump to conclusions too quickly, rather look for patterns, knowing that when we are under stress or are upset, we tend to unconsciously use the left ear, and thus the "left mouth," to delay the moment when the information reaches our brain (remember, the left ear is slower).

To determine which mouth and consequently which ear is dominant, Tomatis recommended first asking about things that people love to do, because non-threatening questions put one at ease. Questions might be about a favorite hobby or pet, an upcoming trip or a visit to friends or relatives, but in any case, something that makes people relaxed and happy. Observe how the person tilts her head: is her right ear slightly above the left one or below it? After checking how the person tilts her head, look for the way the corners of the mouth move, to the right or the left, whether it is slightly up or downward. Is there a dominant trend toward one side or the other or is movement more random?

Pay attention to the voice as well: is the voice clear, the timbre good, with a variety of intonations that match the mood of the person and the topic under discussion? Or is the voice flat, hesitant or monotonous, and the face without expression? The first voice is likely to belong to a right-eared person, with the corners of the mouth tending toward the right. The second voice most likely belongs to a left-eared person, with the corners of the mouth turning toward the left and often downward.

Also consider the eyes as you observe. I have often noticed that left-eared children turn their eyes toward the left as they consider what words to use, as though these might appear in that visual field to help them express what is painfully difficult to say. One might almost get the impression that they are about to look over their shoulders in search of the words that escape them.

Finally, take the personality of the person into account: if she is levelheaded, she is probably right-ear dominant. If she tends to be fairly emotional in her reactions, the left ear is probably dominant.

Parents, teachers, therapists, or others might learn much from observations like the ones above. Children, who process sensory input very slowly, are overly reactive or too emotional would benefit from strategies taking their laterality into account. Doing so can probably prevent conflicts and arguments that make matters worse rather than solving them. When we understand that a child is not lazy but rather processes information slowly, we can stop being overly moralistic when she does not do too well in school.

We Speak with our Ears

In the Fifties, Tomatis did many experiments showing the impact of ear dominance on vocal quality. In one of his experiments, he asked a famous singer to sing into a microphone connected to a headset that allowed him to hear himself. As long as he could hear his voice equally in both ears, his voice was unchanged. Then, Tomatis cut the sound to the left ear, leaving the singer to hear his voice only through his right ear. The effect of controlling his voice with just his right ear was not very dramatic yet the voice became lighter, the sounds more precise. Things changed dramatically, however, as soon as Tomatis cut the sound to the right ear, so that the singer could only hear himself with the left. Under the control of the left ear, the voice lost its timbre, its sense of rhythm, and was suddenly out of tune. All the vocal qualities that had made the singer famous were gone. The change made him appear stiff and puppet-like. Tomatis repeated the experiment with actors and observed the same changes. Cutting the sound to the right ear, thus, inducing left ear dominance, slowed the rhythm of their speech and, in some people, caused them to stutter.

Tomatis' conclusion, that ear dominance determines vocal quality, received ample support from his experiments. Since the right ear has a shorter route to the language center in the left brain, more of the high frequencies arrived intact. Because the voice can only produce what the ear hears, there is more beauty and timbre in the right eared voice.

The second mechanism linking right ear dominance to vocal quality is a feedback loop between the ear and the larynx. This cybernetic loop allows the ear to continuously check the parameters of *vocal* production and make corrections if needed. The feedback loop connecting the right ear to the larynx is shorter and therefore faster than the feedback loop for the left ear. So the corrections can be made instantly, allowing the voice to maintain its flow. Control of the larynx by the left ear delays corrections, causing the voice to lose rhythm and flow.

The reason why the left feedback loop is slower than the right is due to the fact that the left branch of the recurrent nerve, connecting ear to larynx, is longer. Although the difference in length and thus the time delay is slight (roughly 25 milliseconds, about the time it takes to pronounce a syllable), it is enough to explain why left ear dominant people speak more slowly and control poorly their voice when singing.

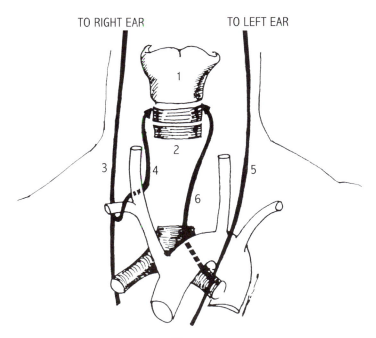

Figure 8: The two Recurrent Nerves[32] 1: Larynx, 2: Trachea, 3: Right vagus nerve, 4: Right recurrent nerve, 5: Left vagus nerve, 6 Left recurrent nerve

The nerve connecting both ear and the organs of speech is called the *recurrent laryngeal nerve* and is a side branch of the vagus nerve. The **right** recurrent laryngeal nerve goes fairly straight from the right vagus nerve to the right side of the larynx, passing under the subclavian artery. The **left** recurrent laryngeal nerve, on the other hand, takes a longer route due to the location of the heart, passing all the way under the aorta to reach the left side of the larynx, making this branch about 17 inches (50 centimeters) longer than the one on the right.

This results in two types of voices: "the right voice" that follows the right recurrent nerve and "the left voice" that follows the left recurrent nerve. Because of the length of the left feedback loop, the "left voice" favors the emission of low frequency sounds and inhibits the production of high frequency sounds. As a result the "left voice" contains mainly basses and does not have a good timbre. The opposite is true for people who have "right voices." Additionally they benefit from the power of charging their brain by stimulating it with the high frequencies contained in their voice.

Once the right ear assumes the leading role, the quality of the voice improves. This is even more obvious when a right ear dominant person is temporarily unable to control his voice with his right ear. One day, Maria Callas, the famous opera singer, walked into Tomatis' office complaining that she could not sing well because she could no longer control her voice with her right ear. Unable to zoom in on the sounds of her voice, she could not produce them accurately. That, in a nutshell, is the role of the right ear: a powerful monitor for the sounds we hear as well as those we produce.

The right ear does not develop this ability overnight. In babies, dominance has not yet been established. When a baby starts to vocalize in the crib, his voice reaches his left ear later than his right one, creating an echo. No wonder his first words are ma-ma and pa-pa. If the right ear works well, it begins, over time, to assume a leading role, as it is the first to hear the sounds. The right ear also starts to entrain the left feedback loop to work faster, so as to get rid of those annoying echoes. In the end, both ears should receive auditory information at the same time. This requires the fibers of the left recurrent nerve (the longer one) to work faster than those of the right recurrent nerve, allowing the two cords of the larynx to work in sync. Tomatis argued that this is possible because the fibers of the recurrent nerve seem to work at variable speeds. Just as the speed of the left recurrent nerve adapts itself to the timing of the right, the left ear entrains with the right, increasing the focus of the latter.

Shifting Sides

The number of learning disabled children and adults suggests that acquiring right ear dominance and the perfect zoom can be difficult. Would, for example, a child who is left-eared, left-handed, left-footed and left-eyed be at a great disadvantage compared to his right-oriented counterpart? This is far from certain: if his laterality is clearly established on the left, then the mechanisms of learning can build on a stable foundation.

More problematic for a child is being right-handed, right-footed, and still left-eared. This type of mixed lateral dominance is commonly observed in learning disabled children. We see it as well as in those who have severe language delays, are non-verbal or have autism.

In such cases, the task at hand is to develop right ear dominance. Tomatis achieved this goal by gradually shifting more and more of the sound to the right ear. Teaching his patients to start listening to their voices with the right ear began with reading aloud into a microphone connected to an Electronic Ear. This system is set up so that the voice comes almost exclusively back to the right ear. It is also enriched in the higher frequency band.

Audio-vocal exercises, as Tomatis called this activity, reinforce the
right ear → left brain → larynx → right ear
feedback loop, the shorter one as we know by now. The exercises over a period of time establish gradually a better audio-vocal control under the lead of the right ear.

Sometimes shifting from the left to the right ear seems to make switching from left to right-handedness easier. At times this is the right thing to do; on other occasions it is not. It all depends on the circumstances. When kids become left-handed because right-handed development was disturbed either at birth or during the first years of their lives, shifting to the right hand is like returning to the initial program, and might be advisable.

Guy Baleydier, a French speech therapist who worked with the Tomatis Method, reported some interesting examples of this shift.[33] At the point in the program when left-handed children started to do the vocal exercises described above, he asked them to write something using their right hand. If they refused, he did not insist since it would have been therapeutically ill advised and would only have increased resistance. Yet many of these children intermittently used their right hands without being aware of it. Mr. Baleydier took advantage of this natural ability and gave the children the choice of learning to write using both hands. If they agreed, he had them draw something simple at first, then more complex things, then letters, and so forth, promoting the use of the right hand. Some of these children shifted hands naturally without the trauma experienced by so many left-handers not so long ago when parents and teachers insisted on the switch.

Six months later, during a follow-up visit, Mr. Baleydier checked which hand they were using when writing. Most were now using their right hand. Mr. Baleydier asked them to write with their "new" hand the first verses of the last poem they had just learned in school (memorizing and reciting poetry are part of the French curriculum).

When the child finished, Mr. Baleydier asked them if they still remembered how to write with their "old" hand. For most, this was not really a problem. He asked them to write the same verse as before but now with their left hand. The results were quite telling: the text written with the left hand contained more spelling mistakes than the one written with the right hand. Even more surprising was the fact that the text written with the left hand usually showed the same types of spelling mistakes that were made when they were left-handed. This difference is all the more baffling since the time lag between the two writing samples was merely minutes.

An important observation is that each type of sidedness involves a different linguistic dynamic. Right ear dominance confers an advantage, left ear dominance a limitation. Lateralized right ear dominance promotes the mastery of language. When lateralization is not established, language problems develop quickly. Additionally, the lack of lateralization prevents the formation of a strong body image that supports the self.

THE BODY IMAGE

It is through our bodies that we play the little music that makes our lives so distinctive. "The human body is the instrument of language and the human language is the sound that makes it resound," wrote Tomatis in *The Ear and the Language.*[34] Yet it takes many years to prepare and train our bodies to become instruments of language. It begins as we rise to our feet, ascend to a vertical position and adopt the listening posture, which together transform us into an antenna for emitting and receiving messages. In addition, a subtle but decisive transformation takes place almost unnoticed: the gradual implementation of the lateralization process that not only affects the choice of a dominant hand or ear, but also orchestrates our progressive mastery of language. These various transformations shape a growing sense of identity on which the "sense of self" is established. We then become aware of our own whole being, instead of being only aware of different body parts as they are excited by various sensations. Still, consciousness would not emerge from the myriad of bodily sensations without the orderly progression described above.

The first primitive mental perception of the body as a separate entity probably starts at the skin level. From the day of our birth, we are bathed in an endless sea of vibrations: those that we produce when we cry, babble, laugh or scream and those that surround us. All these vibrations strike our skin, making us aware of the external limits of our bodies. Meanwhile, the vibrations of our voices, resonating along our spines and through our arms and legs, torsos and skulls, indeed, through our whole skeleton, delineate another border, this one from the inside out. Our skin is the frontier between inside and out, the body and the rest of the world.

A mother's touch and the feel of her skin against ours, augments our first impressions. Her voice enfolds us, echoing her caresses on our skin, helping us develop our emerging sense of self. The voices of our mothers are of course not neutral: they carry a whole range of emotions that resound deeply within and contributes to our own process of humanization. Even before we can raise our heads to look at our bodies, we have representations of them through the vibrations we receive and perceive through touch and sound. This tactile and sonic envelope, whose content is yet unknown, is enough to start the perceptions of a body scheme, leading to a sense of self.

Body scheme and body image are two different but related concepts. The *body scheme* is the awareness of our body and its parts. It is the basic awareness you get when vestibular and visual integrators work well together. In other words, the body scheme tells you that you have a head, two legs, two arms, a chest, fingers, toes, etc… and that you know where they are in space. Your body scheme and mine are alike because we belong to the same species. Yet, if we were limited to this body scheme, life would be about as joyful as watching X-rays of various anatomical parts at a radiology clinic. Fortunately bones and body parts don't fully describe us.

Thanks to our uniquely human capacity, a whole range of emotions soon vitalizes the body scheme. The *body image* that results is a mental representation of the body that transcends our physical boundaries. This is a psychological representation of ourselves, resulting from our history and molded by our relationship to others and society. Because it is as much an internal as an external process, it is unique to each one of us. This representation is changeable and can be perfected through a variety of techniques, in support of our goals and aspirations. As this image takes shape, we become an instrument for communication.

A violinist I worked with summed it up very well. Once he realized that his violin had become fully integrated into his body image, he said to me: "I don't have to think about the bow or my fingers anymore. I just focus on the sound and it leads my movements effortlessly. I can go deeper into the music and communicate with the public more deeply than ever."

What is true for the musician is true for the dyslexic child when he starts to develop a stronger body image: he evolves, becoming a child who can now make sense of his environment and interact more effectively with it. A strong body image, capable of efficient interaction between the self and the world is so essential that religious traditions emphasize it, although they usually advocate ascetic practice as a means of achieving it. They obviously have more lofty spiritual goals in mind. For now, it is sufficient to say that a good body image is the condition for a fruitful and harmonious dialogue, without distortion or false representation, between the self and its environment.

The development of a good body image can be disrupted by a weak body scheme. Autistic children, for instance, have a poor body image because they lack body awareness. Nor are they aware of their relationship to their environment: they bump into things even after noticing them. To the casual observer, they appear as if they were out of their bodies. Often, they lack the conceptual foundation that would allow them to give shape to their body which they drag with them, so to speak, as if it were a mere appendage. Without having the language needed to label their experience, express their feelings and talk about their body, body perception stays weak, resulting in a poor body image.

I have often been struck by the reaction of autistic children when asked to do seemingly simple audio-vocal exercises. Typically, they first become very agitated and refuse to talk into the microphone. Hearing their own voices via the right ear seems to precipitate a state of panic. Listening to their own voice (or, for that matter, any voice) via the headphone scares them, almost as though it penetrates their insulation and threatens their being with dissolution. Observing their reaction of panic strongly suggests that their voices are not clearly perceived as being theirs, but rather as the voice of a stranger intruding on their autistic world. Their voices are not wholly integrated in their body scheme or body image. Keeping a determined silence is probably the only way of reconstituting a distinct boundary between inside and outside and, thus, maintaining a fragile sense of self. It usually takes many attempts and some failure before they can accept that voice as theirs, letting it inhabit them and becoming part of their body. When the initial avoidance wanes, they usually take to the microphone with increasing pleasure, sometimes becoming little chatterboxes, spouting words that no one dreamed they knew.

One of these autistic children—a fairly high functioning one—made me realize that speech contributes to the representation of the body scheme. The resonance of the voice through bone conduction may be essential in establishing this. As usual, I had asked that child to do some vocal exercises. Though it was not the first time, he was still quite hesitant. I sat with him and we listened through the same Electronic Ear, so I could monitor his voice as he repeated words recorded on a tape. He and I wore the same type of headphone and vibrator, so I heard and felt his voice the same way he did.

At first, he dutifully repeated the words but soon appeared to warm up to the exercise, speeding up his response so he could repeat the same word two or three times within the allotted time. His voice grew bolder, sending stronger and stronger vibrations to the transducers on our heads. His body leaned ever closer to the microphone, his mouth kissing it, the words becoming louder and louder. Suddenly, his lips parted and, before I knew it, he had the big mike in his mouth, repeating words with great enthusiasm. He would not let it go. I hurriedly took off my headphones because I could not stand the intensity of the vibrations on top of my head. It felt like the electrical charges I had experienced as a child while trying to creep under an electric fence.

The child seemed blissfully unaware of the unbearable intensity of the vibrations: indeed, he loved it and could not get enough of it. He could have gone on and on, totally oblivious of his surroundings. At that moment, he was no longer out of his body. Instead, he discovered that using his voice created a vibrational connection between the outside and inside of his body. For the first time he realized his body was an instrument that could be controlled, and that speech made it play. In fact, the more he played with it, the more he perceived his body and the better he became at expressing himself. He soon forgot all about repeating words and launched into a long, meandering story with no end in sight. He was not only integrating his body scheme but, with obvious pleasure, was breathing life into it, strengthening his body image and ultimately his sense of self. Mastering his body-instrument made a fuller expression of his humanity possible.

The story of this autistic boy also illustrates a more general point. Typically, children who are non-verbal or have severe speech problems have poor lateralization and an insufficient body image. This concurrence confirms the proposition that speech and lateralization help shape our body image. The boy's awakening began when we trained him for right ear dominance. In this context, we may look at lateralization as an organizing process that leads to a better use of language. In fact, listening with the right ear seems to organize all the mechanisms of speech while shaping a more definite body image. Increasing control over body and speech puts us in charge of our lives, allowing us to interact with our environment in a harmonious way. In short, we are coming into our own.

Because we are so immersed in a "bath of language" to quote Tomatis, we constantly react to vibrations made by others in ways that alter our body image. When I work with depressed people, for example, I often notice that I start to slump in my chair and my voice becomes somewhat lower and slower, suggesting that I unconsciously mirror the posture and voices of my clients. Without a doubt, the way they see themselves influences me.

Tomatis illustrated this point very well with a story in *Écouter l'Univers*.[35] Once, when teaching at the University of Potchefstroom in South Africa, he examined a sixteen-year old boy who was extremely bright but who stuttered terribly. This young man could not talk without sudden jerky movements. Several professionals and a translator were present during the interview. They soon found themselves imitating the young man's jerky movements. So compelling was his body image, so contagious his movements, that it spread to everyone around him without their awareness of imitating him. Worse yet, the translator began to stutter!

We do not have to experience such extremes to know that others affect us. We use many words and expressions that describe quite well how sounds mold and sculpt the image of our bodies: a word will go straight to our heart, another will send a shiver all the way down our spine, and just an intonation is sometimes enough to give us goose bumps. A person who emits "bad vibrations" may jeopardize our sense of self. Under his influence, our shoulders may hunch over, our breath may become labored, and we may loose the verticality that centers us; sometimes, it may even diminish our voices, causing us to drop a few notes and become hesitant. On the other hand, there are people who have "good vibrations." Such people inspire us and, under their influence, we straighten our posture to vibrate on the same wavelength, causing our voices to become fuller and more articulate. Then, two perfectly aligned human antennae dialogue with one another in complete harmony. At that moment, we feel magnificently well withing ourselves. There is no gap between our body and body image. We have finally achieved a flawless listening posture.

Summary

To summarize our progress to this point, I will briefly note the different elements that contribute to the development of the human antenna. They are:

- The ability to stand completely upright;
- The addition of the cochlea to the vestibule;
- The increased ability to analyze sounds;
- The freeing and reshaping of the mouth organs to accommodate speech;
- The link between ear and voice;
- The lateralization process that facilitates speech;
- The transformation of the body into an instrument that can speak and sing.

These elements are the basic building blocks of the human antenna, designed to receive and send messages.

This development follows a long evolutionary process. There is an immense passage of time between the moment when a fish moved from water to land and the moment when we started to walk the earth and talk with other human beings. We may wonder whether this evolutionary process will continue and what the next stage will be. As we have seen, all of us echo this evolutionary process during prenatal and infant development. Some of us have been more successful at it than others, but we can all progress further if we exploit and refine our listening potential. Fulfilling our evolutionary potential requires that we continue to learn. However, as we have seen, glitches in the functioning of the human antenna preclude learning under ideal conditions. That is why it is important to look a bit more closely at some of the glitches, often reflected as learning disabilities, which affect a fairly large segment of the population. It is, in fact, difficult to experience wellness while struggling with a disability day after day. The key to overcoming this sort of handicap is to learn to listen more effectively.

Part III

The Learning Ear

Daily life at the Mozart Center

PRELIMINARIES

We have already touched on several of the reasons why auditory processing difficulties impair our ability to learn. In the preceding chapters we discussed the mechanics of listening. It is now time to illustrate how these elements come together and play a role in some of the learning difficulties children and adults face. To that end, we will examine how our ears are involved in Autism as well as in both Attention Deficit Disorders and Dyslexia. Autism represents certainly the greatest challenge compared with the other ones. It makes it very difficult for autistic children to learn and progress at a normal pace. Some of the characteristics of autism, though, are not too different from some of the characteristics observed in more benign cases: they are only more extreme. Considering first autism can provide us with valuable insights to understand better the common learning difficulties. Finally, in the closing pages of this chapter, we will look at the challenge posed by the study of foreign languages, in which our ears also play a fundamental role. Indeed, many who are not dyslexics in their own language feel somewhat or even totally dyslexic when confronted with the task of mastering foreign idioms. Like dyslexics, they feel that they do not have a gift for language. It is a gift, though that better ears allow us to open.

Being able to learn contributes enormously to our wellbeing. Strangely enough, wellness and learning are not often thought of as complementary. Learning is generally considered a category apart, reserved for teachers, university professors and the vast number of learning specialists trying to resolve irritating mysteries often lumped together as learning disabilities. Yet, children or adults who deal with one of these disabilities know all too well the price they pay on a daily basis, psychologically, emotionally and physically. All aspects of their lives at home, school or work are sadly colored, often making them believe that they are lazy, weird, stupid or incompetent. It affects their relationships, their vision of the future and their chance to succeed in an increasingly competitive society. Those with learning disabilities are not few in number but rather millions who go through life feeling ashamed of themselves, simply because they cannot learn easily.

Learning difficulties of children are usually diagnosed by the second or third grade and, if not properly treated, keep influencing their lives into their adult years. Yet, these people are as bright as anyone and are, in fact, often intelligent, hard working and may become very successful. Those who succeed need little reassurance; they set a glowing example of courage and perseverance for those whose efforts are less fruitful.

As for the autistic children, the search for strategies that improve their chances to learn and, thus, their condition, is imperative. Here again, the Tomatis Method suggests that improving listening allows significant gains.

AUTISM

Autism is a developmental disorder usually diagnosed during the first three years of life. It is characterized by impairment in social interactions, as well as in verbal and non-verbal communication. Theories about its origin are various and conflicting. It occurs in approximately 15 out every 10,000 births. It is four times more likely to show up in boys than in girls and it has been found throughout the world in all racial, ethnic and social backgrounds. The number of children diagnosed with autism continues to climb. So far, there is no cure in view.

Autism comes in many forms. There is little similarity between a low-functioning autistic child who has many sensory integration problems and no language, and a high functioning child who displays a social aloofness and awkwardness but functions well in other areas of life. Still, the difficulty in communicating and the problem of sensory integration are present in both cases, but to varying degrees.

Parents whose children are diagnosed with autism experience a terrible tragedy. Their sense of loss is intense, even though they try to mask it to others. Their commitment to the care of their child is often exemplary and they should be commended for it, as unsung heroes who never make it to the limelight. Because diagnoses are made early and early intervention is the best strategy, they are often caught in an endless cycle of therapies. Needless to say, the pursuit of a cure puts stress on the family and on its financial resources.

The autistic child too is put under stress because he needs to learn skills necessary for normal development, but he has little skills to do so in the first place. If we remember how difficult it is for non-autistic children to learn the most basic skills such as walking, acquiring speech, communicating or writing, then we may come to realize the daunting challenge facing autistic children. No wonder that there is no quick fix and that it takes sometimes years of therapies and hard work to bring about long-lasting changes. So, autism is a developmental and communication disorder but it is also a learning disorder.

To communicate and learn better, the autistic child needs first of all to learn to listen well. Listening, as we know it now, implies more than just pricking up the ears toward a sound source, but it involves the whole body in an effort to reach out and communicate with the outside world and the inner world. It also implies desire, which is often lacking in autistic children. That is why Tomatis believes that autism is also a listening problem.

In his book on opera-singing, *The Ear and the Voice*, Tomatis explains in details how singers must be able to control their bodies all the way down to the smallest proprioceptive sensation, to produce a sound of perfect quality. The same applies to all of us as we grow up: we need to learn to play our body as if it were an *instrument* to ultimately produce language. Unfortunately, autistic children often cannot do so.

Tuning up the body

Many autistic children suffer from sensory integration problems. Consequently, their brain is unable to organize sensory information in a satisfactory way to achieve optimal performance. Part of what they see, hear or feel does not make sense to them. This lack of sensory integration interferes with their ability to learn or to behave appropriately. Since sensory integration is the foundation for many skills necessary to function well, it makes sense to start with a good tune up of the sensory functions. Without it, the body is unable to play as an instrument.

The Learning Ear

In a previous chapter, I have already described some of the consequences of a faulty vestibular integrator, such as poor muscle tone, poor sense of balance, lack of coordination between the two sides of the body, lack of coordination between the eyes and the body and difficulties in motor planning. Additionally, when the vestibule is not positioned correctly, the cochlea is also not positioned for optimal sound analysis. As a result, those children are slow in processing auditory information and slow when they talk. If we remember Tomatis' word that "when man speaks, he speaks with his entire body," we can see the benefit of treating vestibular disorders first, because it improves significantly sensory integration and prepares the ground for mastering language.

Autistic children often suffer from sound hypersensitivity. The result is auditory defensiveness. From Tomatis' perspective, the reason for sound hypersensitivity is to be found in the way hypersensitive kids perceive sounds: they primarily listen with their body (skin, bones) rather than with their ears. If many autistic people feel continuously assaulted with sounds, it is because they listen *predominantly with their bodies, that is, through bone conduction*. Indeed, they do not have the ability to *filter out* background noise and *tune in* to what matters. This experience, as we will see, is not unique to autistic children, but their sensory response to sound is more extreme and, thus, their hypersensitivity is higher. As a result, those children may burst into huge temper tantrums, due to the frustration of having to deal with a constant flow of incoming sounds. If they scream, they might just be trying to mask the sounds that hurt so much. Repeating the same words, phrases or sentences might be another way to soothe themselves against the onslaught of sounds bombarding them.

Hypersensitivity may explain too the unusual ability of some autistic children to perceive sounds beyond the usual auditory range of most people. I still remember a mother wondering how her 10-year old son could hear a plane flying high in the sky, when they were having lunch with all the windows closed and the television on. And still, when they went out to check, the plane was there, a minuscule speck in the blue sky. In an article published in 1991 by *The Journal of Autism and Developmental Disorders*, Albert a 13 year-old boy reports that he could hear a train approximately 5 to 10 minutes before it passes near his home. "I can always hear it, mommy and daddy can't, *it felt noisy in my ears and body*" [Italics are mine]. Like other autistic children, Albert seems to have what the authors of the article, Laura Cesaroni and Malcom Garber, call "reliable premonitions of powerful auditory stimulation." This clearly shows that the auditory system is able to send out a warning signal to prepare the child to the incoming sound while blocking as much as possible that overwhelming stimulus. It is that ability of the ear to filter out overpowering auditory information that needs to be restored to convince the autistic child to listen better. As long as she is hypersensitive to sounds, she has no desire to listen, because listening means pain. Reducing hypersensitivity increases the desire to listen and, thus, supports the desire to connect with the social world—a desire that autistic children sorely lack.

Tactile defensiveness is also another sensory integration problem observed among children in the autistic spectrum. It may also be linked to sound perception. As we have seen earlier, a simple touch of the skin receptors, according to Tomatis, is enough to make the muscles of the hammer and stirrup react as if they were responding to a sound. But, in that case, the touch may hurt or be too much, driving the autistic child to resist touch.

Finally, sensory integration might be hard to achieve when there is confusion between sensory channels—a frequent disorder among autistic children and children with severe developmental delays. In the same article quoted above, Jim, a 27-year-old autistic man reports that "auditory stimuli interferes with other sensory processes, I have caught myself turning off the car radio to read a road sign, or turning off the kitchen appliances so that I could taste something." Jim reports that sounds are often accompanied by vague sensation of colors, shape, texture, movement, scent, or flavor. It is, concluded the authors, as if information was received in several modes though the signal comes from one source." Such confusion is no doubt very detrimental to any form of learning or to any normal functioning.

As long as sensory integration problems persist, it is difficult for the autistic child to progress. A good functioning of the sensory functions of the body is a prerequisite for further development. Tomatis remarked to me once that "while the vestibule may work well—for instance, some autistic children show a great sense of balance—the peripheral functions of that system do not." Trying to improve those functions is the first and necessary step leading to a lessening of the autistic symptoms.

First Results

Each autistic child is different and responds differently to the Tomatis Program. Not surprisingly, the first changes take place in the area of sensory integration. In some cases we see the first results within a few weeks whereas in others it may take longer. Progress is never a straight line. There are still bad days and good days. To make a fair assessment of the changes, it is best to look back over a period of a few months.

Those changes result from training the ear to respond better to auditory stimulation. One of the goals is to reduce the response of the body and to make sure that the ears become the main entrance to sounds. In others words, the goal of therapy is to reduce the hypersensitivity of the bone conduction response and to improve the performance of the air conduction response, so that the ears can filter out irrelevant information and dampen its impact when necessary. The Electronic Ear, the electronic device developed by Tomatis allows working directly on both the air- and the conduction responses. Here is the way it works: the child listens to "gated music" through headphones while playing or resting. "Gated music" refers to the fact that the music switches continuously between two channels: the first one emphasizes low frequencies sounds, the second high frequencies sounds. This gating mechanism trains the muscles of the middle ear to work harder, so that the ear functions better, that is, perceives the sounds of the entire audible spectrum more accurately. Additionally, a vibrator is located on the top of the headphones and touches the skull. It sends the vibrations of the music through the skull and, from there, to the bones of the body. In doing so, it progressively decreases the response of the bone conduction in relation to the air conduction response. The sound reaches the vibrator before reaching the ear. That delay is called "precession" and can vary in length. Since autistic children have a longer time response to sound than other children, the precession at the beginning of the treatment is very long and is progressively reduced to force the ear to process the information faster and faster. It is an efficient, gentle and non-intrusive way to begin to alleviate some of the problems that characterized autism. The great advantage of it is that it works simultaneously at improving vestibular functioning, sensory integration and auditory perception.

Usually, symptoms of vestibular dysfunction are the first to decrease. Muscle tone and sense of balance get better, coordination and motor planning improve, and posture becomes more erect. Overall, children appear more alert and more aware of their surroundings. They also seem more secure and more willing to try new tasks. As for sound hypersensitivity, it is also their behavior that indicates a lessening of that problem. As one mother observed once: "He can now hear the vacuum cleaner or mixer without losing it." Being less fearful of the sounds in his immediate environment, the child starts to feel less threatened and may appear more willing to connect with what happens around him. Consequently, there might be less temper tantrums and less repetitive behavior to mask any potentially hurtful sound or noise.

As autistic children also become less tactile defensive, their desire to reach out increases and they often become more affectionate. For example, a child may come and sit on her mother's lap without being prompted, expecting clearly to be held and cuddled. Often, too, those who are picky eaters may start to accept a greater variety of foods, including foods with different textures.

For those who make little eye contacts, they may start progressively to look people in the face or take some interest in what is going on around them. "When we are driving," a mother said, "he now looks out of the window. He never did it before."

All those signs of changes show a progressive awareness of other people and of the world at large. A better functioning of the vestibular system leads also to a better awareness of the body and strengthens the body image, out of which the self emerges. Overall, the child is better prepared to listen: a prerequisite for further progress.

THE MOTHER'S VOICE AND THE DESIRE TO COMMUNICATE AND SPEAK

Listening rests on the strong desire to use one's ears to pay attention. The autistic child does not seem to have such a strong desire. He may hear without listening. As we have seen, hearing and listening are two different processes, one is passive, and the other one is active. For instance, when we are absorbed in the world of our thoughts, we have no desire to listen to the music on the radio and tune it out. This small "autistic" experience is generalized in autistic children. It is not the "tuning out" that is exceptional but the "tuning in." Restoring the desire to "tune in," to listen, is the key to restoring communication with the external world and with the self. This, of course, is made easier when the body works as an instrument that has first received a good tune up, so that it processes information more efficiently.

The desire to listen and communicate goes hand in hand with the desire to speak. The desire to use the voice is not different from the desire to use the ear: both are connected at the physiological level. The ear-brain-larynx link is essential in producing language, but it can only be put to work if the desire to communicate exists. So, by creating the desire to listen, we also lay the groundwork for using expressive language.

Finding how to awaken this desire was Tomatis' first priority. In his search for a solution, he came upon a very simple idea: to use the mother's voice. As we will discover further on, the fetus can hear his mother's voice and react to it. Tomatis hypothesized that this might be the first attempt to dialogue, the first step in the listening process. In doing so, the fetus experiences his first emotional bond, a blueprint for others bonds at a later stage of development. Tomatis thought that using the mother's voice as a therapeutic tool might improve the desire to listen. And because that desire may have been lost at any age, he thought best to start all over, that is, at the moment when the child is still in the womb. Doing so, the child might be able to replicate the different phases of the listening process.

Trying to reproduce the mother's voice as it sounds in the womb presented Tomatis with some technical difficulties. Since Tomatis believed that the fetus could only hear the high frequencies, he used a filter to remove the low frequencies sounds of the voice. As such the voice does not sound as it sounds in reality: nevertheless, some children are able to identify it as their mom's voice. When the mother's voice is not available, a recording of filtered music of Mozart is used, since his music is the one that gives the best results.

The outcome was amazingly encouraging: children, who had shown little affection, if any, were suddenly affectionate with their mother and developed a stronger bond with her. That attempt to socialize is extremely important. It serves as a blueprint for establishing relationships with others once the child has established a secure base with the mother. His autistic isolation can finally start to break down.

Tomatis' idea of using the filtered mother's voice for therapeutic purpose was certainly original, especially at a time when the scientific community thought that the fetus could not hear. It turned out to be also one of his most controversial ideas. Some perceived it as an attempt of blaming the mother for the autism of the child, which was not the case. To make things worse, when *The Conscious Ear,* Tomatis' autobiography, was published in 1991 in the United States, one of the translators replaced the word "schizophrenic" by the word "autistic." That error had wide consequences, since it occurred in a passage where Tomatis was describing the behavior of the mother of a schizophrenic young man. In the translation, it appeared as if he was describing the behavior of the mother of an autistic young man. In a short time, the idea that Tomatis was blaming the mother for the autism of her child spread in the public and among professionals. When I discovered the mistake in the spring of 1993, I alerted Tomatis. He was outraged by the mistake that attributed to him a view that did not represent his thinking on autism. Unfortunately, there was little he could do, especially at a time when his health was failing. In a letter, dated June 17, 1993, and sent to Tomatis practitioners in the United States, he clearly stated that "the mother has nothing to do with the autism of her child."

As far as I know, Tomatis has never fully presented his view on autism, even though he wrote eleven books and countless articles over a fifty-year long career. Autism was a puzzle for him as it is for most people. Although his ideas may have appeared controversial when he put them forward, he was sure of one thing: the mother's voice could greatly help the autistic child awake from his autism. The results supported his belief.

Tomatis not only believed that the mother's voice was an emotional nutrient for the child during pregnancy and after birth, but that it also prepared him to develop the ability to talk. We know that the ears of the fetus are already functional when he is five months old. In a later part of the book, we will see how the intonation, the rhythm, the timber, the inflexions of the mother's voice, may set the stage for acquiring the "mother's tongue." There is no doubt that the fetus—no pun intended—follows a full immersion course to learn a new language. For instance, he reacts five times more to a sound at 2,000 Hz than he does to a sound at 500 Hz. This is significant because the human ear is especially receptive to sounds between 1,000 Hz and 2,000 Hz, where many of the language frequencies are located—Tomatis calls it the language/communication zone. The logical conclusion is that the fetus has already a keen ear for the sounds of language. By hearing them over and over in the womb, he is quietly preparing himself to produce them later on. It is a long and passive phase but a necessary one before he can start practicing. For that reason, the therapy designed by Tomatis is made up of two parts: one, called the passive phase; the other, the active phase. The first one is dedicated to tune up the ear and the body, so it becomes an instrument with which one can play optimally, the second is dedicated to learning to play, that is, to use language to make that instrument resound. It is clear that the autistic child is deficient in both and has to learn to do both.

The transition from the passive phase to the active phase is not always easy. I have described in the previous chapter how autistic children might experience a state of panic when they listen to their own voice being fed back to their right ear, because of the perceived intrusion of the voice in their inner world—a voice that they do not identify as their own. It is only when they accept the voice as being their own that they can gain a progressive mastery of the language. It is important to underline the role of the physical vibrations of the voice in shaping the body image and strengthening it. The more they use their voice, the more they learn to use their body as an instrument. This, in turn, reinforces the desire to use the voice, creating a dynamic that is not different from the one observed in babies who vocalize, listen to the sounds they produce, adjust them to match the sounds of the language spoken around them, in an on-going fine-tuning that leads to mastering speech. It is that dynamic that the active phase of the Tomatis Method tries to recreate in order to support the autistic child as he attempts gradually to gain control over his voice and, later on, over speech.

I believe that it is the active phase that makes the Tomatis Method very different from other methods of auditory stimulation. We know very well that we are not going to sing well if we do not practice. The same is true for speech. It is through practice that we can master the feedback loop between the ear, the brain and the larynx. If the Tomatis Method had only a purely passive component, it would not achieve the goal of establishing an audio-vocal control that allows speech to flow with ease. While some of the compact disks sold on the market can be quite enjoyable to listen to, they only engage our passivity—and that may be why some of them are very popular. Bringing about permanent change requires more than just being passive. We need to be an active agent of that change. That is true for the autistic child, or for the teenager suffering from a learning difficulty. And here again, we encounter the essential difference between hearing and listening. Most methods address hearing only, while the Tomatis Method, being more comprehensive, addresses both hearing and listening.

The Course of Therapy

The course of therapy is never straight. Autistic children are not different from other children: they react at their own pace, according to the severity of their condition and to their own personality. Tomatis himself used to say that a case that appears easy at first may turn out to be quite difficult. He wanted to underline by this the unpredictability of the pace of any therapy—his own brand included. As can be expected, progress comes in small steps, especially when the sensory systems do not work properly. That is why it is best for parents to consider the progress over a period of a month or two rather than on a daily basis. It takes time for the nervous system and the brain to integrate, reorganize and digest such intense auditory stimulation, and to implement cognitive and behavior changes. In fact, parents who cannot wait to see the result should remember how much energy and time it takes them to change in themselves a habit or a behavior. Even more so for the autistic child, who starts with such heavy handicaps and developmental delays!

Some of the reactions of the child may distress the parents. Their concerns are quite legitimate, especially if the child manifests some unusual behavior, wants to follow more strongly his usual routines than before or tests the limits imposed on him. Some parents may feel that their child is "regressing" instead of improving. I rather prefer to call that period a period of transition. Indeed, transitions are difficult for anyone, including autistic children. As the result of the auditory stimulation, they may start to feel that their known world is slowly falling apart. They try to resist the pull to change by sticking even more to their old ways or by bursting out in temper tantrums. This is usually a *temporary phase*, often a preliminary one to real improvement, but it can tax the patience and the strength of the parents. Still, it is a natural phase: in times of change, we feel insecure, anxious, confused, or even disorganized. It is as true for the autistic child as it is for his parents. Those parents should feel comfortable to talk about their concerns with the child's therapist. Tomatis would routinely propose to parents a free program of auditory stimulation to help them to relax and feel more energetic in order to help them to go through this phase of transition. In fact, when the child changes, it is the whole family system that changes.

Signs of improvements show little by little. Often, parents report that their children develop a stronger presence. They comment: "he is more together;" "she is more tuned in." "She pays more attention:" "he makes more eye contacts;" "she looks people in the face now." However small the changes at first, the trend is often upward, especially when parents look back over a period of a few weeks or months. Autistic children also seem less hypersensitive to sounds and more willing to be touched as sensory integration improves. It is also during that period that they become more emotionally expressive and more demanding. It is their way of expressing feelings as they come out of their autistic shell and it should be accepted as such: a little step in the right direction. As we have seen, they may show spontaneously more affection. At this stage, it is important for parents not to try to elicit such expressions of affection, because the autistic child is only able to express those sporadically at first. It is better to let him get closer than trying to have him show affection on demand, which he may feel like a scary intrusion into his own world. He has his own time-table, and it should be respected. Affectionate behavior will increase as he becomes more tuned in to the people around him.

Autistic children who are afraid of transitions and stick to a very rigid set of rules and behaviors may start to alter those progressively and show more flexibility. Hand flapping, repetitive body movements and self-destructive behaviors decrease also. Finally, language may develop in different ways. Receptive language improves before expressive language. For autistic children without language, vocalization increases and may develop in a sort of babble: the first step in acquiring speech. For children who have language skills, parents notice that they speak more clearly, use longer sentences and more appropriate words. They may also become more personal, using correctly personal pronouns ("I," "You"). Receptive language improves too: "She looks me in the eyes when I talk to her. Her comprehension is much better." The teachers of the children involved in behavioral-based therapies often report that the children focus better and for longer periods of time. Their rate of success in doing drills or exercises is also increased. As their desire to communicate and their ability to do so expand, they handle social situations, including in the classroom, much better. Instead of isolating themselves, they may seek the attention of others and try to reach out. The periods of isolation diminish and the autistic shell slowly melts away.

Healing is not an easy process for the autistic child. It is a long and arduous path for him as well as for his parents whose strengths and resources are constantly put to the test. It is also a challenge for the therapist who wishes to bring about positives changes. The Tomatis method is certainly not a cure for autism and none of the professionals using it claim to perform miracles, but it can significantly improve the functioning of the autistic child.

Listening and the Therapeutic Process

There is still a therapeutic tool that is worth mentioning, because it plays an important role in the healing process. It is in fact at the heart of the Tomatis method: it is the role played by listening. While it is clear that the method can relieve many of the symptoms that affect autistic children, it is also a preparation to listen better, to practice deep listening. Many people think that the autistic child, being cut-off as he is from the external world, is unable to listen deeply to what goes on around him. It is a wrong idea and, maybe, a form of prejudice. I have witnessed in my office instances where autistic children were in a state of deep listening as if they were in a state of deep trance. I believe that in those moments healing was taking place. I do not imply that the child was cured of his autism afterwards, but he looked and acted differently: in short, he was more present or, like some parents put it "more together." In those moments, the child appeared to have fallen in a deep meditative state as if he were listening to an inner voice in the midst of the silence surrounding him. Words do not describe easily that state. The first time I observed it I had a sense that the child was surrounded by some kind of womb-like bubble vibrating with the energy of life itself. The child stayed very quiet, almost motionless, in a deep state of consciousness characterized by profound silence. It is not, though, the silence observed when two people stay quiet because they have nothing to say to each other. It is a silence filled with an enhanced awareness of who the child is—and it might be the first occurrence that he finally gets in touch with himself, which in itself is a huge step forward for an autistic child. At that moment, awareness fills his body image and he becomes fully human. I call those moments of transformation "the moments of silence," but, as I have said, words are inaccurate to describe this phenomenon that is nothing else than the birth of awareness in a child who cannot function properly because a limited consciousness of himself and of others.

Still, to the casual observer, that state of silence may appear once more as the usual withdrawal from the world so typical of the autistic child. I believe it is not. My own subjective experience is that the walls of the autistic shell are no longer hard and solid but have become porous, letting the world come slowly in. It is like seeing the clouds finally opening to let the sunshine in. Those, of course, are images that try to account for the experience of seeing the child entering a state of deep consciousness. He is so quiet—so unusually quiet—that the first time I observed that phenomenon, I felt that I had to intervene: surely something wrong was going on. In fact, it was not something wrong that was happening but something *new*—something I learned to recognize as an important step toward healing. If I had intervened at that moment, I would have broken the deep dialogue that the child was having silently with himself. I would not have *listened* to him, but *intruded upon his thoughts* and prevented the necessary reconnection with himself that is essential for healing. It is a very fine line to walk: our first reaction is to jump to the rescue of the child because his unusual state or behavior worries us, so that we feel that *we have to do something*. It is a normal and loving reaction, but it may be a mistake. There are times, like this one, when it is better *not to do anything* in order not to interrupt the healing process. The best that can be done is to listen deeply, quietly, with all your heart, to support the child as he goes, at his own pace, through his own process of recovery. It is not an easy task because we need to train ourselves to identify those "moments of silence" that I have tried to describe. It is worthwhile to learn to identify them, since they might give us an opening to communicate with the autistic child, as he slowly emerges from his condition. In so doing, we exercise the power of deep listening—a power that good therapists have learned to identify as a potent therapeutic tool and that parents can use too. We create a space where child and listener—be it a parent or a therapist—can finally meet face to face and see each other the way they are without fear. That moment of truth is what parents have been waiting for: the moment when they do not have to look at their child as an autistic child. All the therapies and the progress made along the way have prepared the ground for that moment of recognition, but it would not occur without deep listening.

A LOOK AT DYSLEXIA

Dyslexia affects millions of Americans, both children and adults. Many adults are ashamed to admit that they are slow readers and prefer avoiding reading altogether. Their inability to read may well impair their chances of living up to their intellectual potential and often limits their choice of careers. They are likely to take jobs that probably do not reflect their level of intelligence but require little if any reading. They may drop out of school or never finish college to avoid the humiliation of failing, just because their reading is not up to speed. They know all too well that their chances of succeeding are limited because "good jobs" are reserved for those who have adequate reading and writing skills. Many anxious parents foresee the worst when their child fails to read at a normal level. Children's inability to readily master the written word often becomes the forerunner of increasing social difficulties as they grow up. Dyslexia has often become a social stigma and it greatly impairs those who have to live with it day in and day out.

When I entered first grade, I could already read, write and add. It seemed quite natural to me: I had spent the four previous years in a preschool run by Catholic nuns who never asked themselves whether there was an appropriate age for learning to read. So they introduced the alphabet at a leisurely pace. No one labeled us as delayed if we didn't learn to read in three months, as may be required of today's first graders. It was first of all a game. I still can remember swaying from side to side while sounding out loud the mysterious alphabet whose letters, we were told, looked like a snake, a cane, a hat and, yes, a camel and dromedary (the camel, as everyone knows has two humps like the **M** and the dromedary only one like the **N**).

The association of movement and image with sound was powerful: it allowed me to learn with my whole body rather than with my intellect alone. The letters of the alphabet were not abstract concepts: they had faces, stories, and sounds that resonated in different parts of the body and elicited gestures. I quickly learned that behind the faces of the alphabet, there were other faces: the ones found in stories that take you to magic kingdoms to meet strangers who soon become your best friends and share with you dangerous and exciting adventures. Learning to read, then to write was a joyful experience, never a pain. I believe that mastering those skills was easy because it was presented as a game and that no one was going to rush me if I was not getting it right away.

I am sure that Sister Marie knew little if anything about the role of the vestibule and the cochlea in the process of reading. Instead, her method was intuitive. She probably ignored that the vestibule leads the eyes, controls the muscles of the lips and the jaws — indeed, all the muscles of our body — and imbues us with the sense of rhythm but she instinctively knew the tremendous value of involving our bodies in the learning process.

Perhaps, this is why great orators seem engaged in a dance: their words flowing in concert with their movements. They play with their body as it were an instrument that amplifies and carries their voice. A child with dyslexia, in comparison, appears clumsy and has a flat and hesitant voice. He has not learned to play his song with his body, since he has a poor perception of his body image. He is also usually poorly lateralized and uses his left-ear as the dominant one, losing the right-ear advantage. In short, his body is poorly attuned to process language quickly and smoothly.

Sister Marie made sure that we began with the most basic steps in processing sound. When our bodies were in tune with the sound, then, and only then, did we start to put sounds and letters together. And we practiced fine tuning the ear-eye-voice connection out loud for a long time.

Some parents may be mystified that a son or daughter who is very good in sports and has a great balance and coordination may still have dyslexia. Their appraisal is right regarding *gross* motor skills but often *fine* motor skills are not equally good. Such a child may easily catch a ball on the playing field but still have messy handwriting. When children use a balance board as part of their treatment, we often find that some of the accomplished but dyslexic athletes initially have trouble doing even the simplest exercise. For instance, while on the balance board trying to maintain their balance, they are unable to stretch their arms out from their bodies to catch a ball. Some throw it at shoulder height to keep it within their field of vision. If we ask them to catch the ball at the level of their belly button, they normally miss it, since they are unable to coordinate eyes and hands. Complaints that this is difficult are frequent. No wonder that learning to read does not come easily in the midst of these many challenges.

Reading is a complex process requiring that ears and eyes work together within a precise time frame. As the eyes see the letter, the ears register the corresponding sound. In other words, the vestibule leads the eye from letter to letter and the cochlea translates letters into sounds. Ideally, both operations should happen almost simultaneously. Although even in good readers there is a slight delay between them, it is so short that decoding is easy and reading is fluid. The trouble starts when the delay, also called *latency time*, is too long to allow for the synchronization of eyes and ears.

To make things even more complicated, each sound lasts a specific length of time. For instance, a pure vowel like "aaaahh" may stretch over 100 milliseconds (a tenth of a second). The initial "b" vibration in the sound "ba" lasts only about 40 milliseconds before switching to the "ah." On the other hand, the "m" in "ma" lasts 100 milliseconds or more before the "ah." Moreover, sounds link to other sounds and the transition from one to the next needs to be rapid. So, the ear has to constantly adjust to rapid changes. When it cannot process the sounds rapidly enough, sequences of sounds cannot be properly identified. This time lag impairs the synchronization between the eyes and ears, keeping the right sound from being put together with the right letter. Without the sound, the letter has no life and meaning cannot emerge. Dyslexia is often a frantic process of guessing, hoping for a miracle and taking a chance on finally uttering a sound in the hope that it will fit the letter of the alphabet stumbling across on the page.

No less important is the fact that each sound corresponds to a specific set of frequencies. Take Mary's struggles, for example: learning to read is difficult for her because she is unable to automatically and correctly analyze those differences in frequency. Still, the teacher expects her to link letters with sounds, lumping several together to yield syllables, words, and finally sentences which yield a specific meaning. She might be able to identify a single sound, but what happens if two sounds are almost identical? After all, there are no pure sounds in nature: all are complex, each one containing a fundamental tone and higher frequencies known as harmonics or overtones. It is key and critical for Mary to identify these overtones that resonate with fundamental tones throughout the sound spectrum. For example, the only difference between a V and an F is the type of overtones. However, Mary's selectivity is closed beyond 1,000 Hz, so her ear is unable to accurately discriminate between the overtones of V and F, leaving them sounding the same to her. Her difficulty learning to read can be traced to her inability to discriminate between two nearly identical sounds that lie beyond 1,000 Hz. Mary can certainly hear globally but the information she perceives lacks accuracy.

Because of these complexities, it is not surprising that dyslexia affects spelling. Sometimes, a child learns to compensate, and manages to read, but his troubles surface as soon as he has to spell words. He may write the difficult ones over and over to fix them in his memory. This strategy usually does not work because it leaves out the child's hearing, and he relies only on his eyes. When he has to write the word/sound, he is confused because the word and the sound are not integrated into one unit. He pauses, racks his brain to "see" the right spelling on an imaginary screen behind his eyes; the right word, mixed with hundreds of other words is stored in his memory but he ends up, more often than not, writing randomly or repeating earlier mistakes because of his lack of auditory accuracy.

I have often witnessed children trying to memorize a list of ten or twenty words for a spelling test. The words are not embedded in any kind of context and are mostly in the singular form. Dyslexic students may pass the test as long as they are asked to spell the words on the list. If the same word appears in the middle of a sentence, in a different sonic and visual environment, these children are unlikely to be able to read or spell them. Reading and spelling exercises would meet with more success if children were asked to sound out the words first to facilitate the integration of letters with sounds.

Here is a case in point. Benjamin is a wonderful kid who has severe dyslexia. One evening, I walked into the playroom and found him doing a spelling exercise. He was copying a list of ten words in a column. He simply had to fill the blank in front of each word written neatly by the teacher. Benjamin, I have to admit, is a real artist. His handwriting is beautiful. It is a welcome change from the frequently messy and often unreadable handwriting that I observe in general. Given some lessons, he could become a master in calligraphy. I congratulated Benjamin for doing such a neat job. He responded with a beaming smile. He was savoring the moment: he knew only too well that he rarely did such a good job when dealing with words. I then made the mistake of asking him to sound out the words he was writing so beautifully. His smile vanished, his body seemed to shrink, and he sat silently with hunched shoulders looking despondently at the first word on the list: FOG. His lips moved silently, emitted a whistling sound followed by a rumble that quickly died. Benjamin had not the foggiest idea no pun intended, that he was trying to make out the word: FOG.

Having long passed the learning phase of reading, parents and educators too often forget the process by which letters come to represent sounds. They respond only to the visual part and forget the importance of the auditory. Reading aloud is, for most people, a reminder of the struggle to read, a necessary step to quickly pass on the way to real reading: the silent kind. In other words, the child shows his mastery of reading with silence! Unfortunately, the slow learner going at a snail's pace is rushed through the practice of reading aloud without time to reach true mastery. He is deprived of the chance to use his body as a sounding board to integrate sounds correctly, before linking them with the visual perception of the letters on the page. Not only does he stumble when reading but also multiplies his chances of making spelling mistakes.

The effects of dyslexia are not limited to reading and spelling. They permeate the dyslexic's experience. They undermine self-esteem and shatter the sense of wellness of the struggling reader.

Just imagine how you would feel if you were a dyslexic and had to bring home a report card that dispassionately pinpoints your lack of reading skills or shortcomings? By then, how many times have you heard that reading is the key to success? How often were you told that "you are lazy" and that "you don't try hard enough?" "If only you could be like your sister" a frustrated parent at his wit's end might add. You feel ashamed. You dread the family scene that flares with each report card. The verdict is always the same: "Not good enough! Try harder!" And you try. You feel like a beginning swimmer who barely manages a few strokes before sinking. You drown in an ocean of words. You cannot make out the headlines in the newspaper, the signs on a bulletin board or the terms of your math problem. School reports are a nightmare. Upcoming tests send you into depression. You live like a foreigner in your own land. You feel you must be word-blind.

Deep down, you know that you are smart. You have wonderful ideas but their explanation gets stuck in your throat. You do not have the words to make them known to the world. When you try, you do it using a broken language. You fill the space between the words with uncomfortable silence. Gestures finish your sentences. You mumble, your shoulders hunched. You feel the words slip away. You seethe while your smart sister speeds all the way down the page as you struggle through the first paragraph. You feel it is unfair and still bury your rage. You are too ashamed to let your feelings show. Your parents drag you from one specialist to the next. Classroom tests are not enough, others test and test and re-retest you! You hate the so-called specialists who promise to "fix" you. Although they may reassure your parents, they don't reassure you. You haven't finished last week's homework and more is piled on your plate. Your lack of verbal abilities is taxing you to the max. Any progress you make is small and slow. You are still behind, old enough to know that you are "delayed." You are tired of trying. The alarm clock in the morning announces another doomsday. You feel like giving up. Who cares about the grades? You slip into rebellion or silence. Your future is slipping away fast. You feel depressed and bored to death. You start dreaming of exotic places, where no one has to read or go to school. Maybe you smoke pot or drink alcohol to escape the harsh reality of the world that seems to close in on you. Your relationship with your parents is strained. They think that you are irresponsible, the "bad boy" of the family. Slowly, you drift away. You see yourself in slow motion in a movie that you do not direct. You gang up with others like you. Your lack of self-esteem opens you up to bad influences. You are desperate to be loved and admired. You would do anything to prove yourself to your peers. Newspapers are filled with kids like you, waking up in jail when the deal went sour. They are not labeled "dyslexics" anymore but drug dealers, delinquents, criminals, sometimes murderers. 95% of those in jail suffer from some kind of learning disability. The statistics never appear in the headlines. Still, for you, the awakening will be harsh. Where will you go from here?

This, of course, is the worst scenario. There are many others. You may just withdraw and stop trying to tell others how you feel, because you are convinced that it will get you nowhere. You won't be able to translate the reality of your inner world, the beauty of your dreams, and the intensity of your feelings into words. The words stay locked inside, hard to bring forth. You go through life telling others as little as possible. You are not lying or trying to hide anything but have internalized your failures so well that you do not even think that you need to put your feelings or the experiences of your daily life into words.

Your parents may send you to see a therapist to get the words out of you because, they say, you never express your feelings. But therapy only works if you know how to "talk about your feelings" and you never did. You give up therapy like so many other things before. You probably feel that you didn't try hard enough but how could you? You grew up with this learning disability. You learned to compensate and take the easy way out. You may finish high school and eventually go to college, repeating a class, dropping a difficult course, trying to act like an average student just getting by. You stay away from jobs that confront you with paperwork or writing reports. You are not even aware of the degree of your avoidance. It is as if it is bred into your bones. Your learning disability has become so much part of you that you take it for granted. It is the way it is. It is the way you are. It is your life, your identity. You feel trapped: the future has no opening for you. Deep down, you feel such a failure that you don't want to try anything new. You are bored, depressed, overtaxed: life makes too many demands on you. You may settle for a life that does not overwhelm you.

Yet you may well consider yourself lucky if you still have a burning rage within. It may give you the desire to fight the odds. You may want to prove every one wrong: parents, teachers, and specialists. You tell yourself that Einstein, after all, was dyslexic. And so you work harder than everyone to reach your goal and join those deemed to be "successful." But even success does not always satisfy you: too often it appears to have been built on quicksand. If you succeeded this time, you tell yourself, it was just luck. You are quick at discarding your own efforts. Today's success may become tomorrow's failure. You will never do enough. You may become an overachiever out of low self-esteem. You always have a sense of being on stage, being watched by others like that first day in the classroom when the teacher asked you to read a paragraph aloud and you failed miserably. You may have forgotten this sad memory but its searing effect on your life continues. Otherwise, why would you avoid reading, except when forced into it?

As one can see, dyslexia cannot be reduced to the inability to master the mechanical aspects of reading. It permeates the entire existence of the person suffering this disability. Paul Madaule, who was dyslexic as a child, coined the term "dyslexified world" to describe the mental universe of the dyslexic. The term enlarges the traditional description of dyslexia and shows what is beyond its academic consequences.

Unfortunately, parents, teachers and professional are not always aware of this. The word dyslexia prevents our seeing beyond the narrow limits of its definition. Being clumsy, having a poor body image, being insufficiently lateralized, are still not commonly linked to dyslexia because these difficulties are not part of the accepted definition.

We are unable to connect the dots to reveal the larger picture emerging from a myriad of little facts that pertain to the physical, cognitive and psychological domains and appear unrelated but are interdependent. I often feel that a diagnosis is like a stone falling into water. We are so focused on the sinking stone that we do not see the enlarging circle of ripples on the surface. They are part of the phenomenon yet are invisible. The intense focus on the "problem" may explain why so many remedial strategies fail.

They generally just do that: focusing on the problem to fix it. While the ambition is certainly laudable, it may actually amplify the problem. Just remember how Benjamin reacted when I asked him to read the word "fog" aloud. His body sank, he mumbled a wild guess and fell silent. He was not only ashamed but also fearful. He'd have loved to sweep his problem aside, pretending it did not exist. It was a universal strategy: all of us want to save face. We all want to escape wounds to our self-esteem by denying rather than acknowledging difficulty.

The traditional reeducation of the dyslexic unfortunately focuses on the problem, as I unintentionally did by asking Benjamin to read aloud, rather than on the underlying causes. The emphasis on symptoms rather than causes is like seeing the tip of the iceberg and believing it is the whole iceberg. A remedy that emphasizes the language aspects of the problem only reinforces the dyslexic's belief in his inability to master language, adding to his sense of shame. Symptoms can be very persistent because most treatment entails acknowledging a deficiency of which we are ashamed. Focusing on a symptom may give it a life of its own: it looms so large that we feel defeated by the mere idea of fighting it.

LISTENING AND ATTENTION DEFICIT DISORDERS

What is ADD / ADHD?

These days, everyone seems to be talking about Attention Deficit Disorder, ADD for short. There is also ADHD, a variation of ADD that stands for Attention Deficit Hyperactivity Disorder. Books, TV shows and newspaper articles have familiarized millions of people with the ADD syndrome. Everyone seems to know the signs of this rapidly spreading "disease" marked by inappropriate degrees of inattention, impulsiveness, and hyperactivity.

The list of symptoms defining ADD or ADHD is worth reading. I have just added a series of somewhat ironic questions that cannot be found in the *Diagnostic and Statistical Manual of Mental Disorders*[36] where the list comes from. The questions (shown in *italics*) are intended to slow down your reading of the list and give you reason to think about the ambiguous nature of some of the symptoms. Do these symptoms describe normal behavior in a young and perfectly normal child? Are they indicators of a child under stress or one who has been cooped up or restricted too long? Or do they, as suggested in the manual, capture the essence of what an ADD or ADHD child is all about? If you really want to engage your critical judgment, you may want to read with a bright and curious youngster in mind. Here is the list; it may apply to your child ... or even to yourself:

- OFTEN FIDGETS WITH HAND OR FEET OR SQUIRMS IN HIS SEAT.
  How long has he been seated in the first place? Does he fidget and squirm when listening to a captivating story, or only when his teacher is repeating those boring multiplication tables, which he already knows by heart, for the 10th time?
- HAS DIFFICULTY REMAINING SEATED WHEN (YOU) REQUIRED (HIM) TO DO SO.
  But does he follow directions from others?
- IS EASILY DISTRACTED BY EXTRANEOUS STIMULI.
  A bee in the room, a passing fire truck, etc...?
- HAS DIFFICULTY WAITING HIS TURN IN GAMES OR GROUP SITUATIONS.
  What are the other kids involved in the game doing at the same moment? Does he have trouble when he is about to lose face? Does he then wish to end the game in the quickest way possible?
- OFTEN BLURTS OUT ANSWERS TO QUESTIONS BEFORE THEY HAVE BEEN COMPLETED.
  Has she heard that question too many times? Does she often get passed over, and what child does not in these overcrowded schools? Does she want to be sure to seize an opportunity to shine?
- HAS DIFFICULTY SUSTAINING ATTENTION IN TASKS OR PLAY ACTIVITIES.
  How many times has he been asked to do the same thing or play the same game? If activities are too repetitive and become boring, his brain is likely to opt out.
- OFTEN SHIFTS FROM ONE UNCOMPLETED ACTIVITY TO ANOTHER.
  Are those activities really interesting? Are they worth completing?

- **HAS DIFFICULTY PLAYING QUIETLY.**
  Children intensely engaged in games are naturally exuberant and enthusiastic, except those who are unusually shy or autistic. I would worry much more if I were the parent of an abnormally quiet child.
- **OFTEN TALKS EXCESSIVELY.**
  Such children may be just curious, amazed by life or eager to share their enthusiasm with everyone.
- **OFTEN INTERRUPTS OR INTRUDES ON OTHERS.**
  They may be rude, but so are many adults who are not diagnosed with ADD. You may want to check what kind of manners are taught or seen at home and school.
- **OFTEN DOES NOT SEEM TO LISTEN TO WHAT IS BEING SAID TO HIM OR HER.**
  Beware of this one! Little Johnny may be doodling on a piece of paper while the teacher talks because, in doing so, he cuts off the background noise in the class, allowing him to concentrate on what the teacher says. I still remember a so-called "space cadet" who could quote almost everything her teacher had said, using just that strategy.
- **OFTEN LOSES THINGS NECESSARY FOR TASKS OR ACTIVITIES AT SCHOOL OR AT HOME.**
  But who does not?
- **OFTEN ENGAGES IN PHYSICALLY DANGEROUS ACTIVITIES WITHOUT CONSIDERING POSSIBLE CONSEQUENCES.**
  One child wanted to mix garden chemicals to make "bombs" because his dad had shown him how to build one during his monthly visit. They were actually going to the desert to explode those home made bombs.

You have probably noticed that this list of *symptoms* is based on *external behavior with little reference to context*. What may go on in the life of that child or adult that could explain the external behavior is not taken into account. The consequence is that these so-called *symptoms* are too general and clearly ambiguous. As a psychiatrist friend of mine once argued: "Many of the signs of ADD can fairly apply to bright, curious, independent youngsters. The list of symptoms itself implies that there is only one kind of normal child: the quiet, silent child who does not make waves and is rarely seen. All the others are basically considered as a pain in the butt. I think that this particular way of looking at and diagnosing children says more about our society as a whole than it does about those children. The paradox is that the same signs that we bemoan in children are precisely the ones we identify with success in adults: a certain ruthlessness, a desire to create new things, a go-getter attitude." That is precisely why some specialists think that the diagnosis done by some experts "is very fuzzy, a sort of catch-all category that casts a wide net on a variety of symptoms not necessarily related, and thus should be discarded."[37]

What you may have noticed in the list above is that what changes a behavior into a symptom is its frequency; but, how often is often is open to question.

Some believe that ADD is a neurological syndrome whose cause might be genetic. However, some of them admit that, "the exact mechanism underlying ADD remains unknown. There is no single lesion of the brain, no single neurotransmitter system, no single gene we have identified that triggers ADD."[38] Obviously the fact that the cause of ADD is unknown makes a diagnosis of ADD uncertain. Another complicating factor is that the signs of ADD come in various degrees and might be present in one setting, such as school and not in another, such as home.

I once got a call from a mother who described her son as "the worse hyperactive, attention-deficit kid on the planet." On the basis of that description, we in the office were bracing ourselves for the appearance of a monster. Instead we met a polite, fairly balanced and inquisitive boy who was suffering from dyslexia. His mother, on the other hand, was hypersensitive to sounds and other sensory stimuli, and was consequently easily distracted. Not surprisingly, she could not take too much stimulation at once. What appeared to us as fairly normal behavior in her son was really too much for her due to her low threshold of tolerance for stimuli. Her sense of her son being hyperactive made total sense from her subjective perspective. Still, an objective tool like the TOVA (a tool for testing variable attention) would have established a more reasonable diagnosis than the subjective feelings of the mother.

In his book *Blaming the Brain*,[39] Elliot S. Valenstein, a professor Emeritus of psychology and neuroscience at the University of Michigan, quotes Howard Morris of the National Attention Deficit Disorder Association, noting that many physicians use the drug Ritalin as a diagnostic tool. They assume that, "if Ritalin works, then you've got it and if it doesn't, then you don't." Valenstein adds that it can be misleading to draw a conclusion about the cause of a disorder, based on the effectiveness of the medication that alleviates the symptoms. "Children are assumed to have a biochemical abnormality because Ritalin, an amphetamine-like drug that is a psychomotor stimulant, produces a "paradoxical" slowing of activity and increases attention span in these children."

According to a study by Judith Rapoport[40] from the National Institute for Mental Health, the response of ADHD children to amphetamines is not paradoxical at all because it also decreases activity and increases attention span *in normal children*. She concludes her study by stating that while there may be some minimal brain damage in a subset of children with ADHD, the assumption that they have a biochemical abnormality has no foundation in hard evidence. Nevertheless, an estimated 6 millions schoolchildren (two or three in every classroom) in the United States take their daily dose of Ritalin or other prescribed stimulants for ADHD. To add to the mystery of ADHD, the syndrome is diagnosed ten times more often in the United States than in Europe, and the Japanese report few cases. But, as John Carman, a San Francisco TV columnist puts it comically, "It's in the brain, and scientifically, we know more about armpits than brains."[41]

I don't want to leave you under the impression that I do not believe that ADD and ADHD do exist. However, because of my clinical experience, I do believe that it is often over-diagnosed, and that medication may be overprescribed.

Treatment Options

While the causes of ADHD are elusive, it remains important to do something for the children and adults who are suffering from its symptoms. If we look more closely at the list of indicators, they may all boil down to listening related problems. When we blurt out answers to questions before they are completed, interrupt the activities of other people, do not follow instructions, monopolize the conversation because we talk excessively, we **are obviously not listening**. Listening requires that you first have mastery over your body and the way it interfaces with the environment: fidgeting hands, squirming in one's seat, inability to wait one's turn and being easily distracted are all signs that this has not been achieved. Your brain is not going to focus well if it needs to expend a lot of energy managing bodily functions that should no longer require conscious control. Moreover, if you are sensitive to sound, light, or the minutest environmental stimuli, chances are that you will have trouble attending to a particular task, especially when you feel bombarded by a tremendous amount of information all at once. One of my clients, a highly oversensitive woman, put it very well by comparing this bombardment to "a piece of sandpaper scratching her skin."

Good listening requires, first of all, that all the various functions of our body be synchronized: in fact, *good listening requires good sensory integration*. The debate about ADHD rarely focuses on a lack of sensory integration as one of its possible causes. Jean Ayres, the pioneer of sensory integration, pointed out that poor sensory integration could lead to both hyperactivity and poor attention. She states in *Sensory Integration and the Child*[42] that these problems arise when the vestibule does not function well: "A well-modulated vestibular activity is very important for maintaining a calm, alert state ...The vestibular system also helps keep the level of arousal of the nervous system balanced. An under-active vestibular system contributes to hyperactivity and distractibility because of its modulating influence."

So what would cause the inability of the vestibule to integrate sensory information? There are two possibilities, and in both the cause is insufficient sensory-integration:

THE VESTIBULAR SYSTEM IS OVERLOADED BY TOO MUCH INFORMATION. To deal with the onslaught of information, we may "tune out" entirely. This coping strategy is likely to lead to a diagnosis of Attention Deficit Disorder. To address this issue we have to restore the client's ability to selectively "tune out" some of the sounds, and "tune in" to the information that is essential to learning and acquiring social competence.

THE VESTIBULAR SYSTEM DOES NOT RECEIVE ENOUGH STIMULATION for the brain to function optimally. In this case, we make up for the lack of stimulation to our brain by stirring things up, usually through body movement: fidgeting with our hands if we are children, jumping up and down on the sofa in the living room, running through the aisles in the supermarket despite disapproving customers. If we are adults we might employ compensations such as running twenty miles a day, going bungee jumping, always on the move, led by a thirst for excitement. When activity abounds, experts usually diagnose Attention Deficit Hyperactive Disorder. In this event, however, treatment strategies should include appropriate increases in brain stimulation.

In any event, things are not often so clear-cut: it is quite possible that sensory overload and lack of stimulation alternate, leading to an alternation of the two types of behavior just described.

In Tomatis' view, improving listening skills is a priority in the treatment of ADHD or ADD, since one of the main complaints about children and adults who have ADD/ADHD is that they do not seem to listen. Or, that they hear well but are poor listeners. Listening, we may recall, involves the ability and the desire *to tune in* to relevant information as well as the ability *to filter out* unwanted information. In short, listening depends on smooth sensory integration. Unfortunately, the filtering mechanism does not work that well for ADD and ADHD children or adults.

Listening Tests of people with ADD and ADHD clearly shows that their filtering mechanism does not work well. The Listening Test is a diagnostic tool devised by Tomatis. It looks like the hearing test performed by an audiologist when she is checking your ears. Normally, the audiologist tests your responses to sounds delivered to your ears through headphones. This part of the exam checks your air conduction response. More advanced testing checks the response of your bone conduction. As you may remember, sound travels quite well through bone. In a normal listening test, the air conduction curve should be above the bone conduction curve.[43] This means that you preferentially hear with your ears (air conduction), and only secondarily with your body (bone conduction). So, as sounds pass through the ear on their way to the brain, the ear filters out irrelevant sounds, like background noise, and dampens sounds that are too loud.

When you look at the Listening Test of an ADD/ADHD child,

you observe most of the time that **the bone conduction curve is higher than the air conduction curve. This means that an ADD/ADHD child preferentially listens with the body (bone conduction), rather than with the ears (air conduction).** In this case, sound goes straight to the brain without any filtering or dampening. The child is thus constantly reacting to and distracted by any new stimulus. In general, when bone response is higher than air response, we encounter a form of hypersensitivity to sound, in other words, an inability to filter out unwanted sound when needed.

What does that mean in practical terms? Just imagine that you are deeply involved in a conversation with a friend when your son slams the door of the living room. Your body shudders instinctively (bone conduction response) before you realize that it's the door. Had you seen your son slam the door, your reaction would have been different because you would have had time to anticipate the banging and thus your ear would have been able to dampen the sound to a comfortable intensity. In the first case (you didn't see your son), the bang was perceived directly through your bones. The bang arrived to your brain without any warning signal. That is why it produced a reflex reaction of your entire body.

People with ADHD or ADD react in much the same way as you did when the door banged. The main difference is that their body reacts to almost everything, even the most miniscule stimuli that you would not even notice. They primarily listen with their bodies instead of with their ears. That is one of the reasons they are so reactive and tend to act without thinking: they cannot filter out irrelevant information to focus on what matters at the moment.

While most of the focus is on the negative side, I do believe that there is a bright side to ADD or ADHD, and the Listening Test reflects those positive aspects. If your perception is that sensitive, you'll perceive things that escape most other people. You are more likely to come up with new ideas, feelings and perceptions that are somewhat out of the ordinary, which may raise your intelligence and creativity. Parents often agree that their ADHD child has a great imagination, is smart, creative, curious, even adventurous, but it is hard for them to think about that when they have to deal with the day-to-day management of their child's behavior.

Rightly so, parents often complain that their ADD/ADHD child "is lost in his own world! He does not listen! He is all over the place!" But these children have no other choice than being lost in their own world, not because they consciously want to escape the outside world but because they feel too much of its impact. The "lost child" is often just trying to dampen that impact by withdrawing into a protective bubble; the hyperactive one, on the other hand, may resort to motor agitation to reach the same goal, to mask the unbearable noise in his environment.

Beginning to really listen is not without risk for an ADD or ADHD person. Day by day, they are bombarded by more stimulation they can handle and thus experience the world as a difficult place to live in. When they start to listen, they re-enter the world differently and need to overcome their fears of it. People with ADHD, for instance, need to slow down and stop running on nervous energy. Tomatis uses Gregorian Chant to advance that goal, since it has a calming effect. These chants work well with many children, but the ADHD child often fights its appeasing impact at first by increasing his hyperactive behavior while listening to it. It is as if he feels that the music imposes a rhythm on him that is quite foreign. Hyperactive behavior only subsides gradually as sensory integration improves. The end result is often a child or adult who is quite different from the way they used to be, as the examples of Tom and Jeff clearly illustrate.

Tom and Jeff: Two Case Studies

Tom

Tom was eight years old when I first met him. He had all the classic symptoms of ADD and did his best to demonstrate them during this first meeting. His parents felt that "he had never awakened." For them, he was lost in his own world, only reaching out when he needed something. Academically, he was behind in reading and writing. He was overall a pleasant child, but the frustration he experienced at school was turning him into a bully. Emotionally he was very immature and had a short-fuse. Although his parents were trying hard to keep him on track at school, he would forget either to do his homework or to turn it in. By the end of the day, he could not even remember what he had done in school. His parents were at their wit's end, desperate enough to try about anything.

I explained to Tom's parents that they should not expect overnight changes or miracles. It would take some time before they could see the first results. Remembering an expression used by Dr. Bob Roy, a Tomatis practitioner in Regina, Canada, I told them to look for "windows of attention" that might be a little bit broader than Tom's usual attention span. With this advice, they might start to notice subtle changes.

By the end of the first fifteen days of treatment, the parents reported that there had been some moments when they felt Tom had been able to pay more attention. He had focused on a book during the weekend and had turned in an assignment on time. He also seemed to follow the rules of the house somewhat better. During the three week break that followed, the parents continued to observe that Tom sustained his attention for longer periods of time. They had been delighted to find out that Tom had done some work on his own at school. He also remembered the rules more consistently. He was now experimenting with cursive, a first for him. His father noted that he was more able to express his feelings and the two of them have had some surprising discussions. By the end of second phase of the program, a block of ten days, Tom's mother confirmed that he was listening more often. "He is computing what I am saying," she observed. He was doing better in baseball, a sign that his vestibule worked better and that sensory-integration was improving. Finally, at the table, he would tell about his day at school in lengthy details.

The breakthrough came a few weeks later when his mother found Tom doing his homework on his own at seven o'clock in the morning. She stopped by my office to announce triumphantly: "My son finally awoke!"

Tom's progress continued through another block of 10 days of treatment taken two months later. By now, he had developed a better image of himself and felt more confident. He was proud of his new ability to play baseball. At school, he did far better than he had ever done. The teacher told him: "Tom, you have matured so much! You are not silly anymore!" His awakening delighted his parents. "He is with us now!"

Still, Tom needed to catch up at school. Summer was coming and we thought that Tom could use some of the time to study with a private tutor. Now he was ready for extra attention in previously difficult areas. Not only could he focus his attention but also he was able to perceive sounds and reproduce them correctly. His progress in reading, writing and maths were very rapid. To spur on his new abilities to learn, he also got a ten day "booster" in our office. When school started, he was well prepared. The teacher felt that he had almost caught up and that he was now operating closer to his age-level. For his parents, the dream of a "normal child" was finally close to reality. Was still Tom an ADD child? The question had no meaning for them anymore: Tom was "awake" and doing well.

Jeff

Jeff, a thirty-year-old single man, had a different type of awakening. He presented all the signs of Attention Deficit Disorder without hyperactivity. His lack of focus, his forgetfulness about ordinary things, and his inability to organize the tasks at hand: all affected his daily life. Although he lived by himself and had a steady job, he was still quite dependent on his mother and her partner who lived one hour away. He could not easily learn new things at work, readily got lost when driving and was mildly learning disabled. A hearing test performed by an audiologist showed that Jeff had "an entirely normal hearing sensitivity" but had a *"central auditory processing problem deficit characterized by difficulty in focusing his listening when there is a competing signal or background noise."* Stated differently, this meant that Jeff's bone conduction response was higher than his air conduction response. In short, he heard too much through bone conduction and thus could not screen out the ambient noise which resulted in constant distraction. This accounted for Jeff's difficulties in learning and remembering things. He used memory lists (but lost them, or forgot that they were in his pocket) and a calculator/memory watch for day, date and phone numbers to boost his memory. He reported that he was easily distracted by cars passing by and by feelings within himself as well. Distraction was the key word in summing up Jeff's behavior.

When Jeff came back for his second block of therapy, he spontaneously reported that things were getting better. He no longer needed to look at his watch to know what day it was, nor did he use a list to go grocery shopping. He also wasn't bothered by ambient noise anymore: "I don't have to pay attention to them. It is like a filter. I still can hear, can see, but I don't get easily distracted." He felt better and much calmer, which helped him, he believed, to pay better attention. Shortly after this, Jeff lost his job but handled the situation very well. His mother was impressed that he was not crushed by the news, as she would have expected him to feel. Jeff found another job almost immediately and felt very pleased with himself. For him, the most important thing was that now, "When I wake up, I know where I am and which day it is. I am not lost. I can speak my mind. I don't get easily distracted."

Conclusion

What had happened that made Tom and Jeff function better? It is fairly simple: their listening programs had slowly desensitized their hypersensitive bone conduction responses. Not listening through their bodies as much made it possible for them to filter out extraneous environmental stimuli. The result was an enhanced ability to pay attention, a requirement for optimal learning. It also deeply affected their personalities. Tom's mom put it quite well when she described her son awakening from his state of inattention. As long as both of them were defenseless against the constant onslaught of stimuli, it was impossible for them to start to live an "awakened "life in which their personality could blossom. Tom, as a child, did not yet have a clear awareness of who he was, but Jeff was aware that he was not the person he sensed he could be. His Attention Deficit Disorder not only kept him from connecting with the world around him, but also prevented a deeper relationship with himself. That lost connection was what hurt him most and made him, at times, feel worthless. His treatment put him back on the road toward wellness. While he had still a long way to go, he was at least hopeful that his life would improve.

If we assess the results of the Tomatis Method, the prognosis for people like Tom or Jeff, who have Attention Deficit Disorder *without* hyperactivity, is very good. For reasons that are not yet clear, the treatment may take longer for those who have Attention Deficit Disorder *with* hyperactivity. After seeing many hyperactive children finally calm down to the great amazement of their parents, I remain confident that the Tomatis' work is extremely valuable even for those who have a high level of hyperactivity. Ron Minson, a psychiatrist and Tomatis practitioner in Denver, reports that he has been able to eliminate medication in some cases and in others to reduce the amount previously used to keep behavior in check. Overall, the lives of these children and adults have improved enormously.

THE GIFT OF LANGUAGES

Understanding dyslexia sheds a new light on the difficulties that many of us experience when we want to learn foreign languages. Few of us have a knack for languages; many of us get easily discouraged and claim that we are not gifted enough and will never be able to learn Spanish or Japanese, for instance. We feel dyslexic, so to speak.

While in the past it may not have been as important to learn foreign languages, rapid changes in our society have made it crucial to learn at least one foreign language. Consider Betty and John whose son has married a Mexican woman and who have now enrolled at age fifty in a college program to learn Spanish so that they can communicate with their new family on the other side of the border; or Mary whose husband was transferred to Beijing by his company to run their Chinese operation; or Ray who runs a landscaping business in the Central Valley in California and employs Spanish-speaking people almost exclusively. Mary may decide to live within the confines of the community of expatriates in Beijing and learn just enough Chinese to get by, but Betty, John and Ray have practical and urgent reasons to speak and communicate in a foreign language. Such situations are likely to multiply as globalization intensifies and the wave of immigrants gets bigger and bigger. Anticipating this trend, one of my retired friends decided to learn Spanish. "What for?" I asked. "Well," he said, "I figure the people who are likely to take care of me when I am very old will only speak Spanish. I want to be able to understand them and to talk with them!"

As we will see, most of us shy away from learning foreign languages because our ears are not adapted to the sounds of the language we are trying to learn. We need, so to speak, a new ear: one that will be able to accurately pick up the sounds that do not belong to our native language. Auditory reconditioning can give us the new ears and the associated posture we need to successfully master a new language. The following chapters contain some pointers on how ears can be reconditioned.

The traditional way of teaching languages focuses on words, grammar and sentence structure. Yet how can you memorize words you can not even hear well? Like putting the cart before the horse, this puts the language student in a similar predicament to dyslexic children and adults who cannot process sound as quickly or as precisely as needed.

Comparing dyslexia with the challenge of learning new languages is quite interesting. Both are listening problems. Could it be that a dyslexic has an ear that corresponds to a language other than his own, and that he would not be dyslexic when speaking that language? In fact, according to an article in the journal Science,[44] *"the country where the dyslexic is raised and the nature of the language spoken may play a role in the severity of the disability."* Tomatis has often stated that one can be dyslexic in one language and not in another.

Ever heard of an "Ethnic Ear?"

Even before we were born, we were immersed in sound. We perceived the sounds of our mother's voice in the womb. We learned to recognize her voice, her timber, her intonations, the rhythm of her speech and through them the language that we will claim as our mother tongue. Our mother's voice programmed our nervous system and brain to its cadence and characteristic sounds even before we were born. After birth, our knowledge grows quite rapidly as a result of the sonic bath containing the voices of our parents, family and community members. This is how we developed what Tomatis called our "ethnic ear," one that is specialized in picking up the frequencies of our mother tongue.

In *The Conscious Ear*,[45] Tomatis recounts how he discovered that there was a variety of ethnic ears. This occurred to him when he was treating a group of singers from Venice, Italy. All had the same problem: none could pronounce the "R" with the tip of the tongue. Instead, they all pronounced it like an "L." That was odd, he thought, because the great Italian singer Caruso pronounced his "R" perfectly. When mulling over this apparent difference, Tomatis had an "Ah-ha" experience. He suddenly realized that Caruso was born in Naples and that all Neapolitans roll their "R's." Venetians, on the other hand, all have the same problem in pronouncing the "R." As the voice reflects what the ear perceives, he concluded that Venetians have some kind of selective deafness for rolling "R's" that results in a selective "mutism." Neapolitans do not have this particular deaf spot. Later tests confirmed his hypothesis. If there were different "ethnic ears" within a country, it would be logical to assume that there might also be a certain type of ear for each nationality: a French ear, a Spanish ear, a Japanese ear, etc... So, he started to analyze the various languages, and indeed found mayor differences between them.

Before delving into the differences between languages, we'll first examine why there are ethnic ears. We'll do so by looking at an example. Have you ever wondered why a piano and a violin sound so differently? Well, when you strike a key of a piano, you generate a tone. At the same time, however, several other tones, called overtones, are produced. The overtones are much less intense than the base tone, so you will mostly hear the base tone. When you play the same base tone on a violin, different overtones are formed. Therefore, a violin sounds completely different from a piano. One of the reasons a piano and a violin create different overtones is that the soundboards are so different. A piano has a large, heavy, flat soundboard, while the soundboard of a violin is a small, delicate case, creating different overtones.

Like musical instruments, all languages use the same base tones, ranging from 125 Hz to 250 Hz. Our soundboard is our mouth cavity, and the overtones depend on its shape. So, the overtones depend on how we open our mouths, how we position our tongues, and how we protrude our lips. You may have already guessed that people use their mouths differently when speaking different languages. Hence, overtones differ from language to language, tending to densely group in selected areas of the acoustic spectrum. Their location along the spectrum varies in ways that are specific to each language.

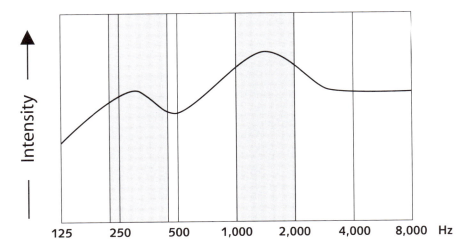

Figure 9: Frequency distribution of the French language

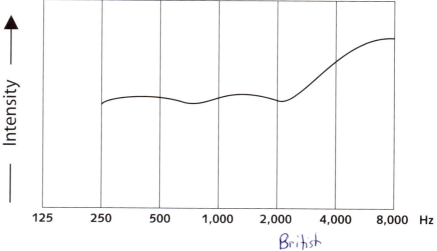

Figure 10: Frequency distribution of the English (British) language

For instance, the French language is rich in frequencies between 1,000 Hz and 2,000 Hz, and therefore the French hear these frequencies quite well. English, on the other hand is rich in frequencies between 2,000 Hz and 12,000 Hz, and the English ear is thus attuned to these high pitched sounds. The English ear is thus **not** attuned to the French overtones, and vice-versa. The French, therefore, have a hard time learning English and the British find it equally difficult to learn French.

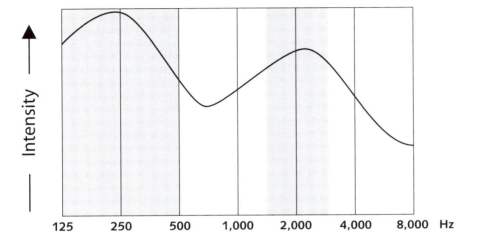

Figure 11: Frequency distribution of the Spanish langauge

Spanish uses predominantly low frequencies, from 150 Hz to 500 Hz and those from 1,500 Hz to 2,500 Hz. Therefore, Spanish speakers have great difficulty learning languages that are rich in high frequencies such as English. Not so for Russians, however: they hear well between 125 Hz and 12,000 Hz and are well adapted to learning languages because their auditory range is so wide that they can easily identify the sounds of other languages. The same is true for the Portuguese people who, for the same reason pick up languages easily.

People of the United States share the English language with their British counterparts but they do not share the frequency distribution. American English is rich in mid-range frequencies, between 800 Hz and 3,000 Hz with a peak around 1,500 Hz. The peak at 1,500 Hz explains why people of the United States often have a nasal voice. French has the same peak at around 1,500 Hz, which explains the presence of nasal sounds in French as well. It would be advisable for French people to learn the English spoken in the United States (rather than British English) because of this similarity. Instead, the French educational system emphasizes the British pronunciation that is so foreign to French ears that many French kids never dare open their mouths to speak English.

An often overlooked complication is that languages not only use different frequencies, but also differ in the length of their syllables. Pronouncing words within the right time frame is the second most important factor in speaking a foreign language well. On the average, according to Tomatis, it takes about 75 milliseconds to pronounce an American English syllable, much longer than the emission time of French syllables (roughly 50 milliseconds). If you are a citizen of the United States who wants to learn French, for instance, you will have to learn to pronounce French syllables more quickly.

What happens is very similar to what happens with vision. If you gaze into the distance, then focus your eyes on a nearby object, there is a transition period which allows your eyes to adjust and identify the nearby object. This transition time is measurable and has a parallel in hearing. Transition time in auditory processing is used by the ear to check each syllable, one at a time, before it is emitted, allowing for the speech organs to adapt and respond to the feedback from the ear. This time lapse is precisely the time it takes to produce a syllable. Another way of saying it is that this is the time it takes to listen to oneself.

The national or ethnic education of the ear impacts not only our language but also our posture. Shifting from one language to another means literally shifting from one physical attitude to another. "When I give a German ear to a Frenchman," wrote Tomatis, "I see him raise his voice, force his words out through his throat, and stand up straight—exactly what an actor would do when asked to play the part of an officer in the German army."

The Road to Success

Tomatis' concept of an ethnic ear is helpful to understand that we are not necessarily at fault if we have a hard time mastering a foreign language. We may simply not have the right ear for learning the new language. It is no wonder that learning a new language is difficult if we cannot correctly hear what the teacher says!

Tomatis believed that the first step to mastering a foreign language is reconditioning our ears so that we can accurately perceive the sounds of the foreign language. To prime our ears, we need to bathe them in the unfamiliar sounds of the new language. Once we hear the sounds of the new language well, our pronunciation will automatically improve. For that reason, it is always better to have a native speaker as a teacher or, better yet, to go to and stay for a while in the country whose language we want to master.

When I was fifteen years old, my parents decided to send me to Germany to improve my German. I had studied German for three years and was an adequate student. Nothing had prepared me for the initial shock of meeting my host family: they had seven kids, ages one to fifteen, two grandparents and an aunt living together. From early morning to late at night, I was surrounded by voices, children firing questions, expectations of immediate answers, and adults trying to share the experience of their lives with me. It was a cacophony of voices and sounds that I painfully pieced together, sometimes one word at a time. While this type of language training was hard on me at the time, it was nevertheless the best I ever had. When I returned, I was suddenly the star of my German class. My words flowed easily and difficult elements of grammar fell into place. I was starting to be able to express myself "like a German." It felt exhilarating and I made rapid progress.

Throughout my stay in Germany, I had been bathed in the sounds of the German language. My host family conditioned me in the same way that they were conditioning their six-month old baby.

Through that short period of conditioning, my stay was only a few weeks long, I had started to acquire the German ear that none of my French-born teachers had been able to pass on. I finally started to fathom how it felt to speak like a native. Or, to be more precise, now that my ears were accustomed to the sounds of the German language, it was easier to reproduce those sounds that my upbringing in the south of France had not prepared me for.

Not everyone is able to spend an extended time abroad to learn a foreign language. Fortunately, thanks to progress in electronics, there are much faster and easier ways to master a foreign language. Even when you don't have access to an Electronic Ear or can't afford the cost of a program, you can use modern technology to immerse yourself in the sound of the new language at a fraction of the cost of going abroad: just watch foreign TV stations that satellite and cable stations beam into your home every day. Or watch DVDs of foreign films using the original sound track. Ideally, you should dedicate some time each day to listening to a foreign broadcast while continuing to learn vocabulary and grammar in a more traditional way.

When you first listen, you are likely to understand little and wonder about the effectiveness of this type of passive learning. If you persist and are patient, you will notice that, after a few weeks, you'll start to recognize the words more easily, stitching them together into complete sentences. This is your proof that your ears are becoming tuned. After two or three months, you will understand entire dialogues regardless of the speed at which the actors or the news anchors speak. Twice in my life I used this passive way of learning through this media: I have found it extremely efficient, even if, at times, I had to resist boredom or the frustration of not understanding. A day comes, though, when you suddenly realize that you are getting it: from then on, you'll advance by leaps and bounds. You may even surprise yourself by spontaneously using words that were passively stored in your memory. What is more, your teacher may praise you for your pronunciation and your seeming ease at speaking a language that you may have thought you could never master.

In the introduction of this book, I recounted my experience in in improving my accent using the Tomatis Method. Now I want to report a few of the successful uses of the Tomatis Method to help other adults and children to learn a language more quickly and effectively.

In 1976, a class of 30 high school students in Coomen, Belgium, was divided into two groups. The Listening Test had determined that students of both groups were well balanced regarding their listening abilities. None of these French-speaking students had previously learned English. The first group was taught English as usual for the entire school year. The other group received the Tomatis training for three months first, followed by six months of regular English lessons. At the end of the school year, an independent judge tested all students for comprehension as well as for pronunciation. The Tomatis group clearly outperformed the control group. More significantly, following the summer vacation, the two groups were tested again, and the difference had become even more pronounced. The Tomatis group retained what it had learned, while the control group forgot a lot. The authors of the report observed that the Tomatis students remembered and comprehended their lessons more easily and were not afraid to express themselves verbally, in stark contrast to the control group.[46]

This Method has also found its way into the business world. In 1995, during a Tomatis conference in Neufchâtel, Switzerland, a representative of Eurocopter, the second largest manufacturer of helicopters in the world, reported that the Method was used by his company to train its employees, its pilots in particular. The program was such a success that it has been in full swing for several years. It reduced the time it took the employees to master a foreign language and consequently saved the company a lot of money. A side benefit was that 83% of the participants claimed that their communication skills had improved and most felt that they were more efficient in their work. In short, they had become better employees.

Since that time, the Method has attracted other European companies who needed to boost the language skills of their employees in order to compete in the worldwide market more effectively.

Learning a language can be fun rather than a drag. We are not just learning a new language, but also new ways of thinking and feeling that make our lives more interesting. New advances in technology have made this easier than we could have expected thirty years ago. Tomatis' findings should also make us feel less guilty about past failures in learning new languages. After all, we are not stupid if our ears need to be tuned to a different pattern of frequencies than the one in use in our native language.

Part IV

The Listening Test

PRELIMINARIES

Each day is filled with opportunities to opt to listen, or to turn a deaf ear to the world around us and within us. Some of these decisions are totally unconscious. A sound may trigger a bad memory of an event, or a voice may remind us of a person that we do not wish to remember. Instantly, a defensive mechanism screens out the uncomfortable memory.

We strive, on the other hand, to "hear" from parents, children, friends traveling or living some distance away. We are "all ears" for the good news and ready to show our support when we receive bad news concerning them. Our ears are "open" to these people because we love them, we have a genuine interest in them, and they strike a chord in us. Thus, we are ready to listen to them.

"Hearing," wrote Tomatis,[47] "gives no indication of conscious engagement ... Hearing, the result of a perception in answer to an external stimulus, is purely reflexive. Listening, though based on an external stimulus, must be internally and intentionally pursued. Specific components such as input, choice and filter come into play. The element of consciousness thus becomes the essential factor on which the difference between hearing and listening rests. *Though both functions evolve together, listening is on a higher plane since it is specific to man in his human evolution* [author's italics]."

In fact, added Tomatis, this is very similar to what happens with vision. There too, "are different levels of efficiency ... One may have perfect sight ... the best retina in the world ... but that won't tell you whether or not he can see well enough to aim a gun. It doesn't tell you either whether he can paint ... For that reason, we hold that a poor [hearing] curve *used well* can give the subject listening potential superior to that of many people with good hearing ... There is a dimension of attentiveness ... an investment of self in listening ... and an awakening of consciousness that takes over the hearing act itself."

Deep and continuous listening is rare. Sometimes we listen with great interest but often our listening is sketchy, fragmented, driven by circumstances or personal interests. Not too long ago, I interrupted one of my friends telling a story about something that had happened to her. That story reminded me of another story: *my* story, that is! I suddenly burned with the desire to interrupt her, and in fact blurted out impolitely: "That's exactly what happened to my aunt!" Was I still listening to my friend who was telling us *her* story? Of course, not! I had switched to *my* story: it was so much more interesting! I was only listening to myself! None of the experience of my friend, which could have enriched me and opened up new perspectives, was to penetrate the closed world of my ego!

We all do the same at times. The force of habit may direct us to conclude a conversation by a "nice talking with you," but in reality we have only been talking for ourselves. We are not so different from the checker in the supermarket, who asks a very friendly but automatic, "How are you doing today?" and immediately proceeds to scan grocery prices. We know all too well not to respond that we are *not* having a good day.

Our ears are equipped with filters. The outer ear is, of course, a physical filter channeling sound toward the inner ear and sharpening our hearing. In addition, our ears become psychological filters as a result of what has happened to us during our lives. Listening is highly selective and is primarily an automatic function. It also depends on circumstances. There are days we only accept data that are pleasant and fairly commonplace, rejecting material that is uncomfortable or threatening; in short filtering out anything that does not fit with our pre-existing frame of reference and may force us to alter it. The saying, "there are none so deaf as those that will not hear," captures this selectivity perfectly

Early in his career, Tomatis began to wonder whether there was a way to scientifically account for that difference between hearing and listening. Would it be even possible to test someone's ability to listen? As a trained audiologist, he was not inclined to attribute psychological implications to the audiograms of people whose hearing he was testing. Audiometry, he was taught, was an objective science on which subjective factors had no influence. His experience with factory workers exposed to intense noise quickly changed his mind. One of his tasks was to test a group of thirty employees three times per week, for several years in a row. By looking at the trends in the audiograms, he realized that patterns displayed by some employees were changing for no discernable reason other than their hope of getting a pension for hearing impairment due to loud noise exposure. "I was surprised," he writes in *The Conscious Ear,*[48] "to discover that a perfectly sincere individual, but one who secretly wanted to be diagnosed as deaf, was able to lower his auditory threshold by ten, twenty, and even thirty decibels. Motivated by the prospects of a pension, the subjects cheated in good faith: that is subconsciously." Clearly, there was more to audiometry than the objective science that had previously been noted. Tomatis' observation raised new questions: How should this data be interpreted considering the subjective responses of the subjects?

One day, one of Tomatis' assistants noticed that he made spontaneous personal observations about the mood or energy level of the factory employees as he tested their hearing. "How do you know this?" asked the puzzled assistant. Tomatis answered, pointing to the test in front of him: "It is right here."

Scientists like to talk about the defining moment in their research. The assistant's question and Tomatis' answer was certainly such a moment. If there was truth to be found in Tomatis' answer, it required a long and careful investigation to transform this intuition into accepted facts. Part of this process was to establish a strong distinction between hearing and listening. This led Tomatis to develop the Listening Test, "which measures psychological dimensions, somatic data, and the quality of interaction between the person and his or her sonic environment." Although the Listening Test looks like a hearing test to those without special training, it is not hearing that is tested, but the psychology that underlies hearing — a point often emphasized by Tomatis.

I witnessed the power of the Listening Test at the beginning of my training while sitting in Tomatis' office. One of his assistants introduced a family who had traveled a long distance to consult Tomatis. Their eight-year old son's performance at school had deteriorated significantly over the last few months. The Listening Test had already been performed and the background information gathered by a Listening Therapist. Tomatis merely glanced at the test and choose to directly address the somewhat intimidated child who sat between his parents. *"So you think a lot about death, do you?"* he asked the child. The boy's posture changed at once. He sat upright as if hit by a bolt from the blue. His eyes were suddenly bright. He looked Dr. Tomatis right in the eyes and nodded.

I'll leave you to imagine his parents' face. They exchanged bewildered glances over their son's head, quickly followed by a sigh of resignation. They told Tomatis that a grandfather, who was very dear to the boy, had died a few months earlier. His death had brought great pain to the family. It had upset their son so much that they thought it was better to ignore his questions and not to talk about the death. They were afraid that an open discussion could disturb him even more. Grand-pa's death had become taboo but silence could erase neither the pain nor the questions. Tomatis' direct question had reopened the wound but had also given them a chance to express their feelings. By the end of the consultation, there was not only a palpable sign of relief among all of them but a renewed sense of trust as well. Undoubtedly the child's questions would now be answered.

Meanwhile, Tomatis also addressed the issue of the son's learning difficulties. He did so by putting them in the context of the grandfather's death: how could the child pay attention in class and succeed while he was so emotionally preoccupied?

I was as surprised by Tomatis' question as the parents were. How did he know that the child was concerned with death? What was the basis for his question? I asked him after the family had left. "It is right there," he answered, pointing to the Listening Test, in the same way that he had done many years before when he answered his assistant. I am not sure that I was entirely able to grasp his explanation but what I had just witnessed was credible enough to convince me that the test was in fact a psychological assessment. I was forced to conclude that the way we respond to sounds has a psychological basis.

I do not want to imply that the Listening Test can show about everything there is to know about a person. My colleagues and I are always glad to corroborate our findings with the findings of other assessments performed by other professionals. There is also a matter of context: life does not take place in a vacuum. I once evaluated a person who had cosmetic surgery performed on her face a month earlier. I knew that this was likely to temporarily result in elevated bone conduction response and that I needed to factor this into my understanding of her Listening Test. Had that surgery not occurred, the interpretation of the same test would have been quite different.

Still, the Listening Test conveys a wealth of information regarding aptitudes, personality traits, mood, energy level, behavior, learning abilities, and reflects the impact of life circumstances on the listening abilities of a person. I once told a client that it was like an X-ray, giving a **general** reading of her at this moment. Since clients often feel vulnerable and exposed under the therapist's questioning, therapists should interpret the results of the Listening Test in a tactful and timely manner. They should also support the test interpretation with a rationale instead of appearing to pull a rabbit from a hat — a narcissistic attitude that prevents the establishment of a good therapeutic relationship.

People certainly deserve an explanation and they rarely fail to ask for it. It is this explanation that we want to explore now. I do not pretend that it will make you a Listening Test authority. My purpose is more modest: I want to give you a way of understanding how your perception of sounds may condition personality traits and behavior, and conversely how your personal history influences your perception of sounds.

THE IDEAL LISTENING CURVE

To evaluate listening rather than hearing, Tomatis needed to define a new set of objective criteria. They had to be observable, measurable and verifiable like the criteria used in conventional audiometry. So, the first thing he needed to do was to define the ideal listening curve. As you will see, it differs substantially from the one used by audiologists.

In audiometric exams, the audiologist is mainly interested in determining the presence or absence of a hearing loss. She does so by determining the minimum auditory threshold of a set of frequencies ranging from 125 Hz to 8,000 Hz. For each frequency, she looks for the softest sound you can hear. In other words, if she needs to increase the intensity of the sound to 30 decibels before you hear it, 30 decibels is your minimum auditory threshold for that frequency. She then charts your responses on an audiogram; she notes the frequencies (hertz or Hz) on the horizontal axis and the intensity (dB or decibels) on the vertical one.

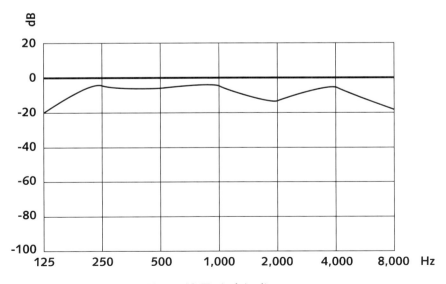

Figure 12: Typical Audiogram

Audiometers are typically calibrated in such a way that the zero decibel line represents normal hearing. The further down from the zero decibel line (0 dB) your score is, the more severe your hearing loss is.

Thus, when an audiologist sees a curve that is almost flat, hugging around the 0 dB line, she will congratulate you that your hearing is fine. Tomatis would agree, but he would add that although your *hearing* is perfect, your ears are not ideal for *listening*.

According to Tomatis, the Ideal Listening Curve looks as follows:

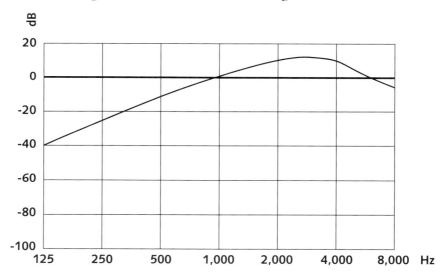

Figure 13: The Ideal Listening Curve

As you can see, the curve ascends as it approaches 2,000 Hz, with a slope of about 6 to 18 decibels per octave, and then shows a dome between 2,000 and 4,000 Hz, followed by a slight decline. "On a purely physical plane," writes Tomatis, "it shows the response of the ear when it functions well." It constitutes "a sort of physiologically ideal curve worth aiming for. It does not follow, however, that once you have acquired this ideal curve that you will attain consciousness … but I believe that there is a physico-acoustic curve that is necessary for the process of listening."

Using the ideal listening curve as the reference point, Tomatis developed a way of interpreting the Listening Test and, based on that, came up with a rationale for a whole array of seemingly unrelated phenomena. For instance, he found that the presence of an ascending curve between 500 Hz and 1,500 Hz indicated an appreciation for music while the flattening of the curve in this area indicated exactly the opposite. A drop between 1,000 Hz and 2,000 Hz predicted singing out of tune. If the curve ascended correctly up to 2,000 Hz, then dropped sharply, the singing voice was still correct, but not beautiful, since it had lost its harmonics. Working with thousands of clients, Tomatis was increasingly able to infer learning and psychological difficulties from the Listening Test, as well as somatic troubles and personality traits — in short, facts that the classical hearing test is not able to determine.

This brings up the inevitable question: why doesn't everyone have the ideal listening curve? Indeed, Tomatis asserted, "all infants have it potentially when they come into the world. But the dramas of life, the affective assaults, the parental or social prohibitions and sometimes physical suffering cause some children to close off from the world of listening and communication. No longer willing to listen, distortions and fade-outs become common; the response circuits are lengthened to enable them to withdraw from those who make them suffer, from those they do not want to encounter. They then remain prisoners of these tricks and evasions, which, at one time, permitted them to defend themselves against the aggressions of the outside world. They find themselves locked in behind closed doors, which they can no longer open. The Listening Test highlights these distortions or deficiencies in relation to the ideal curve, which everyone can potentially attain. Treatment, then, becomes a matter of rectifying these distortions and eliminating these deficiencies through appropriate techniques designed to liberate people imprisoned by the chains of non-listening." [49]

"Acquiring this ideal curve requires balancing the interplay of the two muscles of the middle ear [the hammer and stirrup muscles], thus allowing constant regulation of the internal pressure of the inner ear ... It so happens that the whole auditory apparatus, from the external passage to the internal vesicle, corresponds to that ideal curve. It is really one of the many marvels of nature that the human ear is made, adapted, and modeled for hearing and listening. Distortions, especially blockages that become established, and lapses in listening impede motivation, prevent exchange, disturb dialogue and ultimately disrupt communication. Those who have not experienced or enjoyed true listening cannot imagine what distortions cause them to miss. It is so difficult to relate to the environment when one must constantly correct (on the cortical level) the distortions that complicate our existence. Hearing and communication become infinitely easier once one has ears that are harmoniously open to the external world."[50]

ADMINISTERING THE LISTENING TEST

Like the classical hearing test, the Listening Test is performed using an audiometer emitting pure tones between 125 Hz and 8,000 Hz. The only difference between a standard audiometer and the one used by Tomatis is that they are calibrated differently. In particular, the bone conduction curve is shifted downward by a few decibels, just to make the interpretation of the test easier.

Most audiologists measure auditory acuity at the following frequencies: 125, 250, 500, 1,000, 2,000, 4,000 and 8,000 Hz. These frequencies are spaced apart by one octave. The Listening Test measures in addition at 125, 750, 1,500, 3,000 and 6,000 Hz, to get a more refined auditory representation. Getting readings half an octave apart yields significant additional information.

As in standard tests, the Listening Test measures the acuity of both ears separately. Tomatis practitioners also measure the acuity of the bone conduction on both sides, by placing a vibrator on the mastoid bone, just behind the ear.

The goal of the Listening Test is to determine several parameters:

> **MINIMUM AUDITORY THRESHOLD**: That is the softest sound that the person being tested can hear for each frequency. The volume is progressively increased by increments of 5 decibels till the client signals that he heard the tone. *Contrary to classical audiometric protocol, the tone is not repeated if the subject did not hear it.* This is in line with the fact that the Listening Test is a test to measure *"conscious attention"* simulating what happens in real life. For that reason, the client is not prodded into paying attention to the sound.

SELECTIVITY: The Listening Test also determines whether the subject is able to discriminate sounds of different pitches. We only test selectivity for air conduction. The client has to listen to two consecutive sounds that differ in pitch and decide whether the last one was higher or lower in pitch than the previous one. The test is repeated several times to cover the whole spectrum.

SPATIALIZATION: The bone conduction response reveals how the client localizes sounds in space. He is asked to raise his hand on the same side as he hears the sound, and, if he is not able to locate it, to raise both hands. A typical reaction in the latter case is: "I hear it in the middle" or "I hear it on both sides."

LATERALITY: Finally, the test determines which ear is the leading ear. To test the degree of lateralization, Tomatis developed a device called an audio-laterometer. This device makes it possible for the client to listen to his voice via a headphone. The clinician can vary the intensity on either the left or right side. In this way, he can deliver the sound to either ear, making the client listen preferentially with the right or left ear. If the clinician tries to reinforce the dominance of the right ear, but the client continues to use the left to process language, then he knows that the client is left lateralized and he can even calculate the degree of laterality.

As we study the psychological meaning of the Listening Test, we will look more closely at these different parameters. They will, in fact, be the thread that guides us through the labyrinth.

THE MEANING OF THE AIR AND BONE CONDUCTION CURVES

Earlier, we introduced the concept of the ideal listening curve. This concept is somewhat more complex than it seems at first, since it involves, in fact, two curves, one for air and the other for bone conduction. If Tomatis hadn't calibrated his audiometer differently, the two curves might be on top of one another. With recalibration, they are separated, so the air conduction curve usually lies above the bone conduction curve. As we will later see, *the air conduction curve should ideally always be higher than bone conduction curve.*

The air conduction curve, according to Tomatis, defines the manner in which we listen to the external world. Not only to the blue jay in the backyard or to the rustle of maple leaves in the park, but also to the voices of our children, spouse, boyfriend, co-workers, bank clerks and waiters: the list could go on and on, since most of us are naturally social creatures craving human contacts. The air conduction curve is thus a fairly good barometer of the way we respond to the external world from a listening standpoint. It defines our social response: *our external listening.*

The bone conduction curve, on the other hand, defines the manner in which we listen to ourselves. Sounds traveling through bone resonate throughout the inner space of our bodies and echo through our organs. As we have already observed, it is through our own voice and the voice of others that we form the first inkling of separation between the world inside and the outer world. The voices of others are, of course, the one we perceive through air conduction, but our voice is the ones that we perceive through bone conduction. It is by listening to our own voice that we progressively learned to focus on the sounds we were producing. Self-listening teaches us to emit sounds, to organize them into words and sentences, projecting them to the ears of others. These words and sentences resonate throughout our bones, indeed our whole bodies. As we shall see, our bone conduction curve reveals how we engage with our body: whether we accept, reject or belittle it, even whether we are likely to develop psychosomatic ailments to silence the voice inside. But bone conduction is also the channel that reflects our internal dialogue: our thoughts, our emotions, our feelings, and our most intimate fantasies, all of which constitute the rich soil of our inner life. It is thus the conduit for self-listening (or *inner listening*) provided that we are willing to engage with ourselves, instead of turning a deaf ear to our own inner dynamic. In short, inner listening is the path to consciousness.

Were it not for Tomatis' recalibration of his audiometer, ideal listening would be displayed as a single curve with the air and bone curve overlapping. Moving thus in tandem harmony, social listening (air) is not disturbed by the distortions of the ego (bone), and inner listening (bone) is not disrupted by the intrusion of social life (air). This ideal is rarely achieved. Instead the curves representing each one, ear- and bone conduction, overlap, criss-cross, peak or drop, defying interpretation by an untrained eye. And yet, there are ways to interpret the Listening Test, if we divide the listening curve into different zones.

THE THREE AUDITORY ZONES

Tomatis and other professionals, who have studied the Listening Test for many years, agree that the audiogram for each ear can be divided into three zones. Respectively, they are:

The body zone:
located between 125 Hz and 1,000 Hz.
The language/communication zone:
located between 1,000 Hz and 2,000 Hz
The creativity zone:
located beyond 2,000 Hz

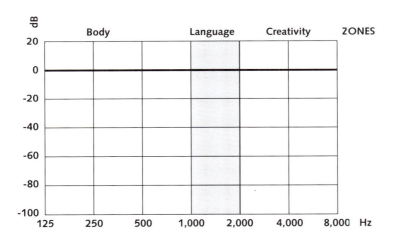

Figure 14: The three auditory zones

The body zone (between 125 Hz and 1,000 Hz) corresponds to the vestibular responses to sounds. As you remember, the vestibule controls the movements of our bodies and responds to low frequencies. It is the ear of the body, so to speak. Perception of sounds in that zone evokes mainly gut reactions. These are visceral, instinctual, and mostly unconscious and affect our whole being. So it is said that the body zone is also the zone of the unconscious. Tomatis used to joke that you just need to play the drum around someone, to quickly see the "ape" in him, which is that animal-like part of us that is also part of our evolutionary heritage.

The language/communication zone (between 1,000 Hz and 2,000 Hz) is the area where we find a great deal of the higher harmonics contained in the spoken language. It is the ultimate conversational zone because this is where even sounds of low intensity are perceived well. It is, moreover, the *zone of logic*, as language requires logic. When you want to communicate, you cannot put the words of a sentence in the order you wish, but you have to follow the implicit and logical rules of syntax. Finally, *our ego* manifests itself through our ability to master language and communicate our thoughts or feelings. Consequently, the curves in this area can provide some indications about the strengths and weaknesses of the ego.

The creativity zone (between 2,000 Hz and beyond) is the domain of the highest harmonics. These are the ones that stimulate us, energize our brain, and thus boost our ability to memorize and learn easily. This does not occur without a broadening of the mind and therefore requires an ability to intuitively perceive things that otherwise would have stayed buried in a morass of material facts. It is, therefore, the *zone of intuition* that is essential for those pursuing an intellectual endeavor or an artistic career. Intuitive experience is often equally the entrance point to spiritual life, and thus this zone can also be called the *spiritual zone*.

Tomatis has also described this zone as the *affectivity zone*. This is related to the fact that we first perceived high frequencies when we were in the womb. These belonged to our mother's voice and became even clearer and more abundant at the time of birth, when we were suddenly propelled into a world where sounds travel through air. For this reason, very high frequencies always stay linked, although most often unconsciously, to our affectivity.

From a spiritual standpoint, these high frequency sounds lead us to believe in an afterlife or in a world beyond the limits of our earthly existence. They call for the creation of a new reality, be it a child to be born, a scene painted on canvas, a musical composition or the deepening of one's spiritual life. This is the zone that resounds with our highest ideals and aspirations. In Freud's terminology, it would be the *zone of the superego*. Overall, responses in that zone may indicate a higher level of consciousness.

Awareness of the three zones provides us with a kind of map. Like a detective in a mystery, we now have some clues to begin to understand the psychological make-up of the person being tested. When we try to sum up the main psychological traits of a friend, a family member or the boss in the office, we tend to often rely on simplistic observations like: "she is totally narcissistic," "he is paranoid," "she is depressed," and "he is a power freak." Such judgments are psychological jargon and fail to grasp the common denominator running through these various observations: an inability to listen. For example, if I have a narcissistic personality, I am so involved with myself that I have little attention left for others, unless they can be used to my advantage. If I am paranoid, I see everyone as a potential enemy. Thus, I see people through the distorted filter of my fears. I often misunderstand social clues: a casual comment from my boss sends my adrenaline rushing, fearing I might be fired. My fear is such that I only read the signs that reinforced it. I cannot afford to listen to other signals, since I need to be on my guard at all times to ward off real or imaginary fears. If I am depressed, the world is perceived through my lack of energy. How can I see a ray of hope in my life if everything looks doomed from the start? All these various conditions, regardless of their symptoms have in common an inability to listen both to oneself and to others.

Evaluating the listening potential of someone yields many clues about their psychological ill or well being. Using the three zones as our compass, we can deduce a series of characteristics that define and capture that person's characteristic behavior.

THE BODY ZONE (ZONE 1)

As you may recall, the ideal curve in the body zone (125 to 1,000 Hz) is an ascending one, with a slope of 6 to 18 decibels per octave. What could we conclude from a listening profile as shown below?

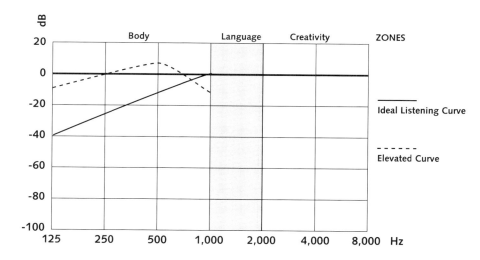

Figure 15: Elevated auditory acuity in the Body Zone

It is quite typical for a child discovering the world through his senses to have an elevated response in the body zone. He needs to touch, smell, taste, see and hear to make sense of his surroundings. When words come, he will be able to step higher on the developmental ladder and start to name, interpret, categorize, and organize the experience of his senses. He won't have to physically touch a chair, his teddy bear or his mother's face to be assured of their continuing existence. They will have become concepts that he can easily retrieve from the recesses of his memory and group into meaningful new combinations. He then moves from a concrete approach to the world to a symbolic approach that considerably expands his mental universe. Not all children will make this leap though. Many will stay stuck to various degrees, at some points along the continuum of development.

The response to the low frequencies in zone 1 tracks this evolution. The more elevated the response, especially in bone conduction, the more likely the child is to continue experiencing the world through his senses and in a very materialistic way. If, on the other hand, the response in the lows is not elevated, the child is likely to move to a less materialistic and less egocentric stage. Rather than being bound to the sensory responses of his body, he becomes genuinely interested knowing people. A drop in the curve in zone 1 corresponds to what psychologists and psychoanalysts call the beginning of "the latency stage" which is often observed in children over the are of 6. If the curves stay high, especially if the bone conduction curve is above air conduction, it is likely that that child will have problems at the vestibular level, often resulting in forms of hyperactivity, lack of attention and behavior problems.

As puberty comes around the corner and hormones rage in the teenage body, the response to the low frequencies in the body zone shoots up again like the S&P 500 during a bull market. Such an upsurge is not exactly surprising considering that the body goes through many changes. The bone conduction responds to that transformation all the more because it is a reflection of what goes on in the physical body. This is a period of intense re-awakening of the senses as sexuality takes center stage. It is also often a period of stark materialism, summed up quite nicely by a slogan I recently saw on a T-shirt: "My kids take me for an ATM machine."

Parents with teenagers know how difficult it is to break through the self-absorption of their sons or daughters. Their attitude is so egocentric (I am the sun, you are the distant planets of my solar system) that a meeting of the minds is difficult, if not impossible. "They do not listen to anything" is the complaint often heard from frustrated parents. What they listen to, what they crave—sometimes through drugs or through loud, pounding music activating their vestibule—is a sensory perception of their body. Of their new body, I would add. From this perception of their body, their new self emerges—a self that is largely in the process of being defined and created through the multiple sensory experiences in which they delight. Listening to others is not the main task of teenagers: they are busy enough trying to understand themselves and the "crazy times" they sometimes feel they go through.

Teenagers should not be pressured into the type of therapy developed by Tomatis unless they have a strong desire to better themselves; otherwise, the effect of the therapy will be limited. Once they feel a desire for improvement, they become more receptive. Probably, by that time they will be somewhat older, and not surprisingly, the listening curves in the body zone (especially the bone conduction) will probably have dropped.

Adults who show elevated listening curves in that zone display the tendencies observed in teenagers: they appear materialistic, reactive, and in search of sensory stimulation. Moreover, when the curves are elevated in the low frequencies, perception of higher frequencies tends to be inaccurate. They are mostly in resonance with their body and its basic instincts, which results in poor listening. This may also account for their difficulties in learning.

The Communication Zone (Zone 2)

Most of the higher harmonics of the language are located in this zone (1,000 to 2,000 Hz), which is the reason for calling it the language or communication zone. It reflects how people relate with themselves and others, and with the world at large. In analyzing the Listening Test we need to remember that air conduction reflects "listening to others" while bone conduction mirrors "listening to one self."

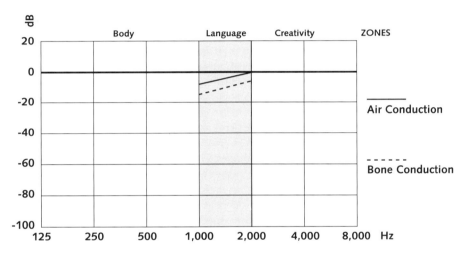

Figure 16: The curves of a good communicator

Let's look at an audiogram of a good communicator (see figure above). Both curves will be ascending with the air conduction curve being higher than the bone conduction. A smooth air conduction curve that is higher than the bone conduction curve reflects someone with a strong desire to engage others in communication. A person with such curves typically delights in social contacts, is likely to be a capable speaker with a good voice, one who can communicate his thoughts effortlessly. As the bone conduction curve is smooth and below the air conduction curve, this person listens well to himself (smoothness of the curve) and doesn't put himself ahead of others (bone below air).

If, on the other hand, the bone conduction curve shows a dip, the psychological profile of that person changes (see figure below).

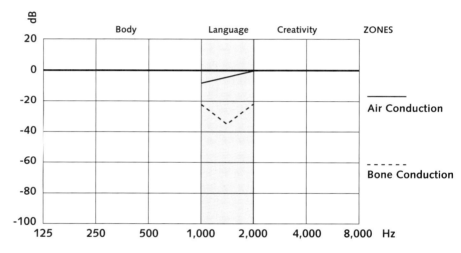

Figure 17: Johanna, sociable, but deep down very shy

Take Johanna for example: on the surface, she is a very social woman who displays the composure of a calm and competent person. She mingles well at parties, works part-time in her husband's office where she manages the staff and is involved in the many activities of her children. This is in line with the smooth air conduction curve. Still, when I point out that she is probably shy and that she would rather stay home than be so socially involved, she readily agrees that this is exactly what she would love to do. She has to make a conscious effort to maintain a facade of social competence. Too often, she feels like collapsing under the strain and experiences bouts of depression. Since I had just met her and knew almost nothing about her personal history, I could only rely on her Listening Test and the ominous dip on the bone conduction curve between 1,000 Hz and 2,000 Hz to make these observations. Her real feelings were not evident during the first part of our meeting since she maintained an easygoing social façade. In the discussion that followed, she verified the information suggested by her test.

If the dip had occurred on both curves, she would not have been able to keep up the social pretense. As a rule of thumb, a dip on both curves in zone 2 is a strong indication that the person has given up any hope of really reaching others and will shy away from social contacts. Small variations in the air conduction curve are precious indicators of the real underlying psychological state of a person in such cases. An ascending or flat air curve will show that the person is still trying to communicate and be involved in the social world. As soon as the air curve collapses, even slightly, the desire to communicate decreases and despair may set in. This is an important cue for the therapist and should not be missed.

Although the depth of the dip may decrease with treatment, the patient is still not out of the woods. I remember the mother of an anorexic young woman being ecstatic after observing some "positive changes" after a few days of treatment. I knew better than to trust what she said since I had her Listening Test handy. The young woman dashed her mother's hope when she told her daughter that she looked better. "I just fake it, that's all! I'd rather be dead!" She was, to say the least, in total agreement with the curves of her Listening Test.

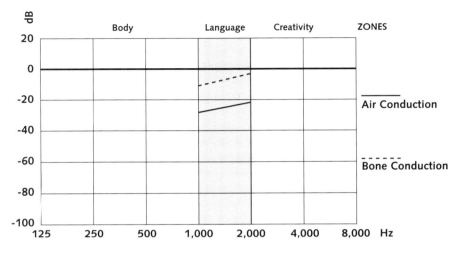

Figure 18: The curves of a poor communicator

Lastly let's look at a person whose bone conduction is higher than his air conduction (see figure above). Such a person mainly listens to himself. He is not really interested in listening to others. In his case, language is used to attack, denigrate, and assert oneself with little concerns for others.

THE CREATIVITY ZONE (ZONE 3)

The creativity zone starts at around 2,000 Hz and continues to the end of the audible spectrum. People who hear well in this frequency range are endowed with a good energy level since they easily pick up the high frequencies that stimulate the brain. The fact that they have good ears means that they have also a good voice, rich in the high frequencies that stimulate the speaker's brain. They tend to be clear-minded, logical, well articulated and goal-oriented and have a good memory. They can normally work long hours because of their high energy level, and often appear to be in a state of flow in their thoughts and actions. They rely on their intuition to develop new ideas, and therefore manifest an inquiring mind that takes creative leaps into new domains. Rarely satisfied with the material world as it is, they have a strong inclination toward spiritual life. This usually goes hand in hand with an altruistic approach to others and society at large. Their approach to life is generally humanistic, less self-centered and, therefore, they often apply themselves to the service of others.

Although this description sounds idealistic, do not forget that the Ideal Listening Curve is, well, ideal. Still, it is certainly an ideal worth emulating. It represents a state of self-realization that we can only imagine when we have a peak-experience.

Stimulating the brain with high frequencies sounds often results in a feeling of joy, a sense of flow, the exhilaration of expanded possibilities in one's life. A musician composed the music of an entire album during the first three weeks of her treatment. One morning, she walked into the center while continuing to scribble the notes of a melody that "was flowing through her" on a piece of paper. She continued to write music during the next two hours without pausing a minute. An aspiring writer broke through his writer's block and was finally able to work towards the completion of a screenplay.

Under the influence of high frequencies, several painters developed a new style, which marked a new phase in their careers.

People who are not necessarily artistically inclined also report an expansion of their creative abilities, a greater trust in their own intuition and overall a sense of self-confidence that eluded them before. The treatment, especially the use of high-frequencies, seems "to spark," as Tomatis put it, a new dimension of being that was potentially there but was not accessible or remained undeveloped.

A drop of the curve in zone 3 does not necessarily mean that the person is void of spiritual life or of creativity. That would be a very literal interpretation of the Listening Test, which does not allow for the context in which a person lives. Older people, for example, commonly develop or renew spiritual interests long absent from their lives. Age can also bring a loss of acuity in the higher frequencies. Here there is an apparent contradiction between physiology and life experience. The example of Beethoven, who composed beautiful music till the end of his career, even though he was deaf, must make us pause before jumping to the wrong conclusions. Therefore, the very real possibility of a hearing loss in zone 3 needs seriously to be taken into account.

If perception of high frequency sounds is so important to creativity, would a curve that continues to ascend in the creativity zone not be even better than the Ideal Listening Curve that drops slightly after 4,000 Hz? Not according to Tomatis. A curve which continues to ascend throughout that zone, after ascending all the way through zone 1 and 2, is a curve that Tomatis would have characterized as belonging to someone who is cut off from his body and from reality. This demonstrates how much caution should be exercised when interpreting the Listening Test: a small variation from the norm can make a lot of difference in understanding or interpreting the results.

A Global View

You may have realized that in describing zone 3, the body zone and the language/communication zone have been considered implicitly. *The general aspect of the entire curve should always be taken into consideration before any evaluation takes place.* Similarly, each zone of each ear needs to be compared with the comparable zone of the other ear.

While the Listening Test is a very important diagnostic tool, it is important to remember the exceptions that prove the rule. Tomatis often emphasized that people who have a poor curve but use it well are actually better listeners than people who have a good curve but lack the desire to listen. One of the best listeners I ever met was a ninety-eight year-old woman who came for treatment of a balance problem. She had a seventy decibels hearing loss, a pair of hearing aids, a very poor hearing curve, but was all ears when listening to others. She maintained a very active intellectual life (books were piled around her small apartment); she was deeply immersed in her own spiritual search and had become a spiritual guidepost for many of her much younger friends.

And so, while the Listening Test indicates many of a person's strengths and weaknesses, it is not the whole picture: there is always more than meets the eye. This last point is worth remembering and will become even clearer as we continue to study some of the other parameters of the Listening Test, the first and foremost being the test of selectivity.

SELECTIVITY

Selectivity is the ability that most of us have to discriminate between tones of different pitch. When listening to two sounds, we are normally able to say which one is higher or lower in pitch than the other one. When this ability works optimally, we can discriminate in a split second without hesitation. However, when we hesitate, it usually indicates that we are having some difficulties. When we make only a few errors across the frequency spectrum, selectivity is "partially closed." However, if we systematically err for each frequency, our selectivity is "fully closed." In this case, it is not possible to draw any valid conclusion from the Listening Test. Full closure of selectivity invalidates all parameters of the Listening Test.

The more closed the selectivity, the more immature the person tends to be and the more learning difficulties are in evidence. Troubles in this area impede psychological development and affect the ability to organize one's thoughts. The impact of these processing errors can be crippling.

Selectivity, Logic and Sense of Organization

People who have trouble discriminating sounds often have a parallel difficulty in thinking logically. There are gaps in the logic when they present an argument because, more often than not, they are unable to organize their thoughts in a sequential order. It is not that they don't have good ideas, for theirs can be brilliant and original. They may even have tons of ideas, but, when asked to put their ideas on paper, all the brilliance may disappear. They are unable to organize their thoughts into a coherent, logical and meaningful expression. The results often are disappointing. This is equally true for the student who has to write an essay and for the businessman whose career depends on his ability to write well-documented, well-organized reports or give a good presentation.

We are able to identify the sounds of the language because of their particular frequencies. Our ears are always on alert for the slightest sonic variation. Our cochlea scans our auditory range, quickly identifying a sound, comparing it with the one before and the one that follows, piecing them together and threading sounds into words and sentences in an orderly way. Of course, our ears are doing other things at the same time. First of all, each sound is compared with sounds contained in the memory function of the brain, to get an accurate picture of each one. Then, and this is very important, these few sounds that make up our language are selected, screening out the multitude of sounds competing for our attention but which do not add any valuable information. The selection process, thus, rests on our ability to quickly hear the slightest differences in the sounds we perceive, and selecting those that contain meaningful information.

The same mechanism of selection characterizes the thought process. Thinking clearly means being able to screen out irrelevant thoughts, so we are able to select, classify, organize and present our ideas in a sequential, logical order. Language helps us organize our thoughts so we can convey them to others. Communication rests on our ability to quickly process language, which, in last analysis, depends on the capacity of the ear to accurately check the different parameters of sound production. Any lapse in decoding accurately will have a ripple effect on language production and will ultimately affect the way we think. That is particularly true when our selectivity is partially or fully closed. In this case our voice will lack fullness and luster. The same will be true for our thought process that can be described as vague and clouded, if not at times disorganized. A nimble mind is first of all a good ear.

Disorganization is not limited to the mind. It is evident in the physical world as well. A child with closed selectivity is often one who could win first place in a messy room contest (although they don't like it if I state this in front of their parents, who just sigh at the thought of the battlefield waiting for them back home). This is, of course, as true for adults whose messy desks or disorganized work habits reflect disorganized thinking.

SELECTIVITY AND PSYCHOLOGICAL DEVELOPMENT

Lucy left a brief message on my answering machine stating that she had a question to discuss with me. Could I call her as soon as possible? I was somewhat surprised by her phone call since her eleven year-old son, Frank, had finished his program almost two years earlier. I knew from a follow-up session that, to the delight of his parents, he was doing much better in school. What could have prompted Lucy's call? Had Frank's results by any chance deteriorated? Her call gave me no clues about it.

"When we came for the evaluation," Lucy explained, "you asked me if something had happened to Frank around a certain age. I cannot remember which age you mentioned. Would you mind looking over his chart and tell me what you told me then? I will tell you afterwards why I am asking."

A quick glance at the chart told me that around the age of six or seven, Frank's selectivity had stopped opening, possibly in response to something that disturbed him. What? I could not tell. I shared this information with Lucy.

"How strange!" she said. "I just received a letter from Frank's old school on the East Coast. It informed me that one of his previous teachers had been arrested on charges of child molestation. And guess what? Frank was in his class at the age you just told me! I remember how much he hated to go to school. I had to force him to go every morning. Do you think that he may have been molested too?"

I told Lucy that it was way too early to draw any conclusions. After all, I said, it is fairly common for first-graders to *resist* school. They may not connect well with their teacher or they feel bullied by some of their peers. They suddenly have to learn to read, write and keep up with children who display a keener intelligence; they must sit for long hours at a desk, forced to mature, even grow up when they would rather be out playing. Moreover, competition and the sense of falling behind in the rush to master written language can be traumatic, especially if parents and teachers see early faltering as auguring future difficulty or even failure. Furthermore, kids can get sick; a parent may be laid off making mortgage payments difficult and creating a climate of anxiety at home; parents may announce a separation or divorce; a well-loved grandfather may pass away. The list of possibilities is almost endless. While a glance at the Listening Test may generate some hypotheses about a potentially disturbing event that has taken place in the life of a child, it certainly does not tell the whole story and does not fill in the details. For that reason, I told Lucy, I would be cautious, especially in a case where child molestation may have taken place.

She felt reassured by all the possibilities that I laid before her. She admitted that she didn't think that his teacher had molested Frank, because he had gotten hold of the letter and had read it without any sign of being disturbed by its content. Better, she concluded, let the matter rest than to upset Frank with questions that might be groundless and could really disturb him. He was, after all, a well-adjusted child. She could not justify destroying his sense of wellbeing for the sake of her curiosity.

"How could you tell about the age?" she finally asked. I told her that I was neither a fortune-teller nor that could I intuit past events of people's lives. There was, instead, a rational basis for my answer. I explained that learning to listen is progressive and parallels the developmental process. Discriminating sounds is not an innate ability; on the contrary, it is a learned skill that requires time to become accurate.

According to Tomatis, ==it takes about eleven years to fully develop.==

At first, babies perceive sound without discrimination. This is so because the transition from liquid audition to air audition constitutes an extraordinary adaptation. The ear of the baby is suddenly flooded with a myriad of sounds, some soft, others loud, made up of a wide range of frequencies. Just imagine how we would feel if we were deaf and suddenly began to hear? We would most likely feel assaulted by this jumble of sounds and would have a hard time finding meaning in this cacophony. The inability of the newborn to immediately and distinctly perceive each sound might, in fact, be a protective mechanism. His fragile nervous system might not otherwise withstand the onslaught of noise and sounds that greet his arrival into the world.

Selectivity, like a diaphragm, "opens" progressively. ==Low frequencies are the first to be accurately identified and reproduced.== As the child matures, he perceives medium range frequencies distinctly, then high frequencies. Around the age of eleven, selectivity should be open provided that he had experienced no physical or emotional difficulties. At age eleven, a child should be able to zero in on sounds, identify them properly and reproduce them accurately.

When Frank came in for an evaluation, he was nine years old but had a selectivity of a six year old. So, when Frank was six years old, something serious enough happened that made his selectivity stop opening. Again, it was a guess, not certitude. As a matter of fact, Lucy had not remembered anything special during Frank's evaluation two years earlier. Except for a major move a year earlier, the family's life had been uneventful.

Lucy was certainly not insensitive to her son's experience, but what might be traumatic for a young child might be totally inconspicuous to an adult. I still remember being totally shattered by a contemptuous comment of one of my counselors at a summer camp when I was seven years old. He certainly had no clue about the impact of his comment on me. I was too proud to complain about it even to my peers. I kept my anger and shame inside, feeling devastated and depressed for several days. Children do not necessarily lick their wounds in public. No wonder parents may miss the mark.

Lucy did have one clue though: Frank did not like going to school. But why? Was he afraid of his teacher? Quite the contrary, Lucy remembered that he liked his teacher. What he disliked was school! And there were plenty of reasons for not liking it! Frank had a history of ear infections and, consequently, a listening problem that went undetected as long as Frank didn't have to master reading and writing. When he entered first grade, he was suddenly unable to meet the challenge. He withdrew into negative behavior, falling further and further behind, trying to dodge school in order to hide his difficulties. His listening problem became worse and his difficulties at school grew, creating a vicious downward spiral with no visible end. In Frank's case, the school problems were sufficiently traumatic to stop the opening of his selectivity.

Listening is about reaching out, connecting, and making contact with our environment as well as with the inner world of our thoughts and feelings. While we strive to perceive good news and good vibrations, we are likely to turn a deaf ear to any situation that threatens to disturb the modicum of peace and equilibrium that constitutes our comfort zone. When pressure becomes too intense, we feel like retreating into a shell. Like Frank, we cannot take it; we do not even want to deal with the situation at hand. What we do, consciously or not, is to take a step back and buy some time, hoping that the difficult or overwhelming problem will go away on its own.

In short, we want to put as much distance as we can between ourselves and the cause of our discomfort. Distance here does not necessarily mean physical distance, for we may not be able to run away even if we would like to. So we resort to more subtle strategies. When we do not want to listen to someone, we just turn a deaf ear.

You may still hear the voice in the background, but it does not make you upset as it did while you were still listening. You have found a very good defense mechanism to protect yourself. It is doubtful, though, that you've made a conscious decision to turn off the person bothering you. Quite likely the need to protect yourself overrode your thinking and whatever other needs you may have had at that moment. Now, even though the offending voice keeps droning in your ears, the sounds have lost their clarity and sharpness, they seem to come from further away than the spot from which the bad vibrations emanate. That is precisely what a closure of selectivity does: it dims the sounds and make that they are processed slower. That way, we are putting a distance between whatever disturbed us and ourselves.

The closure of the selectivity might be advantageous in certain situations, but after the situation has been resolved and perhaps long forgotten, the closure may persist causing us to suffer from the inability to clearly discriminate sounds. While Frank may have reacted to the stress of learning to read and write in first grade by unconsciously closing his selectivity, he was soon trapped by the very mechanism that once protected him. First grade was long past when we met, but he still could not read well and was quite disorganized. However, he was an intelligent boy and things changed rapidly when his selectivity did finally open.

If you think about it, you might expect that musicians have fully open selectivity. However, musical training is not a guarantee of good discrimination: some musicians and singers make mistakes when their selectivity is tested and are often quite upset about this revelation. One of the singers I treated burst into tears every time we came to that part of the test. She became so distraught that we had to stop the test several times. She had had an especially harsh upbringing and it seemed only human to rely on defense mechanisms to keep the pain at bay. Years later, though, this defense mechanism was still at work, even though the cause of the pain had passed. As therapy proceeded and selectivity progressively opened, terrible childhood memories surfaced and were dealt with, while her singing grew more beautiful.

Auditory stimulation may not always open a closed selectivity. In fact, at times it can even temporarily close an already open selectivity. According to Tomatis, drug addicts often have a fully open selectivity during their initial evaluation. It closes, at least partially, as soon as the program begins. Tomatis explained that this is an unconscious way of protecting themselves from the painful issues they become aware of as the treatment proceeds. It would otherwise be so painful that they could relapse in their drug habit, to erase their overwhelming pain. They need to tackle issues one at a time—a process that parallels the opening of their selectivity.

Dolores offers an exceptional example of the opening and closing of selectivity during an auditory stimulation program. A bright and pleasant woman, her easy-going appearance hid a dark secret: she had been sexually abused as a child and had never recovered from that traumatic, innocence shattering event and its crushing effect on her sense of self. Years of therapy had not banished nightmares about this dehumanizing event. As we worked together, her selectivity slowly opened and her Listening Test improved. But as she began to listen to herself more closely, she also started to complain about the return of raw, intrusive memories. On a hunch, I did a Listening Test almost daily to keep track of her struggle and progress on the path to recovery. One day, she walked in, smiling and relaxed, declaring that she felt marvelous. It was a breakthrough, she thought.

I naively felt that this was the long awaited opening. Yet the next morning, after a very agitated night, she was again flooded with old memories. When I tested her, her selectivity had closed again, as it had been in the beginning. She was back in her protective shell. We discussed what to do next and agreed that it would be best for her to take a break and re-evaluate later if we should continue. In the end, she decided to stop but acknowledged that our work together had facilitated her psychotherapy immensely. This example illustrates how painful auditory stimulation can be at times.

Though I would certainly have preferred to continue working with Dolores, I have also learned, in my work as a therapist, to respect the resistance of my clients. If they resist, it is for good reasons. It is out of the question to strip the defenses from a client to speed up the therapy, as I once heard a self-appointed healer recommend. The use of sound or music for therapeutic purposes must abide by the same ethics that govern any form of therapy. While it is clear, for example, that closed selectivity might interfere with learning to read, it is clear too that closed selectivity might be the psyche's way of protecting our psychological balance—even if the price is some psychological imbalance! Therefore, the practitioner must be prepared to deal with all kinds of issues when selectivity begins to open.

In general, the more selectivity is closed, the more immature the child or adult is. And the more reason for the therapist to be cautious. Because closed selectivity invalidates all the other parameters of the Listening Test, Tomatis compared it to a veil that masks the real self, the "true me." The person is in such a state of confusion that he is unlikely to have real insight about his behavior. Whatever potential (good or bad) he may have, it is hidden and above all inhibited.

Some of my colleagues and I were consulted on a case involving a twenty-one year-old man whose selectivity was totally closed. While other parameters suggested intense potential for frustration, anger and anxiety, the colleague presenting his case described this young man as fairly calm. Knowing that closed selectivity can invalidate all other parameters of the Listening Test as well as insulate from painful experience and thus quell reactivity, we were unanimous in the opinion that our colleague should not treat him because, being primarily an educator, he lacked psychological training to help the client deal with the emotional impact of losing that protection. Numerous clinical observations taught us that the opening selectivity could strip the calm façade, releasing the submerged personality, perhaps unleashing violent or sexual acting out. It is, in fact, quite common that opening selectivity results in a period of confusion between assertiveness and aggressiveness, which requires verbal exploration and support to sort out, especially for children. Parents can be shocked in seeing their "little lamb" act like a bully. Although *this stage is temporary* and things stabilize after a while, family therapy or psychotherapy is an important adjunct in these cases.

All these examples have one point in common: they show that selectivity is an important indicator of psychological responses to life circumstances. Open ears commonly indicate good adjustment. Closed ears suggest the need to reduce sensations and to distance oneself from a source of anxiety, fear or discomfort. It is a good defense mechanism as long as the threat exists, but it stunts emotional growth if it persists longer than the source of the anxiety. Re-opening selectivity is an effective therapy for putting someone back on track to healthier living.

SPACIALIZATION

Several chapters ago we discussed how we locate sound in space. As you may remember, the exact mechanisms are not well understood, but most likely we localize sound using the time and/or intensity differences between sounds reaching our left and our right ears. If we are very skilled in using these mechanisms, we have a very good sense of orientation in space. We can also make errors and declare, for instance, that we hear a sound on the right side of our head when it actually comes from the left side. The following is a more detailed look at the impact such errors have.

Spatialization Errors in the Body Zone (Zone 1)

In zone one, mistakes indicate difficulty locating oneself in space. Typically, the person gets lost easily, even if directions have been repeated several times and even when copied carefully on a piece of paper. Right and left are easily confused. The result is a poor perception of the body. Consequently, the body image is not strongly rooted in the body and hampers the development of a strong sense of self. People who have spatialization problems cannot trust themselves because they cannot provide the information provided by their senses. They have a sense that "something is off" with their body. What is off is their orientation in space. For that reason, they tend to avoid any kind of sport activities where orientation plays an important role. For instance, they have trouble catching a ball, because their depth perception is off. They cannot accurately evaluate the distance between the ball moving in space and their own body, just as they cannot evaluate the distance between the source of a sound and themselves. Actually, they may position their body in the wrong spot to catch the ball.

People with errors in zone one, usually have vestibular problems. They are likely to be cautious, tentative, and somewhat rigid in daily life. Most of the time, they are unaware of the reason they lack confidence in themselves and may attribute it to a "natural" clumsiness or to their personal character: "It's the way I am! I cannot change it!" Such resignation precludes search for treatment or change, especially in adults.

Spatialization Errors in the Communication Zone (Zone 2)

Not surprisingly, spatialization errors in zone two indicate communication errors and impact our dialogue with others. The dance of social interaction literally eludes us, leaving us to wonder which foot to use, and causing us to dance without conviction.

For instance, a spatialization error at 1,500 Hz, right in the middle of the communication zone, denotes low self-esteem and persistent apprehension. Common interpretations of the "Draw a Tree" assessment, used to evaluate self-perception, often confirm the results of the Listening Test. When asked to draw a tree other than a pine, many people with shaky self-esteem draw a palm. "Nine out of ten times that is a sign that the person feels intellectually inferior," says Dr. Bob Roy, a Canadian psychologist and Tomatis practitioner from Regina, Canada. This individual is not necessarily unsuccessful in life. A businessman who had a 1,500 Hz mark on his Listening Test drew the characteristic palm tree and explained to Dr. Ron Minson, from the Center for InnerChange in Denver, that he compensated for his lack of self-confidence by throwing himself into new business ventures. However, the success of each new venture could not erase the deep sense of insecurity that he carefully concealed. He had to prove over and again that he could be successful to counter the vision of himself as a failure. He was quite surprised that Dr. Minson perceived what he so carefully hid from others, yet was relieved to find someone in whom he could confide.

The Chicken and the Egg

The fit between spatialization mistakes and specific psychological traits invariably leads to some questions: are these errors the result of a physical condition leading to a certain psychological response, or is a psychological reaction translated into a physical condition? First, we will exclude cases that are purely physical. For instance, many head injured patients and people who experienced whiplash make these errors. Their vestibule suffered a shock, often resulting in dizziness and feeling disoriented, and followed by a gradual recovery. Auditory stimulation speeds up that recovery process but spatialization errors are still frequent, even after the dizziness has disappeared. Such cases should serve as a warning that not all errors are inevitably psychological.

This being said, there are sometimes psychological benefits associated with not being able to locate sounds. It might be a defense mechanism that keeps threats "out there," in a vaguely defined and delineated space, making them seem less threatening. This strategy is similar to the one used by the ostrich who buries her head in the sand to avoid the danger. The outcome of this often unconscious strategy or fantasy counters the desired goal: now, the danger comes from anywhere rather than from a precise direction. Still, this may be a small price to pay for the brief respite of believing oneself safe. Various other scripts are likely. They come in different shades and degrees of seriousness and may have various reasons. For instance, we could wonder if the businessman with the 1,500 Hz mark had been exposed to verbal abuse as a child or had witnessed verbal disputes.

In that case, the 1,500 Hz mark right in the middle of the communication area might not be a coincidence, since the disturbing dispute impacted listening in that area. There are obviously other possible reasons for spatialization errors, thus it seems good clinical practice to investigate the potential links between spatialization mistakes and psychological states before assigning a cause.

Still, if this strategy of distancing disturbing sounds does not work well, lateralization can achieve the same goal. In this case, left-ear dominance becomes a way to delay the scary or annoying information.

LATERALIZATION

Lateralization, you remember, refers to the fact that we tend to favor one ear in the communication process. We are either right or left ear dominant. The established dominance plays a role not only in our ability to learn, but also influences our psychological make-up. In general, right ear dominant people are likely to be more rational and left ear dominant people more emotional. Still, things are not as polarized as they may appear. Under stress, a right-ear dominant person is likely to shift to the left ear to buy himself a bit of time to process or to push away the stressing factor. That is to say, that lateralization can move back and forth from the right to the left ear under pressure.

In general, left ear dominant people are more influenced by their feelings while right-ear dominant people tend to stay cool and hold back their emotions. The ideal would be an equilibrium that brings together the best of both possibilities: an ability to use reason without excess paired with an ability to be in touch with one's feelings without being overwhelmed by them.

Relationships between two people who are extreme opposites in terms of ear dominance are likely to be explosive, unstable and often end up in separation or divorce. Since opposites attract each other, such relationships are fairly common. It is the traditional couple in which a wife may complain about a cold husband who is neither "in touch with his feelings" nor "understands her feelings." The husband may likewise complain about his wife wasting time (and his time) wanting to talk about feelings that are vague, messy, in short purely subjective—the ultimate insult—and do not fall into a neat category or statistics. His advice to her: "Grow up! Stop kidding yourself and stop being a kid lost in a fantasy world!" In this case, teaching them to listen to each other might be the best way to save the relationship.

The Present, the Future and the Past

We can get a fairly good idea about the lateralization of our friends or children by observing them. Some of the body language characteristics that you want to pay attention to have already been described in the chapter about the dominant mouth. Add to these elements an observation of timing, of the relationship to the past and future. To further develop this idea, picture a casual, imaginary discussion between you and your child (or a friend, if you prefer).

After chatting for a while, talking about a neutral topic, you may want to shift the emphasis to the future, to the projects and ideas he dreams about. It has to be something he looks forward to and stirs his enthusiasm. While he is talking, observe his body language, the tone of his voice, his posture. Has he turned slowly to the right? Is the right corner of his mouth going slightly upward? Are his eyes moving slightly toward the right? Is he tilting his head, moving his right ear upward, as if he were presenting his right ear to the sounds of his own voice, listening to himself as he talks? Is his voice bright, full and energetic? If so, he is probably right ear dominant, but we can't be entirely sure yet.

Continue talking and bring the conversation to a topic that raises his anxiety level: school is a good one for children who are not doing very well in school, but it can be anything stressful in his life. If he maintains his body language, keeping it oriented towards the right and if his voice stays clear, you can be pretty sure that he is right ear dominant. If the stress evoked by the conversation is too great, you may see some fluctuation and turning toward the left, because, as mentioned previously, the best way to respond to stress is to buy some time, using the left, slower ear to process the information.

Let's now look at an alternate scenario. When talking about the future and all its exiting projects, our child talks in a low, monotone voice, his eyes slightly toward the left and his head tilted, with his left ear upward. The left corner of his mouth goes upward instead of the right one, etc. These observations clearly indicate left-ear dominance. When switching to the stressful subject, he will most likely become even more left ear dominant. This is typical of children who have difficulty learning in school. His lack of mastery at processing language quickly and accurately also prevents adequate control of his emotions: it is hard to contain your emotions if you cannot master the language that expresses them, or if you can do so only at the slower rate imposed by the left ear.

The first conclusion from this experiment is that stress tends to move ear dominance to the left. This buys time to deal with the stress as the left ear processes information more slowly. The second conclusion is less obvious, but also has to do with time. You may have noticed that the left ear dominant person did not shift to the right, even when talking about the brightest aspects of the future. He camped in his position on the left, trapped in the habits of his past. This suggests that:

Each ear represents a different time:

- The right ear symbolizes the present and future,
- The left ear symbolizes the past.

Therefore, the Listening Test captures in a snapshot the temporal dynamics of the person caught between past and future. We'll come back to it later. For the moment, we may want to remember that lateralization supports two different types of psychological personalities depending which ear is used as the dominant ear.

Dominance in Disguise

Still we should be careful before making hasty conclusions. As we have seen before, the process of establishing dominance extends over several years. In most cases, dominance is well established by age 6. It is, thus, inappropriate to draw psychological conclusions when observing children younger than six or seven. At an earlier age, it is best to talk of a trend toward one sidedness or the other.

The same caution applies to adults. The following story illustrates how misleading appearances can be. I have a friend who is *entirely* left ear dominant. If we relied solely on that information, we might expect him to make decisions guided by his feelings rather than logic. The basis for that conclusion would be that he is a "right brainer" since his left ear leads. This should preclude mastering language quickly and efficiently, leading to difficulties in learning (and possible dyslexia), in sequencing his thoughts logically and expressing himself clearly. A cursory analysis might emphasize that he is likely to be easily overwhelmed by feelings, adding to his confusion. One may even conclude that his learning problem and his difficulty expressing himself limit his aptitude for ascending the corporate ladder. We might even predict his future as an artist (since popular psychology predicts they are right-brain dominant).

Let's now check this image against reality. My friend certainly expresses himself more slowly than right-ear dominant people. When he speaks, his head clearly turns to the left, as would be expected from someone who controls the flow of his speech with his left ear. And of course, the left corner of his mouth tilts toward the left ear. The physical reality certainly corroborates our hypothesis. The biography does not. Even though my friend went to eleven primary schools, it was not due to learning or emotional difficulties. Instead, he went to so many schools because his father's career required frequent moves. He entered the university when he was barely seventeen and earned a Ph.D. in chemistry. He then worked quite successfully for several international companies, at times managing fairly large teams of people, often scattered over several continents. He was described as fair, caring and considerate but people working under him also emphasized his tremendous organizational skills and ability to analyze complex problems by breaking them down into manageable bits. For someone expected to have difficulty learning languages, he did quite well, and now speaks five of them fluently. So how did he manage to perform so well, contrary to expectations associated with left ear dominance?

The answer is surprisingly simple: my friend is in fact a "right ear dominant person in disguise." He just became left ear dominant when he lost his hearing in his right ear at age 6! By that time, dominance had been established. But he had no choice but to use his left ear. Fortunately, the extraordinary plasticity of the young brain allowed his nervous system to accommodate this new situation. Even though the flow of his speech is slower, as we would expect from a left ear dominant person, my friend acts as a right-ear dominant person. Psychologically, nothing had changed for him.

This should explain the caution against stereotyping and jumping to unwarranted conclusions. If you read the description of my friend carefully, you may have found it strange that I said that he was *totally* left ear dominant. You are right to be cautious: we can never be *totally* right- or left ear dominant unless we have only one functioning ear. Otherwise, even when dominance is established on the right side, there might be instances when people move temporarily to the left. There are also many who do not have well-established ear dominance and often move back and forth between right and left. However, to efficiently process language and use the cognitive functions associated with it optimally, it is best to be right ear dominant. It is also true that ear dominance colors our emotional life, since most of us depend on language to express our feelings

Shifting Dominance

The psychological consequences of shifting laterality are readily observable when training for right ear dominance. In the Tomatis approach, children and adults are asked to repeat words, sing or read aloud into a microphone. Their voice is then processed through the Electronic Ear and is fed back to their right ear. While reading or singing into a microphone would seem to be a fairly simple task, it is one that children in particular often resist, either passively ("I am too tired") or assertively ("I won't do it!").

Two six-year-old girls taught me a great deal about the interface between lateralization and psychology. Donna was a big girl who rarely smiled and was very stubborn, according to her mother, a special education teacher. She readily threw temper tantrums when told no and often behaved in manipulative ways. According to another mother whose child attended the same school, Donna bullied other children during recess. When we started to do microphone work, she first resisted, but then grudgingly consented to "read" stories she made up, based on the illustrations in the books she picked. One day, after more attempts to resist, she began to scream into the microphone. That was new! Anyone would have stopped right away, finding the decibel level unbearable, but she kept blasting her ears. I intuitively felt that she was trying to deafen herself to avoid listening to herself. Under those circumstances, there was no way that she could hear her own voice returning to her right ear! Language was reduced to a scream, to *baby* scream! I walked to her and said:

"Donna! I want you to whisper in the microphone! I want you to stop screaming!"

She looked up at me, her face contorted by rage.

"I don't want to talk in the microphone! *I don't want to grow up anyway!*" she shrieked.

She intuitively understood the connection between lateralization and maturation: I could not have explained it better!

Virginia, the other six-year old, knew deep down that listening with the right ear meant that she could not stay a baby. During our first meeting, she emphatically repeated that she would never be a grown up. "I want to be a baby all my life." When we started to ask Virginia to do some vocal exercises using the microphone, she resisted, first passively and then rebelled openly, sitting with pinched lips, folded arms and eyes fixed on the wall behind the microphone. One morning, she threw a terrible tantrum at the door. She refused to come in. "I know!" She yelled. "You want me to talk into the microphone! You don't want me to be a baby! You want to force me to be a grown-up!" She would not budge even when her mother tried to bribe her with the promise of a toy. I broke the standoff with a suggestion:

"Look! I said to her. You can be a baby *and* a grown-up at the same time!"

The possibility had obviously never crossed her mind! I could see relief on her face. I had freed her from a role that she intuitively knew she could not continue to play. I also knew that she still needed to cling, to some degree, to the feeling of security that staying a baby would give her. It was, after all, her mom's fears that she had been allaying. Her mother had had a terribly abusive childhood and did not want the past to be repeated. She dressed Virginia like a little fairytale princess and treated her like the most fragile and precious object on earth. She dressed herself impeccably, presenting a perfect image, although her life was precarious. Psychologically, she identified more with a dependent child than with a mature and independent adult. If Virginia grew up, her mother could do no less, releasing, in the process, the fantasy that sustained her for so long and which she had passed on silently to her daughter. So enmeshed were mother and daughter that Virginia could not mature without feeling she would betray her mother. Both were caught in this cycle, neither knew how to break it. By giving Virginia permission to be both baby and grown-up, I gave her a way out without her feeling she was betraying her mother.

Virginia dried her tears and walked into the center making no more fuss. When the time came to do her microphone exercise, she struggled through it but persisted to the end. Soon after, she started to show the first signs of a more age-appropriate behavior ... and mother started her own therapy.

FROM BABY TALK TO LANGUAGE

How is it that children intuitively perceive the connection between right-ear dominance and maturation? No six-year-old has, after all, been trained as a psychologist! Still they show great perspicacity. The truth is that children intuitively understand that the mastery of language requires right-ear dominance. It is the fastest way to process the flow of sounds in language. It is also the fastest way to listen to oneself as one thinks or speaks. But one can only speak well when one follows the implicit rules of language. Word order and conjugation of verbs, for example, are governed by very stringent rules. Although the rules of phonetics, syntax and semantics vary from language to language, all of them have rules. Following the rules guarantees that we can communicate with ourselves and others who know the language. Scrap the rules and we are left with a meaningless cacophony of sound.

That is why the young infant has an extended period of passive listening which zeros in on the sounds characteristic of the ambient language. The child's development and his chances of survival are predicated upon his ability to gradually master the rules leading to fluent language. Without rules, speech would have no shared meaning. When the process of mastering the rules is delayed or derailed, thoughts are difficult to put into words. They are fragmentary and hesitant, a likely jumble of words stitched together in unfinished sentences.

Establishing right-ear dominance integrates the code governing language. When words and meaning are finally conquered, independence starts: armed with the ability to make himself understood, the child can set out into the world. Independence is, however, fraught with risks and fears. For some children, clinging to mother, clinging to *baby talk and behavior* is a way of resisting the injunction to grow up. Resistance to growing up, maintaining the illusion that they still need the same care and attention as a baby, is a way of refusing the call of the future. Exchanging willingly baby talk for the rules of language is a symbolic acceptance of a world governed by rules.

The child's self-centeredness needs to give way to the acceptance of others as separate individuals. It is a shift from "listening to oneself" towards "listening to others." *Baby talk*, such as screams, tears, broken sentences, tantrums, acting out frustrated desires, has to be replaced by more socially acceptable ways of expressing one's needs. The child needs to learn to *verbally* communicate its desires and to negotiate them in a clear and logical manner; he needs to learn to respect the implicit rules of language and accept the rules governing social relationships. Growing up also implies giving up the desire for immediate gratification, which now has to be channeled—or sublimated, as Freud would say—in more mature ways.

This can be quite a tall order for some children (or adults who have not grown up). It creates a lot of anxiety and often quite a bit of resistance. Children like Donna and Victoria resist because leaving their baby world amounts to being launched into an unknown and scary world that requires radical change. Continuing to use baby talk indicates listening to the voice of their desires. These children are immersed in a world of constantly changing emotions, living in an eternal present. They are the little princesses of their castle, living in a sort of autistic state, ignoring the knocking on the door. When they begin listening to themselves through the right ear, they suddenly feel expelled from their baby world: the door has finally opened to the external world and it scares them so much that they apply all their energies to close it back and resist the promises of the future.

As language skills develop, children increasingly take their place in the world, taking responsibility for their words and living with the consequences of what they say. Their resistance to participating in that process is a sign of grief, their reluctance to leave the safety and protection of their childish world. Yet, this world needs to fade in order for them to continue to grow and reach a higher level of listening and consciousness. As we will see later, caring support from the parents can play a major role during this transitional phase and facilitate a gradual shift from bilateral listening to right ear dominance. When children mature unevenly, with emotional growth or learning lagging behind physical growth or behavioral autonomy, there is reason to suspect that lateral dominance is not emerging and treatment is in order. And that is precisely the goal of training the right ear to be dominant: activating the feedback loop that leads to a command of the language and accelerate the maturation process. As surprising as it may appear, change can be quite rapid and painless.

It would be inappropriate to use the expression *baby talk* or *baby world*, when talking about adults. Still, there might be some remnants of *baby talk* and *baby world* in the way adults sometimes interact with others. The self-centeredness of some of them, their manipulative ways, their need for instant gratification, their impulsiveness, their fits of rage, their inability to control their feelings, all of which remind us of the emotionalism of a child prior to his acceptance of the world of others. When the behavior is extreme, they are unlikely to listen to others: they just look for gratification of their needs, and others are just the means to get them fulfilled. In a much milder form, they can be adults whose only similarity with the baby world is that they are easily overwhelmed by their feelings. If they are left-ear dominant or if their ear dominance is unstable, trying to establish right ear dominance can help them greatly to get a better hold of their feelings when under stress and to articulate their thoughts more precisely.

Penelope is a good example of this transformation. She was left-ear dominant and highly emotional. This was all the more evident after her husband announced that, after thirty years of being married, he was leaving her for a much younger woman. It was a nasty divorce with a lot at stake, most notably the couple's great wealth. Penelope was feeling that, behind the scene, her husband was trying to deprive her of her due. She dreaded having to see her husband while the lawyers were haggling about money. She began to realize that she had always felt somewhat intimidated by her husband.

We worked for some time to move her from left to right ear dominance prior to the date she had to go to "the big meeting," the one she described as deciding her financial future. What she reported the day after the meeting was quite in line with what other adults report when we move them to right ear dominance. She had felt calm throughout the meeting and able to express her desires and wants in a clear and rational way, quite unusual for her. It was almost a shock to her that she could control herself so well and not feel overwhelmed by a rush of emotions, even when her soon-to-be-ex-husband was trying to get more than his share. She had stood her ground in a manner that surprised even her husband. As a result, he accepted an arrangement that was financially agreeable to her. When she told me about the meeting, Penelope was jubilant.

Like many other adult clients before her, she said that the therapy had been very important in giving her that new confidence and calmness. She had started to feel the change when she began to listen to herself through the right ear. This example, as well as many others taken from Tomatis' clinical practice, support the idea that lateralization plays an important role in our psychological make-up.

To summarize, selectivity, spatialization and lateralization reflect the way we listen or do not listen, to ourselves and to others. They can be used as unconscious defense mechanisms that may have been appropriate at a certain point in our lives but may become detrimental to our personal growth if they last beyond their temporary use.

PERSONALITY AND THE LISTENING TEST

We cannot escape being shaped by the way we listen. Because we tend to listen selectively, using filters to block off unpleasant facts and listening eagerly to what is pleasurable, we constantly reinforce our particular way of listening and thus continuously protect our core personality. This self-reinforcing cycle is hard to change, even when we suffer from negative consequences. So, the way we listen shapes our core personality and our listening profile reveals its strengths and its weaknesses.

How is our personality reflected in the Listening Test? To find out we have to look at the overall shape of the listening curve in each of the three zones. Based on years of clinical observations, Dr. Tomatis identified three main "personality patterns." He called them the "schizoid," "paranoid" and the "depressed" type, respectively. A word of caution is in order here, since these words can easily lead to the conclusion that these labels indicate pathology. That is certainly true in extreme cases, but different words can be substituted to avoid the risk of attaching pathological labels inappropriately. What was called the schizoid type can be referred to as the "airborne" listening type; the paranoid becomes the controlling listening type and the depressed type becomes the depressive listening type. To the original three types described by Tomatis, I have added a fourth one that I have called the "flat-liner" listening type, since the curves of the Listening Test in this case are flat.

You will find these listening styles described below. These profiles are not intended to fit everyone in an auditory "one size fits all." What these descriptions attempt to do is to present some of the most striking features of each profile to give you a feel for each. It goes without saying that life is abundantly diverse and that there are as many different personalities as there are individuals. Looking for commonalities under an ever changing surface is the most we can do for now.

The Airborne Listening Profile

The airborne listening type shows an ascending curve (for both air and bone conduction) all across three zones. Relative to the ideal curve, the Listening Test for this profile is somewhat depressed in zone 1, the body zone. It gradually ascends in zone 2, the language zone and reaches its peak in zone 3.

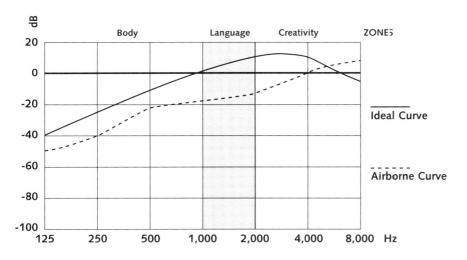

Figure 19: Airborne listening profile

Briefly, the airborne profile describes people who tend to live more in their head than in their body. Metaphorically, their feet rarely touch the ground. Do not ask them to be passionate about the boring and often messy details of daily life. They are most at home in the world of religion, spirituality and metaphysics. Indeed, that is where they feel they belong. As a matter of fact, I have heard a few people with this profile report out-of-body experiences with great delight. If they could "check out," they would do so at once. The earth and the life on it strike them as messy and muddy, something that makes them feel uncomfortable. The world of ideas seems a far safer heaven. People with this profile often feel the need to help others, are altruistic, and strongly respond to the dictates of their consciences. For this reason, they tend to be attracted to groups that are primarily interested in improving the spiritual life of their members.

Nevertheless, it is hard for many of these air dwelling individuals to face the demands of a spiritual quest since they are not grounded strongly enough in their bodies to face the challenges and pitfalls of such a quest. They may pass from group to group, from one set of beliefs to another, shopping around for new ideas in search of something that keeps them safe above the ground. Not being rooted in their bodies, they are often unable to make a firm commitment to a single belief system. They are frequently tourists instead of participants in spiritual quests. This attitude is in sharp contrast to the attitude of the adepts of traditional spiritual practices, in which the role of the body is strongly emphasized. Spiritual practices that are not rooted in the body are unlikely to grow or last very long.

There are many reasons why people avoid being in their bodies. For example, some do not fully live in their bodies because sexuality is a source of conflict. They may deny the intensity of their sexual feelings and perhaps try to channel them in unrelated but compensatory activities. Freud called this process sublimation: a process that he believed could lead to significant achievement in the world of arts, sciences and culture. As paradoxical as it may sound, some may sublimate their sexual desires by throwing themselves into sports. For example, an "air-borne" can become a compulsive jogger to run away from his fear of confronting his sexuality. Although we illustrated the point talking about the fear of sexuality, there are of course any numbers of fears that can cause people to avoid being in their bodies.

The reasons for such fears are numerous. Many people endured sensory integration difficulties as children, including motor problems and tactile defensiveness, all of which can lead to a poor body image as well as a poor self-image. It is difficult to accept being touched by someone if you experience touch as rough and painful. Cultural and educational factors may play a role too: for instance, parents may convey negative images about gender or sexuality, which not only strongly influence our relationship to our bodies but also inhibit our intellectual functioning. If one resides in a body that is frozen, chances are that the mind is frozen as well, at least to a degree, locked in a belief system that acts as a protective carapace.

When the body starts to "thaw" and the person becomes more in touch with it, there is often a surge in the bone conduction response in zone 1 and sometimes in other zones as well. The body and mind awaken to a new awareness of themselves: they finally connect instead of being separated. It is a time of joy, exploration and expansion. It is not without pitfalls, however, and counseling might be required if the ego shows a tendency to balloon and the body leads into a dance that culminates in acting-out sexually.

In other people, inhibitions can be very resistant and the perception of being separated from the body persists. Then the yearning to be touched, cuddled, loved is not strong enough to overcome the fears inspired by the body. Sometimes, those fears may lead to a nervous breakdown or a psychiatric episode. In that event, the term "schizoid" as used by Tomatis is applicable. However, this is far from the kind of air-borne listening profile one typically sees, as is evident in the case of Alex.

Alex was twenty-five years old when I saw him. His psychiatrist had referred him because he had learning problems and had failed his C.P.A. exam. He was a pleasant young man who looked much younger than his age and behaved in an equally immature way. He laughed in a loud and nervous way every time I asked him a question, as though I had just made a joke. This was particularly irritating because every time he laughed, his voice seemed to come from a different corner of the room rather than from in front of me where he sat. It was a disembodied laugh, with a strange ring. It seemed to clearly mirror the split between his mind and body and I started to wonder why Alex was under the care of a psychiatrist. The interview itself did not seem to go anywhere. While he told me of his difficulties in studying, I sensed that he was disengaged. It was as if he were talking about someone else with the same problems. There were no feelings in evidence and our discussion barely scratched the surface.

Things changed dramatically after I did his Listening Test. His curve was low in zone 1, dropped a little in the language zone before ascending sharply in the last zone. The general configuration of his Listening Test immediately raised some red flags in my mind. I was not sure how to approach Alex but I remembered that Tomatis had described his type of curve as a curve that could reflect people's interest in religion and spirituality. It seemed natural to ask whether Alex was interested in religion.

"I go to church every Sunday," Alex confirmed while his laugh resonated in some corner of the room high above our heads.

"Do you think about death?" I casually queried, asking the ultimate metaphysical question.

Alex slumped in his chair, suddenly quiet. My question had struck like lightning. I waited patiently, feeling that we were entering a new territory.

"Yeah!" he mumbled without looking at me. He sighed heavily not sure if he wanted to jump into the fire. Finally, he looked up.

"I am thinking about killing myself. I am thinking a lot about it." Then, after a pause, he added: "Actually, it's not that I want to kill myself. I want to kill my boss! She is always on my back, bossing me around and treating me like an idiot!" His voice had become shrill, full of rage. It matched perfectly the strong ascendancy of his curve in zone 3. Alex himself seemed shocked by his outburst. He could not stay with his anger and immediately retreated. He slumped in his chair, shuffling his feet on the floor, not looking at me.

It was not long thereafter that Alex told me that he never had a relationship with a woman. He had tried but had been rejected. The wound had been so deep that he could not imagine anything but being repeatedly rejected. The incident had reinforced the lack of confidence that had plagued him from childhood. He had been shy and had become even more so. His self-esteem had plummeted. His cover was a superficial, friendly manner that made him seem even more immature. While he continued to dream about a relationship with a woman, his juvenile, almost childish demeanor made this unlikely. At 25, he was emotionally still an adolescent, trying to resolve his sexual identity and getting nowhere. As long as he stayed in this cocoon, close to his family, he was safe. Things changed when he entered the work place. There he had to report to an assertive woman, whose responsibility it was to make sure that Alex followed through with his assignments.

Alex believed that, at work, things went from bad to worse and then went out of control. He was too repressed to act out his fantasy of killing his boss—that bitchy woman whose acts confirmed his belief that all women, with the exception of his mother, were out to get him, to humiliate him like the one he had loved and who had betrayed him. If he killed himself, he thought, his suffering would finally end.

Alex's solution was irrational but not surprising. Many people turn angry when they cannot express themselves and end up becoming depressed. But depression did not concern me as much here as the potential for violence that was evident in Alex's Listening Test. With such a disconnection between body and mind as Alex's listening profile suggested, there is no anchor to ground the thought process. Fantasies predominated and might overpower moral consciousness. Even a simple event may trigger acting out a fantasy, sometimes with catastrophic consequences. Alex's treatment should, therefore, avoid the use of high frequency sound. Because high frequencies energize, they might have given him more energy to act out one of the scenes which he obsessively pictured. Instead, I first used low-frequency sounds to make him feel more grounded in his body and to decrease the underlying anxiety resulting from his "schizoid" state.

There were indeed more urgent issues to address before addressing Alex's learning disability. With Alex's permission, I contacted his psychiatrist to inform him about my findings. As a therapist, I doubt that I would have been able to uncover such a material in one session without the help of the Listening Test. It allowed me to uncover a wealth of information at a glance and gave me a glimpse into Alex's personality and the workings of his mind. Otherwise, I am fairly sure that we would have continued to skim the surface, talking about his learning disability, his failure to take his C.P.A. exam and the resulting anxiety. I would almost certainly have just missed the big picture—and the real reason for failing his exam and finding his personal and professional life unmanageable.

There is a conclusion to this story: as we worked, Alex felt more at ease with his body; the tension in his shoulders relaxed; his whole face lengthened; his posture became more erect. He gradually started to experience more confidence in himself. When he took his exam again, he passed. He looked more mature and responsible and no longer had any desire to kill himself. He was now ready to move on with his life and he did, though still looking for a relationship.

The Controlling Listening Profile

There is a natural need for all of us to exercise some control over our lives. We clearly cannot live surrounded by chaos. Without some resemblance of control, our lives would be totally dysfunctional. The most fundamental way to maintain control is physical: hopefully, we know how to reduce the speed of our car by using the brake pedal. With a very primitive mind, we might try to control others through physical power. In more advanced societies, however, words rather than sheer physical power are used for control, and those who use force instead rarely go very far and often end up in cycles of violence, in jail or even dead.

Language allows us to achieve control over our lives. In fact, words give us the ability to manipulate the events of our lives so we can plan, revise and improve our intentions before putting them into action. Words help us retrieve memories and organize our thoughts, as well as name, analyze and understand our daily experience. Without these abilities, many would find their lives without meaning. This is all the more true of those with a controlling listening profile, indicating a desire for control that goes a little beyond the typical need. If that natural need for control becomes excessive and an end to itself, it might raise to pathological levels, as we may see on the next page.

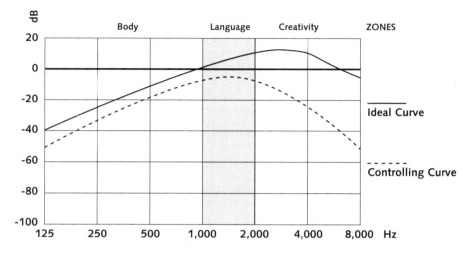

Figure 20: Controlling listening profile

The controlling listening pattern in its pure form is shaped like a dome with its top in the zone of the language and communication, dropping in zone 1 and zone 3. People with such a profile are not very grounded in their body and are also impervious to metaphysical or spiritual concerns. Indeed, those following that path would be looked upon with contempt. Do not expect that they would be moved by a generous cause or would go out of their way to help others. If they are generous, they do so out of self-interest. Their primary concern is for themselves. In fact, they are completely absorbed by their ego. They use their language and communication skills to boost their ego and to protect themselves, from real or supposed attacks. In any case, whatever they say or do is self-serving. They use language to protect or to claim what they perceive to be theirs. They don't use language to engage in a real dialogue. As you may guess, they are not good listeners. The listening curve reflects that they only listen to themselves

In fact, people who need a lot of control, constantly need to assert their authority, since, deep down, they do not feel in charge and are therefore full of anxiety and doubt. They need to exercise perpetual vigilance and cannot relax for fear of being overpowered. They cannot afford to listen to others because they might have to change their mind: something unthinkable for someone who has to know everything better than anyone else.

A super controller is by nature very conservative. He is rigid, unwilling to compromise and may try to control others using fear. Any hint for a need to change is perceived as an attack on his personality; any "criticism" needs to be nipped in the bud. Protection of his fragile and fearful ego is the basic drive of his life. This does not bode well for his relationships. His social life can only be conflicted since he does not trust anyone. His potential for intimacy is limited for precisely the same reason. Mingling with people and participating in social activities are to be avoided unless they are rewarded with a position of leadership.

If air conduction is higher than bone conduction, conflicts with others do not come to the surface in an explosive way. A controller would, in this event, rationalize his feelings and construct a series of arguments to re-establish his authority. He would probably pride himself for being cool and unemotional. If, on the other hand, bone conduction is higher than air conduction, the conflict is divisive, explosive, and potentially violent. In the extreme, the label paranoid fits these moments of crisis.

This is, however, an extreme case. Like all extremes, it sheds light on the more benign cases. The main features of the controlling profile are similar but they are softened. In this event, the Listening Test no longer shows a dome but rather a shape more like a bump with both sides gently sloping down toward zones 1 and 3. The need for control still exists but it only mildly interferes in the social life of the person. This much softer version of the controlling profile suggests someone who still tries to establish his dominance in the domain he knows best: the intellectual domain. Acuity in this zone suggests one who loves the workings of his mind, one who adores ideas and concepts that reduce the complexity of life into neat compartments. People with this profile thrive on detail. Their inquiring minds look for the logic hidden behind the chaos. They analyze, dissect and organize their experiences; they cannot help but rationalize their feelings. Being fully knowledgeable in matters of interest is very important. This profile could lead one to become a sociologist who wants to understand the workings of society in detail, a psychologist eager to comprehend all aspects of human behavior or an engineer who loves to understand how things work in the physical world. Each gets excited about mastering the various components of a problem. Even though others may find people with a controlling profile lacking in warmth or being too reserved, this is not necessarily true: their emotions are more likely to be expressed through language than by physical displays of emotion. A need to control means that one's emotional life is always under the mind's scrutiny and analysis. This entails thinking things through, even one's affections. The need to control can often be irresistible even if, at times, it puts one at odds with partners or friends.

To be comfortable, some people have to feel in control at all times in order to fight the underlying and often unconscious anxiety of loosing control. That anxiety may have roots in either childhood or present life. It is not a well-defined anxiety that can be precisely assigned to an object or a cause, yet it colors both worldview and behavior. In itself, anxiety is not a bad thing as long as it is not immobilizing. Anxiety can go a long way in pushing us to come up with solutions that help us manage our lives and environment. Curiosity, intellectual inquiry, analytical skills are rooted in mild anxiety: why bother to look, examine, analyze things, and inquire about the meaning of life if we are fully content with our lives or if our senses are fully satiated? It is the sense that something is missing in life's puzzle that arouses our wish to control and puts us on the path of inquiry. It is the void inside that needs to be filled—even temporarily—which sends us on a search. The controlling traits that we may find amusing also have a positive side: stubbornness becomes an asset when it is mobilized to resolve difficult problems; analytical minds see all sides of a question; a detail-oriented intellect makes sure that no important aspect is lost. Indeed, this softer version of the controlling profile can lead to extreme productivity and can contribute immensely to the social good.

An urge to control may extend to the desire to control one's body, leading to a love of sports. Here pleasure comes from mastering physical discipline. A sense of power comes from building a strong and resistant body. There is a sensuous pleasure in amassing muscles or demonstrating that they respond well to challenging physical tasks. A strong physique projects a sense of control and power that commands respect. A controller will work at building an image of himself as being in charge. Although he primarily controls through the power of words and a narcissistic display of his intellect, a straight if not rigid posture and a good build are certainly additional assets in achieving his goals. Just remember how we are more likely to be impressed by a speaker with a towering presence than by one who looks insignificant. Exercise helps the controller to relax—at least a tiny bit, since he cannot relax completely out of fear of losing control.

Almost anyone could be a controller. The desire for control comes in all kinds, sizes and descriptions. The need for control can be moderate, very strong, or even quite pathological. You might hate a supervisor, for example, because he checks on the company's employees a bit too much out of a need for control. Control can also come from a trade unionist who wants to reorganize labor relations, or a politician who claims to know better how to lead the country than his opponent. The need to be in charge can come from mothers or fathers, teachers, neighbors, best friends or yourself. The less the sides of the bump drop on the Listening Test, the more likely these people are to use language and communication as a two-way street and the more readily they listen without the intrusions of fear and distortion.

The Depressive Listening Profile

We know all too well how it feels to be down in the dumps. Still, that is way different of being depressed. It also is very important to make a distinction between a passing feeling of fatigue with being depressed. The Listening Test shows the difference quite clearly: in actual depression, the curve is flat up to about 1,000 Hz and then drops in zones 2 and 3; in the case of a person prone to fatigue, the listening curve follows a similar path but rises at 6,000 Hz, instead of continuing to drop. A person with the latter profile may have sudden bouts of fatigue and experience a mild form of depressive symptoms but will bounce back from tiredness fairly quickly. Sound stimulation is warranted here because it will help this individual regain her vitality.

The most striking feature of the depressive listening profile is the big drop in both the language and in the creativity zone. The drop in the creativity zone (zone 3) means that such a person cannot take advantage of the stimulation provided by the high frequencies of surrounding sounds. Since she is unable to hear them, she cannot use them to "charge" her cortex. No wonder that such a person complains of being easily exhausted or depressed!

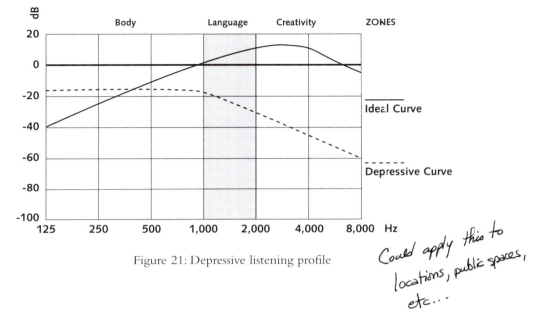

Figure 21: Depressive listening profile

Could apply this to locations, public spaces, etc...

As we have noted, the drop in the language zone (zone 2) indicates a tendency to cut oneself off from social contacts or even from pleasurable activities. It takes energy to relate to family members or friends, as well as to engage in pleasurable and interesting activities. Instead, the impulse to withdraw deprives people of the stimulation and energy gained from being with others. We do spend energy when we engage our friends and relatives in a conversation (in this the depressed person is right), but we gain even more energy when we socialize and enjoy the company of others. A depressed person has forgotten how wonderful and stimulating it is to be absorbed in a fun and satisfying activity. Instead they are brooding about the negative side of everything.

Traditional psychotherapy usually aims at reconnecting depressed people with their loved ones as a way to brighten their lives. This approach is based on good intentions but is not always successful:

often the client can not muster the enormous amount of energy it takes to communicate with others. To compensate for that, therapists often recommend taking small steps, one at the time, as well as some physical exercise (a vestibular activity that stimulates the brain). It may, however, take medication to give a depressed patient the impetus to carry out the recommended activities. Auditory stimulation can be a quite useful adjunct to other therapies or to medication in this regard, since it stimulates the brain while the person is seated or lying on a couch.

Lack of energy is not only mental but also physical. It is interesting to study the listening curve from that perspective. As we have seen, the straight line suddenly breaks at around 1,000 Hz and takes a downward turn. It is like looking at a plane which suddenly loses altitude. Physically, the 750–1,000 Hz mark coincides with the stomach area (to be explored further on). The trunk of the depressed person seems to retract toward her stomach; the head is bent forward, the shoulders and the back are stooped, as if pulled downward by the weight of the head. This is why a depressed person may seem all crumpled up instead of being erect. Even if she tries to sit straighter in her chair, she is very likely to collapse again, bent over her stomach as if it were weighing her down. Most likely, she will also complain of ailments in this area, be it digestive or other problems. This may be an unconscious effort to somatically fix the anxiety in the body. However, these bodily ailments may mask the real source of her anxiety. Children who have school anxieties are often prone to developing tummyaches, which can be a child's version of depression. Displacement of anxiety from the mental to the physical is fairly common but does not resolve the cause of the depression; it only masks it.

In accordance with the results of the Listening Test, voices of depressed individuals tend to be low, flat, colorless, hesitant, somewhat raspy, coming from deep down in the belly. This is in line with the description of the symptoms of depression found in the Diagnostic and Statistical Manual of Mental disorders: *slowed speech, increased pauses before answering, soft or monotonous speech*, slowed body movements, *a markedly decreased amount of speech (poverty of speech), or muteness*" (Italics are mine). Such voices do not contain the rich harmonics needed to generate stimulation for the brain. Remember that our brain is not only stimulated by the sounds coming from without, but also by those coming from within. We know that singers feel quite energized by the sound of their own voices. Though we may not be singers ourselves, still the quality of our speaking voice plays a part in keeping us alert and energized. Aside from medication, auditory stimulation and physical exercises, I often wonder whether the treatment of depression should not include a regimen of drama classes, singing lessons or simple vocal exercises as well.

The Tomatis Method starts with passive sound stimulation to raise the energy level enough to make the clients willing to start using their own voice as an antidote to depression. At first, most clients are reluctant to do so, but become rather eager once they discover the benefits and start to feel reconnected with their former self, the one they thought they had lost to depression.

Even if you don't have access to auditory stimulation, you can easily practice this type of exercise. There is no need to take expensive voice lessons: you just need to open a book and regularly read aloud for twenty to thirty minutes at a time. To do it right, sit straight, and read into a "microphone" made by joining your right thumb with your right forefinger. Hold the "microphone" a few inches from the right corner of your mouth. In fact, Tomatis practitioners recommend doing this exercise daily in between sound stimulation sessions.

Sound stimulation is not, though, a miracle cure for depression. It can certainly help—sometimes immensely—to relieve symptoms of fatigue, anxiety, mild adjustment disorders, sleep disturbances and the general apathy that plagues depressive people. However, *in case of clinical depression, it should only be used as an adjunct to the services of a health care professional.* The utmost caution is required, for instance, when treating people suffering from bipolar disorders. Giving them too much energy when they are in the depressive phase of the cycle could significantly elevate their mood and precipitate a manic episode with unfortunate consequences: lack of judgment, grandiosity, buying sprees, reckless driving, foolish business investments, sexual acting-out, and delusions of all sorts.

Working with severely and clinically depressed people also requires a thorough assessment of the potential for committing suicide. In such cases, auditory stimulation should only and only be done under the supervision of a qualified health care professional, as auditory stimulation may provide the energy necessary to carry out suicidal ideations. Similar caution must be exercised when working with severely mentally ill people.

Bernard Auriol, a French psychiatrist, noted positive results when using sound stimulation with psychotic patients, especially ones suffering from hallucinations, but cautions that the decrease of those hallucinations and a better contact with the environment may also increase the possibility of acting out and auto-destructive or aggressive behavior.[51] It is thus best if mental health professionals are involved from the beginning of auditory stimulation intervention and act as consultants throughout the entire treatment.

Still, there is ample evidence to support the use of sound stimulation with depressed people. Tomatis had not foreseen that application when he started his work. Many of the parents, who were offered listening sessions with the Electronic Ear while they waited for a child, started to report that they felt more energized, more outgoing, and more inclined to socialize. This was quite similar to what they could observe in their children who were undergoing this unconventional therapy. Those reports aroused Tomatis' interest. He began to successfully apply filtered sounds to patients complaining of being depressed. His observations are echoed in a study by E. Deneys,[52] done under the supervision of Dr. Auriol. She examined depressed people pre- and post auditory stimulation, using the Minnesota Multiphasic Personality Inventory (MMPI). She found that auditory stimulation decreased anxiety, depression, introversion, and neuroticism while it increased behaviors listed on the scale assessing ego strength. Auriol concludes that the study, despite some limitations, suggests that sound stimulation helps patients bring their problems to the surface, allowing them to adjust better socially, although their core psychopathology stays unchanged. Still, for clinically depressed people and for those inclined to feel depressed, the improvement suggested by the changes on the assessment is good news. These changes may make all the difference between "feeling in the dumps" and "seeing the light at the end of the tunnel." It is my hope that more research on the effects of auditory stimulation will provide professionals with another tool to fight the debilitating impact of depression.

The Flat-Line Listening Profile

I have added a fourth category to the three originally described by Tomatis and have called it the flat-line profile since this Listening Test shows a perfect or almost perfect flat line (thus its name). This profile suggests that information goes in one ear and immediately goes out of the other. It might be the ultimate way to protect oneself against past, present or future source of anxiety. If you assume this indicates poor listening, you are dead right. What is a person with this listening profile like? It is difficult to say. If you cannot put your finger on it, do not be disappointed: your indecision reflects the indecision characteristic of those with this listening profile. They do not seem able to make choices easily: it would take an energy that they have in short supply. For the same reason, there is little motivation for doing anything. They may start one thing and abandon it almost immediately for another that will most likely again end up in the garbage can of aborted projects. Flat-line listening is associated with speech that is slow, broken by pauses, full of incomplete sentences and a low, monotone voice. This person does not have an ear for music and it is no wonder: his preference is probably limited to rap, rock or industrial music "which is no music, man, and that's the point" as a teenager with a flat curve, once put it to me.

An individual with a flat-line profile usually has little knowledge of himself: he is likely to be seen as floating on the wind. He does not know what he wants and seems to be unable to articulate his preferences. His ears do not analyze sounds well and, consequently, he doesn't analyze things in detail or depth. Indeed, he is likely to pretend that nothing is happening to preserve his peace of mind. Cut off from himself as much as from others, he is an enigma to himself and to others. Sound stimulation for him is often like everything else: it typically doesn't make enough of an impression to make a difference. In short, he is difficult to work with because he does not see the point of changing. Changing requires dissatisfaction with one's life and he is not really unhappy (nor happy for that matter) and, thus, has no desire to improve. Changing too requires some imagination regarding the future, but he has little of that. This profile is often seen in teenagers who have a hard time growing up.

Outwardly, this type of listener may appear to be a nice, well-adjusted kid. However, under the smooth flat surface of his air conduction curve, the bone conduction curve might indicate resistance, anger, anxiety, frustration, depression or a desire to be loved, yet little of this pattern emerges into the open. Even if it did, he would have little desire to look into it and to go deeper. Relationships are shallow, interests are few. Academically, he does not do very well, may suffer from dyslexia and has trouble remembering things accurately. He is easily tired and bored. He tends to follow his peer group and does not make waves. Overall, people with flat-line listening tend to conform. People may find him charming, pleasant and easy-going, but they only see one side of him, or rather the surface. Parents, in the case of a child or a teenager, may complain that he always needs to be pushed, especially when it comes to homework or schoolwork. They become irritated by infrequent decisions, his seeming laziness, and his inability to commit himself to anything and may resent the constant bickering that makes family life difficult. If he is an adult, people may feel irritated by his indecisiveness and by his inability to be a team player when the need occurs at work or in the family. How could it be different? He knows neither himself nor what he wants and is not even sure that he wants to know it.

To sum up we can say that the Listening Test gives us the ability to predict, with some accuracy, certain personality traits that accompany some listening curves, but it is important to exercise caution. The profiles presented here are fairly clear: while they are somewhat typical, they were also simplified for the sake of the explanation. In reality, a practitioner rarely finds such a pure type. They are all intertwined, like the different traits of our character in real life. A good deal of practice is necessary to figure out the general outline of the personality under study and to apprehend the inner dynamic at play. It is clear, though, how our perception of sounds says much about how we feel and behave. The listening profile not only reveals some aspects of our personality but also reflects how well we feel physically, as we will see in the next chapter.

LISTENING TO THE BODY

Another new piece of information is worth exploring here. Each frequency of the auditory domain seems to resonate in a specific area of the body: the low frequencies in the lower part of the body, the higher frequencies in the upper part. This led Tomatis to propose a scale linking various body organs and specific frequencies of the audio spectrum. This means that we may be able to relate irregularities on the bone conduction curve to specific ailments. As always with the Listening Test, we should always look for corroborating evidence before drawing conclusions. In the event that the Listening Test suggests a certain ailment, the practitioner should refer the client to a medical doctor.

Clients, of course, are rightly surprised when the practitioner pinpoints a physical problem just by looking at what they think is a hearing test. I have quite often observed that sort of astonishment on their faces. A 10 year-old boy, quite resistant to the idea of treatment, thought that I was playing a magic trick on him when I asked him if he had fallen and hurt his right knee, which he had. That remark convinced him more than anything else to agree to do the program.

In the table on the next page, you'll find the correlations Tomatis established between various parts of the body and the frequencies of the audio spectrum.[53] In the next chapter, we'll see a few more examples of ailments that correlate to the Listening Tests.

To complete our exploration, we'll wrap up what the Listening Test reveals, adding one last parameter: the comparison of how we listen with each ear. By taking into account what I will call the "dialogue of the ears," we will greatly enrich our understanding of what a careful analysis of the Listening Test can reveal about our body and mind.

The Listening Test

FREQUENCY (Hz)	BODY PART
8,000	Head
6,000	Head
4,000	Tongue/Cervical Vertebrae
3,000	Shoulder Blade
2,000	Dorsal Region/Larynx/Plexus
1,500	Cervical Back Section/The Lungs
1,200	Heart
1,000	Medial Dorsal Region, The Stomach
750	Pancreas/Liver/Gall Bladder
500	Dorsal Lumbar Junction/ The Intestine/The Elbow
250	Junction Pelvis-Lumbar Region/The Intestine/The Knee
125	The Pelvis and Feet/The Genital Organs

THE DIALOGUE BETWEEN THE EARS

For the sake of clarity, I've described the Listening Test as if only *one* ear had been tested. This is somewhat like testing your vision by checking only one eye and then proposing to apply that data to the other eye. Anyone who wears glasses would rightly be shocked by such a proposal. It is no different with our ears. The full picture emerges only when both are tested. To adequately assess a client, the therapist should compare both the general profile of the curves for each ear, as well as the profile of the curve in each zone with the corresponding zone of the other ear (for instance, right body zone with left body zone, etc.).

In order to better understand the dialogue that takes place between the ears, let's quickly summarize some of our previous findings:

- The air conduction curve reflects our external listening, that is, the way we perceive the outside world and appear to it (appearances or façade).
- The bone conduction curve reflects our internal listening or self-listening. Ideally, the air conduction curve should be higher than the bone conduction curve.
- Both curves should be ascending, forming a dome between 2,000Hz and 4,000Hz before dropping slightly (Ideal Listening Curve).
- A departure from that ideal pattern reveals a listening problem. The discrepancy can be a combination of peaks and valleys with bone conduction overlapping air conduction.
- The right ear represents the present; the left ear symbolizes the past.

A few examples will explain what is meant by a dialogue between the ears better than a long and theoretical explanation would.

Let's first look at how this works at the simplest level, the physical level. Suppose a peak appears on the bone conduction at 1,000 Hz in an otherwise normal Listening Test. This peak indicates an area of great sensitivity. As we saw in the previous chapter, this frequency corresponds to our stomach and thus alerts us to the possibility of some stomach or back problems. Keeping the time value attributed to each ear (present for the right, past for the left) in mind as well, we can develop a time line for that particular problem. There are three possibilities:

- **The peak only appears on the right audiogram.**
  In this case it reveals an *acute* disorder. As you remember, the right ear symbolizes the present and future.
- **The peak only appears on the left audiogram.**
  This indicates that the problem occurred in the *recent past* and is in the process of subsiding, in line with the thesis that the left ear represents the past.
- **The peak shows on both audiograms.**
  Now we are dealing with a *chronic* problem, one that started in the past, continues in the present and may persist in the future.

That is to say that the Listening Test has a temporal dimension that reflects the past, the present and the future of the person being tested. Looking at the chart of correspondences between frequency and organs, it is possible, with some practice, to detect a possible physical ailment and, when needed, to refer the client to a physician for further observation.

In the years of clinical practice in Northern California, I often observed a peak at 1,500 Hz on the bone conduction curve especially during the allergy season when pollen from trees and drying grass fill the air. In those cases, the problem was temporary and the peak only appeared on the right audiogram. However, when it shows on both the left and right audiograms, it indicates a chronic problem and thus asthma is more likely. While this is not to be construed as a medical diagnosis, these may be important indications for treatment and thus warrant referral to a physician.

Comparing the listening profiles of the two ears also reveals whether we are dealing with an acute or a chronic *psychological* problem. Let's look at an example. As usual, we'll first assess the overall shape of the curves before delving into the temporal aspect.

Julia was a traditional "soccer mom," devoted to her children, who also assisted her husband in his large medical practice, volunteered with charity organizations, and was always on the go, helping and taking care of others. Outwardly, she was pleasant, always smiling, always attentive, and always busy. She was someone on whom you could count whenever you needed her. As she put it herself, she seemed to have it all. You could not have dreamed of a better mom, a better spouse, or a better friend. As expected, her air conduction curves on both ears were smooth and way above her bone conduction curves.

On the other hand, a glance at the bone conduction curve on both ears showed a very different picture. The bone conduction curves, which ideally should be smooth as well, followed a pattern of valleys and peaks. Thus, there was a great discrepancy between her façade (reflected by the air conduction curve) and what was going on inside her (bone conduction curve). If Julia appeared to manage exceptionally well in society, it came at a great cost. Indeed, she was constantly compensating to maintain the appearance of competence and self-assurance. Her apparent confidence had little self-esteem to support it. She appeared sociable but felt shy inside. Though she yearned to withdraw, her busy life kept her engaged. She felt like dying inside but no one guessed. While everyone extolled her virtues, she felt like a fake. When I told her during our first meeting that she would probably rather stay home than venture into the world, she heartily agreed. She had little pleasure in life: every task felt like a duty, a constraint that kept her at a distance from herself. She felt life passing by, as though she had little part in it, a feeling often reflected by the large space between air and bone conduction clearly visible in her Listening Test. She confirmed these observations by saying that she often felt tired and depressed.

A deep bone conduction valley in the language and communication zone of *both* ears is a clear sign of a long-standing problem. Had it been only a drop on the right side, it could have occurred as result of a current trauma or stress, a temporary situation that would have cleared up after a while. I suspected instead that Julia's condition might have had an emotional cause and that the resulting drop in the profile of the left ear was then duplicated on the right side as the condition became chronic. I even hypothesized on that first day that she might have been the victim of physical or sexual abuse, but did not bring it up, focusing instead on establishing a good therapeutic alliance. I knew that the time for more personal confidences would come later. In fact, clients entering into therapy rarely verbalize their real problem on the first day. Family therapists, for instance, know well that the presenting problem might mask a much deeper problem. A family may look for help because a child is acting-out in school but it may turn out that the behavior is symptomatic of a more severe dysfunction in the family system.

Though I may well have suspected otherwise, I accepted Julia's description of what troubled her. Her presenting problem, as she explained to me, was a constant weariness and feeling of depression. She was hoping that the program would help her have more energy. It was not long thereafter that she opened her heart and told me a history of sexual abuse and ensuing bouts of depression. Only her husband and her previous therapist knew about it. She was proud that her children had never suspected anything, even less her friends. I acknowledged that sexual abuse had been one of my hypotheses from the beginning of working with her. She was surprised: how could I have guessed? I took the Listening Test from her file and proceeded to explain some of the details of the test that I had not commented on during our first meeting because I felt it was inappropriate. What I had perceived, I told her, were not the details of her personal story, which could not be done in any event, but rather an inner dynamics that she now confirmed.

This is where the value of the Listening Test rests, I told her that day: it allows a faster and more efficient approach to the client's needs. If the Listening Test is correctly interpreted, it cuts through a mountain of details that can sometimes be an obstacle to therapeutic understanding. It helps structure a more organized way of entering the client's life. Still the client needs to tell her story to set the stage for the corroborating evidence of the Listening Test and to flesh out the details to her own satisfaction.

If, instead of *valleys* in the communication/language zone, Julia's test had shown a *peak* on the bone conduction of both ears, crossing over the air conduction curves, the clinical picture would have been quite different. Such a woman would not have been a quiet, shy woman, but an aggressive, difficult woman, reacting instantly to the smallest slight. Unlike Julia, this woman wouldn't draw many people to her; instead, they would fear her, complain about her terrible character and try to avoid her. She would have resembled the controlling personality described earlier, rather than a person you would really want to have for a friend.

On the other hand, if the audiogram of one ear had shown a *valley* in the language area on bone conduction and a *peak* in the same zone on the other ear, the clinical picture would have changed again because of the asymmetry between the two ears. This profile would immediately tell us that this person demonstrates an acute imbalance or unevenness in behavior. She would alternate between sociable and friendly, or shy behavior and a bossy, demanding or angry manner. No one would know the exact rhythm of the dance when relating with such a person, because she probably would not know it either. The alternating attitudes would probably lead people to find her hypocritical, because the contrast in attitude would be so stark. In the extreme, these behaviors fit some of the characteristics of borderline personality disorder.

These examples clearly show the importance of understanding the dialogue between the ears. It is only by comparing the profile of each ear that we can understand what they are telling us about the psychological dynamics of the person tested.

You have probably noticed that, for the sake of simplicity, I have not considered some of the other parameters of analysis discussed earlier, like selectivity, spatialization and lateralization. Each one would have added another layer of analysis; each one would make the task of interpreting the Listening Test, as well as the resulting overall clinical picture, more complex. It is not an easy task to read a Listening Test. It takes time, patience and a long apprenticeship before one can master its fundamentals. I have made it look simple, to a degree, by breaking it down into its different components. Once you try to reassemble them into one complete picture, you might, at first, feel overwhelmed by the complexity of the task. Each piece has to fit into the general picture, but a slight modification of any one parameter may modify the meaning of the whole.

My goal in this endeavor has certainly not been to train you to read a Listening Test, but to give you a feel for it, to make it easier for you to understand how sounds are woven into the fabric of our lives and to show how the way we listen can be captured on a graph. While this may appear to be magic, it rests on solid science. Tomatis told us many times how much he was surprised by his own discoveries. It took him time to see the trees within the forest and to develop a valid, predictable instrument to explore the human psyche. Of course, as at the end of any good study, I need to caution that more research is needed to validate this instrument whose interpretation, it seems, resembles art more than hard science. On this aspiration, we will move on to a different way of interpreting the Listening Test.

SYMBOLIC EARS

For Tomatis, the development of listening starts in the womb and continues through birth and throughout life. It is an ongoing process that stops only with our last breath. The Listening Test conveys, in its own way, some aspects of that journey because, as we have seen, several of its characteristics are time dependent. For instance, selectivity opens gradually and lateralization establishes over time as well. The examples I presented earlier clearly demonstrate that when either process meets resistance, personal growth tends to be delayed or to halt altogether. Moreover, when a child's development gets stuck, the block is likely to be carried into adulthood. In short, if the maturation process that includes lateralization and selectivity does not progress, the child will circle in a changeless present with little chance of moving ahead or flourishing in the future.

A child who is stuck in the past is usually left-ear dominant, leading Tomatis to consider the left-ear as symbolically representing the past. Thus, the left ear symbolizes the world of emotions that characterize the past. Remember, for instance, that immature speech tends to be based on emotion rather than on logic. It is the language of children or adults who cannot find a way to grow up, who prefer to be sheltered by their parents, protected from the dangers and the challenges of life as if they were still in the womb. The two six-year old girls who did not want to grow up refused to talk into the microphone. For them their desire to remain children, nurtured by mother for the rest of their lives, was a compelling fantasy. And so, *Tomatis associated symbolically the mother figure with the left-ear, the past and the world of the emotions.*

As the child matures, we observe that ear dominance usually shifts to the right. The progression from left to right parallels the progression from dependence and high need for nurturing, traditionally associated with femininity, to greater autonomy, logic-based language and living by the rules of society, qualities often associated with the masculine. So, *Tomatis associated symbolically the right-ear with the father figure, the rules of society and logic-based language.*

This symbolism is encountered in many traditions where left is considered synonymous with the feminine and right synonymous with the masculine, with the father seen as representative of the society to which the child will need to adapt, so that, one day, he can become one of its members. There is nothing really new about this framework, except that these archetypal qualities are being incorporated into the study of listening and its development, and that Tomatis found a parallel progression reflected in a comparison of the left and right audiogram of the Listening Test.

The journey is about going from the left towards the right. For Tomatis it is symbolized by moving from mother's caring arms toward the safety of father's embrace; from a world dominated by emotions and affects toward a world where emotions and affects are reined in by the laws governing society; from the use of an emotional-basis language in the direction of a logic-based language; and from childhood to adulthood. It is about meeting the challenges of life, the innate impulse for growing and becoming a person in one's own right. It is about gaining sufficient perspective to look back at the past and be thankful for the roles mom and dad played in helping us become the person we were meant to be from the moment of conception. And it is about listening more than anything else from that very first moment.

PART V

The Psychological Ear

MOTHER CARES FOR HER UNBORN CHILD

LISTENING IN UTERO

Many expectant mothers will happily tell you that they can feel that their babies respond when they talk or sing to them. Not so long ago, modern science dismissed such claims as women's fantasies. This is not so surprising since evidence from science was considered far superior to what people could figure out for themselves. Since the scientific establishment was mostly male, few could claim any direct experience with pregnancy and technology was not sufficiently advanced to validate the claims made by pregnant women.

In the fifties, when Tomatis advanced the idea that the fetus was already listening in the womb, his colleagues criticized him, feeling that he had really gone too far. This was a revolutionary idea at the time and that it faced opposition was not surprising. Even today, most psychological theories ignore the importance of fetal life in child development. Until recently, an unborn baby was still the "witless tadpole" described by the French philosopher Jean-Jacques Rousseau.

"In the old view," wrote David Chamberlain,[54] "babies of any age before birth were though to be unaware, unexpressive, and unaffected by their interactions with us. At the heart of these misunderstandings was the belief that baby brains were so poorly developed that babies could not learn or remember anything, could have no true pain, find no meaning in physical sensations, have no emotions, and no truly human experiences until many months after they were born. Babies in the womb were brainless, deaf, and dumb and therefore it was silly for parents to try to talk to them." Freud and many of his followers, who place the emergence of self-awareness in the second year after birth, echoed this traditional point of view.

Although these views are slowly changing, we need a paradigm shift in psychology and education if we want to give to the unborn baby prenatal care and sensory stimulation that will lead to a balanced and creative life. What happens in the womb during the first nine months of gestation reverberates not only beyond birth but also throughout life. The Chinese, as well as many so-called "primitive societies" who are concerned about giving the expectant mother an appropriate environment and a good climate to foster the coming of a beautiful child, know far more than science tells us.

Babies are very active in the womb. Space may be limited, but there is plenty to explore and learn. The repertoire of activities of the fetus becomes more complex as they get closer to birth. Each skill that is mastered is the steppingstone for the development of another one. During the first trimester, the fetus learns to roll from side to side, turn his head, flex his back and neck, stretch its legs and kick the wall of the uterus. By twelve weeks, he is busily involved playing with his fingers, toes, hands and feet or pulling on the umbilical cord. Touch is an essential tool for exploration.

At four and one half months, the vestibule is fully operative, expanding the range of motor movements. The fetus now turns somersaults, propels himself with legs and feet from one end of the womb to the other and changes sides with graceful pirouettes. It may not seem much compared to our frenetic pace, but these exercises repeated over and again create patterns of activity involving muscle and joint movement. These patterns lead to sensory awareness, which establishes a somatic foundation for learning. At this stage, the fetus acts purposefully and initiates a series of activities which reinforce his sense of competence. He is neither insensitive nor unconscious. We can even say that he has prenatal intelligence, though it is quite different from the adult intelligence we recognize. He has a sensorial intelligence, but his senses are not yet necessarily differentiated. An autistic child, who experiences light as sound and sound as light, may be an apt metaphor for describing the perceptual world of the unborn child. This switching between senses is normal in the early weeks of development after birth. These senses will become differentiated as the neural pathways mature.

The inner world of the womb can be directly explored. It is not an isolated place: the outer world echoes through the wall of the uterus. The placenta itself is not an impenetrable barrier but rather "an organ of transfer which assures that virtually everything which enters the mother will also enter the baby."[55] If we could return to the womb for a few minutes, we would hear a thumping heartbeat, blood rushing through arteries, the stomach rumbling as it digests lunch and the wind-like noise of the air as it fills and leaves the cavernous lungs.

We could also hear, and more importantly, feel our mother's footsteps on the ground as she moved from one place to another throughout the day—a good reason why children love swinging or being rocked in their mother's arms and why adults soothe themselves by sitting in a rocking-chair at the end of a hard day. The metronome-like pattern of the mother's footfall registers distinctly in the vestibule. When movement becomes associated with sound, it becomes rhythm, dance—its cadence infusing tango, salsa, waltz or rock-and-roll. Rhythm is synonymous with beat, pulse, and life. The mother's rhythm coming from her footsteps and heartbeat brings reassurance that life goes on. After birth, the heartbeat also becomes associated with milk, the food that sustains life, and its source, the breast, since babies, as they suck her nipple in a rhythmic fashion, hear the soothing beat of their mother's heart.

The footfall and the heartbeat of the mother are two rhythmic patterns, fairly regular and constant against the background noise surrounding the fetus. If not for the amniotic liquid and the vernix, (a white substance that covers the baby, filling the outer ear and dampening sound), the womb would be an unbearably noisy place.

Still the fetus reacts sharply when the volume spikes and becomes uncomfortable. Mothers report being kicked when they turn the radio up or when a commercial suddenly roars from the TV.

At five months the ear is fully developed and the auditory nerve is completely encased by a myelin sheath that facilitates and hastens the transfer of auditory information. Tomatis believed that the fetus might even hear before the completion of the hearing system, although it might be less efficient. Just as we do not wait until our legs have reached their full length before we walk, we do not await full myelination before using nerves. Even before the vestibule and cochlea are fully operational, the skin's four types of sound receptors appear to act like a primitive ear. As noted by Blum, et al.[56] "a deaf person can be trained to hear with the skin by the aid of special transducers, which adapt the broadband spectrum of sounds and voices to the narrowband spectrum accessible to the skin mechanoreceptors." These skin receptors might not transmit sounds very accurately while in the womb, but once the vestibular system and the cochlea mature and start to function in an increasingly integrated way, sounds will become clearer.

The Mother's Voice

If the fetus hears so much, can he hear his mother's voice as well? After all, many mothers say they communicate with their unborn babies. As early as the late Forties, Tomatis asked himself that question after reading *The Mechanisms of Larynx*,[57] a book written by the English zoologist V. E. Negus. He was especially intrigued by the fact that Negus reported that newly hatched birds belonging to a singing species were unable to sing if non-singing birds sat on their nests. If both the mother bird as well as the adoptive mother bird sing but belong to different species, a robin instead of a blue jay, for instance, the young bird is likely to sing like his adoptive mother: in other words, the blue jay will sing like a robin. This switch is not reversible: even if the blue jay is put back in the nest with other blue jays, he still will continue to sing like a robin. Such observations lead to an inescapable conclusion: the bird's song was conditioned by the mother's voice perceived through the eggshell long before birth.

Konrad Lorentz, the famous Austrian zoologist who received the Nobel Prize in 1973, proved this point brilliantly. He described how, in one experiment, he talked regularly to a brood of duck eggs in the absence of the mother. After they hatched, the ducklings started to follow him every time they heard him speak. His voice clearly triggered this automatic response, providing additional proof that unborn ducklings perceived sounds, leading to imprinting, a primitive form of bonding. If this was true for birds, could it be true for human beings as well? Tomatis found an answer to his questions while working with the neurologist Andre-Thomas who was a pioneer in infant research in France.

Andre-Thomas had developed a test called "the sign of the first name" to demonstrate that a newborn baby could recognize her mother's voice immediately after birth. This was not a fancy test involving sophisticated equipment but an empirical test that never failed to produce the same result. It was performed in the first ten days of the infant's life while the middle ear and the Eustachian tube are still filled with liquid, producing conditions that are very similar to those in utero. During the experiment, the baby was seated on a table surrounded by several people, men and women. One after the other, they called the baby's name. She only reacted when she heard her mother's voice: she turned her head in her direction and leaned toward her. Andre-Thomas saw in that reaction proof that the child became acquainted with her mother's voice in the womb.

Science has progressed by leaps and bounds since Andre-Thomas' simple experiment. His observations have been confirmed with the help of modern technology. Today, there is no doubt that the child hears the mother's voice. But what she actually hears is still a hotly debated question.

Hi-fi in Utero? What does the Fetus exactly Hear?

The fetus not only hears his mother's voice, her heartbeat and the rumbling of her stomach, but also all the surrounding sounds. He hears the voices of other people around the mother, the running of her car's engine as she drives around, the clattering of the plates on the counter when she cooks, or Brahms' string quintets played in the background. As an aside, children who have often heard a piece of music while still in utero often show a special attraction to that piece after birth.

Many uterine sounds are consistent, forming a continuous backdrop that reassures the fetus and contributes to his wellbeing. These neither surprise nor disturb the prenate and, in fact, are barely noticed. In one study, children conceived near Narita, Tokyo's airport, had fewer psychological problems than the ones whose mothers had moved near the airport when she was already a few months pregnant. If unborn children can sleep through noisy takeoffs and landings, we could conclude that sounds, even loud ones, are not disturbing as long as they are familiar. This good news is qualified by the fact that these children weighted statistically less than the ones born in a peaceful environment. Obviously, the fetus' ability to adapt has limits and noise takes its toll as it does on those who are already born.

In this noisy concert, the mother's voice has a special place: it is not entirely predictable—long moments of silence are interspersed with quiet or passionate conversations— nor is it repetitive like the heartbeat. The tone of the voice, the speed of speech, the specific rhythms of the mother's language introduce variety in the midst of familiarity. The ear of the fetus is constantly alert to the small dissonances that disrupt the daily patterns of life in utero. We can imagine, without stretching the evidence too far, that the fetus looks for moments when a new, somewhat unfamiliar sound reaches his ears. Life, after all, can be boring when it follows the same routine day after day. We strive for novelty: it energizes us, it creates new connections in our brain, and it makes us feel alive.

We are also creatures of habit: they constitute the background of our lives and we soon feel out of balance when change stretches us to the limit or pushes us from our regular habits. And so we try to strike a balance between our fear of change and our desire for new experiences. The fetus is probably not very different but the balance between old and new information has to be more tightly kept because the prenate is so fragile. The mother's voice seems ideally suited for this role. Like a symphony in which the theme is first played and then reiterated in different variations, always coming back to the departure point, the mother's voice is music to the child's ear: familiar, reassuring and still fresh and new. We can even imagine that the unborn child pricks his ears in anticipation of the melody of his mother's voice, his first attempt to connect, to bond and communicate with the world outside.

But exactly how does the mother's voice sound to the unborn child? Certainly not like the voice of our mother as we have learned to recognize it since birth. Tomatis believed that the fetus hears mainly the high frequencies of her voice. Several researchers in France seriously challenged this opinion. Feijoo argued that the fetus could only hear the low frequencies and not the high frequencies as Tomatis claimed. Busnel and Querleau introduced sophisticated equipment into the uterus, demonstrating that the fetus grows in an environment where sounds are dampened. Dampening does not mean that the sounds are suppressed beyond a certain range as Feijoo concluded. All sounds are heard, including the mother's voice. They are perceived in somewhat the same way as we perceive external sounds when we wear earplugs.

In the Fifties, Tomatis postulated that the mother's voice is transmitted to the fetus through bone conduction, following the length of the spine. When we speak, the larynx touches the spinal cord, which resonates like a string. The more erect we stand, the better the sound travels down the spine. Opera singers and actors know very well that their voices are more resonant when they stand straight, causing the bony structures of their bodies to resonates with maximum amplitude. If we observe pregnant women, they too spontaneously adopt a more upright posture to counterbalance the weight of the child. This is an ideal posture to transmit the sounds of their voices to the ears of the fetus.

Tomatis originally thought that the vibrations of the spinal cord were then transmitted through the amniotic fluid to the ears of the unborn child. This explanation ran counter to the fact that before birth the Eustachian tube is open and filled with liquid. Consequently, neither the eardrum nor the middle ear can function before birth. When he realized this, he proposed a different mechanism. He postulated that the fetus pushes his head against the posterior wall of the uterus (where the spinal cord ends) to pick up the bone vibration. So the sounds are transmitted all the way by bone conduction, bypassing the not yet functional middle ear. At around eight months after conception, the baby turns upside down and rests his head against the iliac bone. From that moment on, the iliac bone is the transducer (and amplifier) of the sounds of his mother's voice.

In the late Eighties, two French scientists, Dr. Christophe Petitjean and Dr. D. Klopfenstein, studied how sounds are transmitted to the fetus.[58] Dr. Petitjean put a vibrator on the skulls of thirty-eight pregnant women and observed whether the sound reached the pelvis, and if so, what frequencies were transmitted. He also recorded the reactions of the fetus, including the number of movements and its heartbeat.

The results confirmed Tomatis' hypothesis that the mother's voice is transmitted to the fetus through bone conduction. In effect, both the base frequencies and the higher harmonics were picked up. The intensity of the lower frequencies was muted whereas the higher frequencies passed through undisturbed. This is in line with expectations, as bone conducts higher frequencies better than low frequencies.

When exposed to frequencies belonging to the communication zone (1,000 Hz to 2,000 Hz), the fetus moved more frequently than when exposed to either higher or lower frequencies. For example, at 2,000 Hz, the fetus moved five times more often than at 500 Hz. From this we can conclude that the particular acuity people have for the frequencies of the communication zone exists before birth, giving the unborn infant several more months of immersion in the intricacies of human communication and the mother's particular language. Maybe that is the reason we call the first language we speak our mother tongue, since our immersion training in our first language began while we were still in the womb.

Using more sophisticated equipment, Dr. Klopfenstein, head of the Department of Gynecology of a hospital in Vesoul (France), came to the same conclusions.[59] He also showed that the best reception was recorded on the iliac bone and on the pelvis.

What can expectant mothers learn from this research? As we have seen that good posture is crucial in transmitting their voice to their unborn baby. It is not enough for a mother to talk to her unborn baby. She needs to stand erect or sit straight for her voice to resonate optimally throughout her pelvis and reach her baby with the full range of harmonics. The dialogue between mother and child can then unfold: mother's spine is like a cord and her pelvis like the case of a cello—playing beautiful music to the fetus' ears.

The Sonic Birth

As always, Tomatis tried to find a practical application for this discovery. Based on his finding that the fetus mainly hears the higher harmonics of the mother's voice, he speculated that he could help people by having them listen to the filtered voice of their mother, recreating the sound as it was heard in the uterine environment. Instead of keeping the mother's voice as it sounds to our ears, he filtered out all the sounds below 8,000 Hz, thus keeping only the high frequencies, reproducing the sounds of the voice as he believed the fetus heard them. This is a very different experience than listening to regular music. "It sounds like static or scratches" is a comment I have often heard. I even once heard a man declare that it sounded "like a choir of crickets or cicadas." Reactions vary but can be very strong at times. Overall, the filtered voice of one's mother seems to trigger memories of early development in the womb.

One could compare the therapy developed by Tomatis to a process of being "reborn," sonically speaking, but this time free of the difficulties the child may have experienced before. This is a way of giving the child a way to start over again, giving her a new lease on life. Therefore, the therapy passes through the various phases of our lives, corresponding to our journey from the womb into the world. To evoke the time we spent into the womb, the mother's voice is recorded and then filtered in such a way that the high frequencies of the voice (those beyond 8,000 Hz) predominate. This phase is then followed by what Tomatis called the "sonic birth" where the voice is progressively less and less filtered. *The purpose of this process is to mimic the passage from liquid audition in the womb to air audition after birth.* Gradually, the voice of the mother becomes more intelligible as the cricket-like sounds give way to a more full-bodied voice. Soon, the full and clear sentences of a story, usually *The Little Prince* by the French writer Saint-Exupéry, are heard. The moment comes when the child, who has been listening to his mother's voice without knowing it, may jump on his feet and proclaim: "I hear mommy!" For some children, this recognition can have a very profound impact, and may herald the first stage of the birth of their emotional self.

Jack was a seven year-old autistic child when he came to the Center. He had made some good progress through countless hours of behavior modification therapy. He could talk but his language was rarely spontaneous. Short verbal responses, consisting of a few words, a sentence rarely completed, were the result of learning by rote. These were stereotyped answers, showing that Jack had not engaged emotionally. Most often, he did not even look at the person to whom he spoke, a characteristic autistic feature. When we started to play his mother's filtered voice through the earphones, he instantly froze, listening intensely. "Mommy!" he said and he stood still listening as though struck by some wonderful memory. It was clear that the voice had mysteriously broken through the walls that too often surround autistic children and make them so difficult to reach. Jack's mother, Joan, was deeply moved: "He never spontaneously called me mommy! This is the first time!"

During his "sonic birth," Jack became very affectionate. Although he had never avoided physical contact, he was now actively seeking it. He also became more verbal and suddenly started to point out things as he named them. This was a big step. When we point, we are manifesting intent, linking words and the object they name; we acknowledge the reality around us, agreeing on meanings that may elude the child who does not point. Pointing is the concrete manifestation of a thought, a basic step in the development of higher forms of thinking. Suddenly, Jack was pointing to anything and everything, visibly enjoying discovering a world that had always been at hand but that he had barely noticed. It was as if he had been wandering in a fog that reduced the world to a general outline, where people were shadows appearing and disappearing, some familiar, and some unknown. As people and objects started to come into focus, Jack experienced a desire to connect and to emotionally bond with them on his own terms. One day, as they were driving back home, his mother heard him call her: "Mommy! This is Mommy!" She looked in the rear mirror and saw Jack pointing at her, with a broad grin on his face, and repeating: "Mommy! This is mommy!" She was so stunned and elated by his ability to identify her using spontaneous, appropriate words that she almost ended up in a ditch.

The use of the mother's voice can help restore an emotional connection that has been lost. It brings people back to life emotionally and is truly a powerful healing tool. For reasons that we do not know, Jack had become autistic, cut off from the world. His bond to his mother was formal and emotionally detached. Playing back the mother's voice had, in Jack's case, infused the relationship with emotional content without which there is no bonding and little life.

But what happens when the mother's voice is not available? Consider five year-old Tatiana. She was born in Russia at the time of the collapse of the communist regime. Her mother had tried to abort her, but Tatiana had survived and was consequently born two and a half months prematurely. She was immediately abandoned and raised in an orphanage for the first three years of her life. Living conditions were dire: rooms with cribs lining the walls and with too few caretakers to provide warmth and stimulation; toddlers rocking for hours to provide themselves a measure of comfort; small children crying or fighting, sinking gradually into a bottomless despair. Tatiana was lucky to have the same caretaker throughout those three years: she probably would not have survived without the warmth and attention that she received from her. Tatiana was a beautiful toddler with blond hair and blue eyes, but she was almost mute and was handicapped by a clubfoot. Her chances in life would have been very dim indeed, but a couple from the United States, with three boys of their own, fortunately adopted her.

When Caroline, her adoptive mother, flew back to California with Tatiana, she had no idea of what was in store for them in the ensuing years. First, there was the surgery for the clubfooted. Then came the occupational therapy sessions and countless hours of speech therapy. The challenge was daunting: Tatiana only spoke five words of Russian when she was adopted and now had to learn a new language! Though Tatiana was an affectionate little girl, Caroline's fighting spirit often plummeted at the seeming snail's pace of even the best progress. When Tatiana finally managed to learn to speak English, she spoke with a very soft voice, sometimes difficult to understand. Despite her progress over the past two years, Tatania was still quite delayed and her mother wondered if she would ever be normal.

When I met her for the first time, I was reminded of the little "space cadet" that Caroline had described to me over the phone. I had rarely seen such a short attention span in a child: she went through the toys in the playroom at high speed, grabbing one, rejecting it immediately, her attention caught by another one to which she gave the same treatment. This went on for a few minutes till she found a Walt Disney edition of *The Little Mermaid*. The picture of Ariel, the little mermaid, absorbed her totally. She leafed quickly through the book, pointing to each picture of Ariel with delight. "Ursula, the bad witch, is trying to get her," she confided in a very soft voice.

In the following weeks, the same scene was repeated many times. Ariel, the little mermaid, had great meaning to Tatiana who clearly identified with her, but Ariel's life was always at great risk because of the cruel Ursula. I could not help wondering, looking at the pictures of Ariel fighting to survive in the depths of the ocean, if the story was not an apt description of Tatiana's first months of life in the womb. No wonder the story had such power over her! Through it she was able to revisit and conquer the threat of death that she had experienced almost from the time of conception. After all, it was her own mother who had tried to end her life! She had survived, but not without emotional scars.

I asked Caroline to record her voice as if she were Tatiana's biological mother. Whether or not to use the voice of the adoptive mother is a topic of debate among Tomatis practitioners. I am personally inclined to use it when the relationship between the adoptive mother and child is both good and affectionate. The idea is to simulate an in utero experience which is emotionally positive and thus becomes a steppingstone to healthier development. It is a *symbolic* experience in which sound provides good memories which will hopefully supplant the bad. This sonic regression is a form of "re-patterning" that establishes a solid foundation for the future.

Tatiana's reactions to Caroline's voice dumbfounded all of us. She was in the playroom when we started to play the "mother" tape. She was immediately riveted to the spot, listening intensely. She then ran to the parent's room where Caroline was sitting on a comfortable couch. She jumped into her lap, curled up in a fetal position, sucking her thumb and looking at Caroline with an ecstatic expression. For the next half hour, Tatiana behaved like a happy baby while listening to Caroline's voice and looking straight into her eyes. Caroline was, at first, overwhelmed by such intensity of feelings. She had never had an opportunity to nurse Tatiana when she was a baby. Here was a chance that might never return. She faced the challenge beautifully: she and her child were finally as one. She gave Tatiana the love that she had never received as a baby. For all of us, it was an unforgettable moment.

We were even more surprised when the tape stopped. Tatiana stood up calmly, gave a little smile to Caroline and marched back to the playroom. There, she played for the next half hour, listening to the filtered sounds of a Mozart symphony. Nothing in her demeanor gave any indication of what has just happened. She was again a five-year-old sketching Ariel, the little mermaid, with a red pencil. Things changed rapidly when we played Caroline's voice again. Once more, Tatiana ran to the parents' room, installed herself comfortably in Caroline's lap and, once again, was the perfect image of a happy baby sucking her thumb. This lasted till the end of the tape. When the voices of the monks of the abbey of Solesmes finally rose through the headphones, Tatiana got up and went back to the playroom to pencil another drawing of Ariel.

That afternoon, when they went home, Tatiana found a big round basket where the family's dog used to sleep. She lay in it, nestled in a fetal position for a long time. Caroline was concerned but didn't try to stop her. She understood that Tatiana needed to go through this regressive state. She needed to be a baby again since she never had the chance to really be one. Caroline watched and admired her as only a warm and loving mother can. "I know she is catching up" Caroline would say, "but she is much regressed." This did not last long. Soon Tatiana emerged from her regression and showed robust signs of progress. She focused for longer periods and concentrated on one activity at a time. "She is more together now," Caroline would comment with obvious relief. Tatiana continued to mature in the ensuing months. It seemed that a blockage had been removed, one that had hampered her intellectual and emotional development for so long.

A year after she had completed the program, I saw them again. Caroline wanted to make sure that Tatiana received the right type of stimulation needed to sustain her as she was working to master the complexities of reading and writing. She had been very distressed by a report on ABC showing how many of the small children adopted from Romanian orphanages had developed major cognitive and behavior deficits due to a lack of proper stimulation as infants. A CAT scan performed on a small group of these children clearly showed that the language centers and frontal lobes were functioning below normal expectations. These children's development failed to follow biologically determined timetables. In a distressing number of cases, the children were unable to perform simple intellectual tasks or exhibited behavior problems due to failure to form attachments with their adoptive parents. Tatiana was not among these disconnected children: she was loving and very bonded to Caroline though she certainly had some cognitive delays.

Caroline wanted an annual booster to make sure that Tatiana moved forward as she grappled with homework and learning to read. Over the next years, she progressed beyond any expectations that I could have had when I saw her for the first time. "When I brought her back from Russia," Caroline told me three years later, "she was one of the worst off compared to the children adopted by the parents of my support group. Now, she is one of the best!" She was very proud and had reason to be: she had worked hard to bring Tatiana to her current level of achievement. From my standpoint, the stimulation provided by the music processed through the Electronic Ear had prompted Tatiana's brain to establish new connections, making it easier for her to respond to the many challenges of our society. Ultimately, social and intellectual functioning depends on emotional stability: the use of the mother's voice had filled a void that could have been the source of many future difficulties. It brought peace to Tatiana, bound her deeply to Caroline and created a safe and strong foundation for a healthier development.

Playing back their Mother's Voice to Adults

The mother's voice can also have an emotional impact on adults and lead them to a better psychological and social adjustment. Sylvia, for example, was an attractive, bright twenty-five-year-old with a great sense of humor, but the first day she walked into my office, she seemed more like a wounded bird teetering on the brink of disaster. She looked so exhausted that I felt like offering her my arm to make sure that she did not collapse. I first thought that she might have anorexia: her face was very pale and emaciated and the oversized blue sweatshirt she wore did not hide the extreme thinness of her small frame. She dropped into a chair with a big sigh and closed her eyes for a while to catch her breath.

Sylvia had left a small college town in the Midwest for San Francisco in search of freedom and a less conservative lifestyle. Her free spirit and disregard for convention were inherited from her mother, a painter. She was also gifted in the arts: she painted like her mother, wrote poetry and played the banjo. Sylvia was a smart young woman but she had been in trouble for many years. While still very young, she had engaged in a series of relationships that crumbled. She had moved from man to man and from place to place. She had very little sense of boundaries and had trouble saying no to men who used her and then rejected her. She felt she could not live without a man in her life to ease a void that she always felt deep down. By the time Sylvia turned twenty-five, she had had five abortions and was experiencing a nervous breakdown.

The problems that brought her to my office had started two months earlier, just after the last abortion. Her world had suddenly collapsed. A sense of joy and excitement, that usually supported her through good and bad times, had deserted her. She felt lifeless: she stayed in bed for countless hours, unable to eat or even move. She had so little strength that she stopped working. As her depression became worse, she started to think about ending her life. It no longer had meaning for her: life became a succession of days that grew darker and darker. Had she lived alone, she might already have killed herself. Luckily, she shared an apartment a few blocks from Haight-Ashbury with a group of people who kept an eye on her, trying to help her as best they could. They were so concerned that they tried to convince Sylvia to consult a physician. She, however, was adamant: no doctor! And so, she was consumed in a downward spiral of depression.

It was a phone call from her mother, Julie, which finally brought her to my office. Back in Ohio, Julie had followed the news from San Francisco with increasing anxiety. Her husband, Dane, had just returned from a workshop with Don Campbell, a long time advocate of the power of music to heal physical and emotional difficulties and the author of *The Mozart Effect*.[60] Dane had heard Don talk at length about Tomatis' idea that high frequency sound can charge the brain with energy. Maybe this was the solution they had been looking for to help Sylvia. It was alternative enough that Sylvia might not balk at the thought of consulting a professional. By the time Julie called her, she had reached the point of knowing she needed help and agreed to see me the same day.

It was not the best time to start therapy with such a challenging case. I was scheduled to leave for Hawaii six days later for a ten day vacation. I explained the situation to Sylvia and strongly emphasized the need to consult a physician while I was away. She flatly refused, saying she didn't believe in conventional medicine. This put me in a bind since I could neither start treatment nor let her go without help. After all, she had put so much hope in this visit. I was also concerned that her depression would get worse and that she might commit suicide. While we talked, one idea kept running through my mind: why not start her on the Tomatis program for six days instead of waiting? I could arrange for another professional to take over in case of an emergency during my absence. With luck, I might also be able to soften Sylvia's position on mainstream medicine and send her for a physical.

For the next two hours, Sylvia listened to the music of Mozart and to some Gregorian chant. Listening might not be the most accurate word to describe this first session since she fell asleep after half an hour. When she left, she looked a little rested. More importantly, I could see a glimmer of hope in her eyes.

"I slept thirteen hours last night" she announced the next day. "When I got up, I ate a real big breakfast. I could not stop eating." She was quite surprised at herself. After all, she had barely slept or eaten for months. In the next few days, her recovery continued at a fast rate. When I left for Hawaii, she was starting to have a healthier glow on her face and, for the first time in months, she had a sense of control over her life.

When I came back, Sylvia appeared to be a different person. She had not only managed to continue eating and sleeping regularly, but more remarkably, she had found a job and had been working for a week. She now looked to each new day with anticipation. She was slowly coming back to herself and was renewing friendships that she had neglected for months. She had not consulted a physician, she told me with a grin, because she believed that she had now embarked on a journey of self-healing sparked by the few days that she had spent listening to the music of Mozart.

As we worked together, we saw the last signs of depression rapidly lifting. Still, her relationships with men were an area of great difficulty. She was particularly annoyed with one of them, but could not find the strength to terminate this unsavory relationship. Strangely enough, there was a resolution during the sonic birth that we were able to accomplish after we had received the recording of her mother's voice. Sylvia had been working late the previous night and was tired. She fell asleep during the session at the critical moment when she should have been able to hear her mother's voice clearly. Should we wake her up? I hesitated. A child who had a temper tantrum in another part of the Center delayed the decision for a few minutes while we calmed him down. Things had just returned to normal when Sylvia appeared in my office, tears streaming down her eyes. "I was calling you." she said, "but you didn't come." She had on her face the look of someone who had been abandoned and was disappointed. "I didn't hear you" I answered. "But I called you!" she said petulantly wiping the tears from her face with her hand. She had, indeed, called me for help but it was in the middle of a dream and the words for help had stayed in that dreamland. They had never echoed into our world. The dream itself was simple but terrifying: she was trying to open a big, heavy door that stayed shut even when she pushed hard against it. It was a matter of life and death; she could barely breathe and the walls around her seemed to be closing in. She made a final, desperate effort to escape. She crashed her shoulder against the door, which suddenly opened wide. The weight of her body propelled her through the opening. She felt herself falling through a huge, empty space like an asteroid plunging from the sky. It was then that she had screamed my name and woke up, her eyes filled with tears.

As she recovered her composure, searching for meaning in the dream, she was struck by the similarity between the dream and her birth. "My mother had a very, very long labor. I could not come through. I was stuck in the canal. I could not breathe. I was pushing, pushing." She seemed to speak from a trance. Long lost sensory perceptions from a drama that she could not otherwise have remembered were rushing through her mind. These were not vividly recollected memories that were now flooding her, but sensations recorded by the body and stored in its dark recesses. How could it have been otherwise? She had no language at birth to express the primitive and powerful fears and sensations that had engulfed her as she fought for her life. The sonic birth had lead to the dream that so accurately captured the trauma of being born and released the terrifying sensations that she had experienced at the time. "After birth," she continued in a dreamy voice, "I was taken away from my mother for two days. I felt as though I had fallen into an empty place.... a bottomless pit. It was so lonely ... So cold ..." Her body shivered. She fell silent for a few minutes. When she started to talk again, her voice was firmer: "All those men in my life" she said, "I guess it was my way of trying to fill the void. I was so afraid to be alone. Better someone, anyone, than no one."

In the ensuing days, Sylvia broke off her relationship with the man who, she finally admitted to herself, was taking advantage of her poorly defined boundaries. Her recovery was fast. She took a better-paying job managing a coffee shop, organizing weekly concerts and booking the musicians. For the first time in her life, she had a sense of control over the events of her life. There were still hard times, but she no longer felt overwhelmed by her feelings. They seemed to have taken a back seat; she could observe them at a distance instead of being flooded by them and reacting immediately, without thinking. Her sense of boundaries got stronger. She refused to behave as a victim any longer. When we parted, her depression was just a bad memory.

The story has a happy ending. Three years later, I received a phone call from the Midwest. "It's Sylvia! Do you still remember me?" How could I have forgotten her? "I want you to know that I am married to my high school sweetheart. We have a baby. It's wonderful! I have to tell you too," she laughed, "I am a fairly well-rounded person now!" It was a song of happiness. I felt grateful for her call. These are great moments in a therapist's career when we learn that we have made a significant difference in someone's life and that it will reverberate in his or her future in a healthy and positive way. I also felt grateful for the technique developed by Dr. Tomatis without which such changes would not have taken place in such a short time and with such long-lasting effects.

The stories of Jack, Tatiana and Sylvia illustrate the power of the mother's voice in therapy. For Jack and Tatiana, it provided them with a secure emotional base, the fundamental ingredient for healthy and stable maturation. For Sylvia, her mother's voice brought about a release from conflicts that were probably rooted in birth trauma. The dream in front of the door was a metaphor for the feeling of being stuck on the one hand, and the incredible liberation of energy when the door finally opens, on the other. It was her mother's voice that enabled Sylvia to revisit birth and made it possible for her to experience herself as reborn.

I want to emphasize that not all sonic births have such dramatic effects. In most cases, the process goes smoothly and is unremarkable. Children acknowledge that their mother is the one they hear on the tape with a knowing smile. It is a tacit recognition of the important role of their mother in their lives. To children who ask why they are listening to their mother's voice, I explain that their mother recorded her voice out of love for them and because we knew that it would help them to resolve their difficulties in school. They don't question this explanation: it actually makes them very content. It is not uncommon, during these times, to see children shower their mothers with great demonstrations of affection. They deserve it: raising children is not an easy task and is made even more challenging in our fast-paced society.

Music for the Unborn Child

Most mothers want to create the best climate for their unborn children. Good medical care, the right nutrition, solid support from the father of the child, friends and relatives, a decent economic situation, are all elements that help. Some also join support groups, take exercise classes, workshops or seminars in preparation for the delivery and the task of raising a baby. I would suggest that music be added to this list for its soothing, calming effect as the time of the delivery gets closer.

Not all music is good for prenates and their mothers, however. Heavy metal music, rap, rock-and-roll and industrial music are not recommended: the unborn child has no need to perceive the world as a cacophony, buffeted in the womb with each loud beat. Mozart, Gregorian chant, baroque or classical music, lullabies and old folksongs are more likely to decrease the mother's anxiety and please the child's ears as he listens to his first concerts. These choices are not only valid during the period of pregnancy but also for a long time after birth. The child's sensory-systems are easily overwhelmed by loud, pounding music and need to be protected for months and years to come.

Mozart, baroque music and chant are the most respectful of the ways our bodies work. The rhythm of Gregorian chant, for instance,

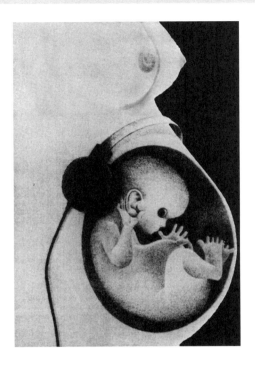

is a very natural one: it fits in with the rhythm of the heartbeat and the rhythm of our breath when we are relaxed. Baroque music has a rhythm of sixty beats per minute, the optimal resting rate for the heartbeat. Common sense should be the rule when it comes to the choice of music. The mother must ask herself: does this music make me feel relaxed or agitated? Do I feel that my baby relaxes too? Listening to serene and beautiful music may be an opportunity for mother and child to listen to each other and communicate. And, of course, talking and singing to the baby should not be forgotten.

Tomatis discovered the effect of his therapy on pregnant women because some of the children under treatment in his Center had expectant mothers. As with all mothers, Tomatis provided a free program to them, to help them relax and understand what their kids were experiencing. As they listened, these pregnant moms told him that they felt more relaxed, had more energy and were less anxious than during previous pregnancies. They attributed this well-being to the music that they listened to in the parent's room. Many of them also reported that, after birth, their infants were quieter and also loved music. Some of the mothers, indeed, swore that their babies could recognize a piece of music or a song that they either had played or sang during their pregnancy.

Based on these reports, Tomatis began to suspect that auditory stimulation might also help pregnant women during childbirth. To research this, Dr. Klopfenstein, head of the Department of Gynecology of the General Hospital in Vescul, France, initiated a pilot study.[61] His findings were nothing short of spectacular. As expected, laboring mothers were less anxious. More importantly though, dilation, the opening up of the cervix so that the baby can pass into the birth canal, took significantly less time, as can be seen in the table below.

Preparation	Dilation Time
Medical Checks Only	4 hours
Exercise Classes	3 hours 30
Exercise Classes + Tomatis	2 hours 30

Dr. Klopfenstein concluded that the Tomatis program enhanced the relaxation response learned in more traditional settings such as classes for breathing and relaxation.

Encouraged by these results, he did a large scale study with 170 expectant women, chosen at random.[62] Again, he saw a significant reduction in dilation time (to an average of 2 hours and 22 minutes). Also, the number of Cesarean sections dropped by over 30% among women giving birth to their first baby. Finally, the Hamilton test, a self-administered test measuring anxiety, showed a remarkable decrease of the anxiety level in the Tomatis group. On average it dropped by 9.15 points, which typically only good psychological treatment can achieve. Dr. Klopfenstein concluded that there was no doubt that the Tomatis Method reduced the level of anxiety of the mothers and, in doing so, created the conditions for a positive experience of pregnancy, in particular during the last two months which are often fraught with fears.

Another study, conducted in 1991 at the Foch Hospital in Suresnes near Paris,[63] confirmed the results observed by Dr. Klopfenstein. Although this group of women followed a Tomatis program less intensely (only twice a week during the eighth month), still the rate of anxiety decreased significantly in the Tomatis group while it increased in the group following a more traditional course of treatment. Labor was also significantly shorter, by an average of 47 minutes, mainly due to the fact that 17% of the women in the Tomatis group gave birth to their babies in less than three hours (6% in the control group). The APGAR test, rating the degree of adaptation of the baby to his new environment, showed that the Tomatis babies recovered better and faster. The Tomatis babies also weighed more since most Tomatis mothers gave birth after a slightly longer gestation period than those in the control groups (about 3 days longer than the mothers who followed traditional preparation techniques).

Statistics are important, but they do not always express the feelings of those who are assessed. When they were interviewed about their experience, most Tomatis mothers reported that they had felt more relaxed, more rested and had more energy, in line with the results of the Hamilton Test. Some mothers, who had already given birth to another child without the benefit of the Tomatis program, reported not feeling as exhausted after birth this time around. Many were ready to go home still feeling relaxed, as if the program's benefits extended beyond the birth of their child.

While the mothers could report their feelings, there was no way of knowing how the fetus felt about the program. No portable phones or fax machines send messages from the womb. But we can listen to what the mothers observed. The data are anecdotal and need more research, but we can discern several trends. First, mothers noticed that their babies reacted differently according to the music played. For example, the solemn rhythms of Gregorian Chant seemed to elicit more kicking against the abdominal wall than other types of music. We cannot say for sure that this "first leg attempt at jogging" is the reason that so many of these Tomatis babies had great strength in their legs, more muscular development and excellent balance, but those observations were repeatedly reported by their mothers. Tomatis babies actually tend to walk earlier and start to show more independence than their peers. They delight in listening to music and can become quite excited when they hear Mozart. "He never stops playing with the dials on the radio, trying to find Mozart," reported one mother of a two year old.

As seven month old infants, they tended to show no fear of water when taking their first swimming lessons. They floated on their backs and stretched their bodies, not even bothered if water filled their ears. They also floated face down, stayed comfortably in that position while the other children clung to their mothers, and tried to get back into an upright position. Marie Ouvrard, a midwife of Vesoul, who did follow-up as the Tomatis babies learned to swim, noticed that the great strength of their lower back made it possible for them to stretch on the water during the first session and to immediately try to propel themselves forward with their legs tight in a dolphin-like fashion.[64] Maybe the jogging movements prompted by listening to Gregorian chant in utero were a preparation for the swimming lessons taken after birth. A good preparation for life too, according to Marie Ouvrard, who observed that these children were more sociable, independent, daring and strong-willed than the other ones. They had what the French call "joie de vivre," an innate propensity to delight in all aspects of life.

A Child is Born

When a child is born, all his senses are summoned at once. Air suddenly fills the chambers of his lungs, the fingers that touch his skin may feel rough, the sweet odor of milk attracts him, lights startle him and make him blink, voices and sounds are louder and probably overwhelming at times. Amidst this onslaught of sensory stimulation, he'll still respond to people's faces and voices as of day one! "A newborn's ability to see and hear in the delivery room" writes T. Berry Brazelton,[65] "may be as important to the 'bonding' process as the act of putting the baby to breast to suckle." The newborn is able to recognize his mother's face though it may not respond as quickly to his father's face. We may hypothesize that the ability to identify the face of his mother is enhanced by linking it to her voice. William Condon and Louis Sanders[66] demonstrated that newborns synchronize their movements to the rhythm of a mother's voice immediately after birth. This has a parallel in the child's effort to link a letter and a sound in the process of learning to read. Both vision and voice deeply shape the future relationship between child and mother. It is through the senses that they learn to communicate. There is nothing more essential to the attachment of a mother to her child than seeing her baby's eyes gaze curiously at her or matching his movements to the rhythm of her voice. Soon, both of them are engaged in an intense, complex give and take dance that fosters communication and learning, establishing a solid foundation for further progress.

A huge body of research and literature explores this complex dance between a mother and her baby. When we sift through the details of many studies, we clearly see that love is vital for this dialogue. Love, as we well know, is as life sustaining as oxygen or food. For the baby, love is a lifeline. He receives it through his mother's touch, hears it through his mother's voice, and sees it in his mother's eyes. He solicits it by his cries, vocalizations, smiles, movements, and by his gaze at his mother's face. He feels one with his mother, unable yet to perceive his body as being separate from his mother's body. It is such a contagious feeling that both mother and child live in a mutuality of love.

Remember Tatiana when she heard her adoptive mother's filtered voice for the first time. She reacted as if on cue by behaving as a newborn, requesting through the play of her eyes, her smiles and cooing that Caroline provide her with the type of love that her biological mother had never showed. What Tatiana was after was that life-sustaining feeling that she had never experienced, having been abandoned immediately after her birth, a birth induced by the mother's attempt to abort. The tone, the inflexions, the melody of Caroline's voice carried the message that Tatiana was unconditionally loved. It is a message that all of us, even as adults, want to hear.

Falling in love is often experienced as becoming one with the other person. It is sometimes described as an oceanic feeling of merging with the other like in the mother-baby relationship. Giving and receiving love makes us emotionally and physically strong: we can grow, mature, and expand together because we mutually support each other. It is when love is missing from our lives that we feel lonely, depressed, and even physically lack wellness. We can feel angry, abandoned, powerless, and sometimes lack the will to live. Life has lost its bright hues and its meaning. The comparison between the mother-child relationship and the love relationship of two adults is no accident. They seem to be mirror images of each other. The relationship between mother and child is, in fact, the basic blueprint for all future relationships as we grow older, and perhaps wiser.

The symbiotic relationship between mother and child cannot, of course, last. If it remained unchanged, we would never have a reason to grow up; we would stay emotionally attached to our mothers in the same way that our bodies were once attached to her through the umbilical cord. Cutting the umbilical cord is symbolic of the progressive separation that will set us on a course of individuation. A mother's failure to attune to her child's every need and desire is actually a necessary opportunity for him to take incremental steps toward autonomy. Here we are not talking about neglect but about small lapses of attention, an inability to immediately respond to the child's cries or needs because the phone is ringing or a slice of bread is burning in the toaster. Little by little, through those little failures of attunement, the child will be forced to realize that he is not one with his mother, but that they are separate individuals.

The Child grows up

We may want to take a pause here and think about the parallels that exist between biological evolution on the one hand, and personal evolution on the other. As we saw in part one, each individual re-enacts, in his first months of existence, the path followed by evolution. The struggle the child encounters in trying to stand reflects our distant ancestors' long forgotten struggle to achieve verticality. His initial inability to talk mirrors the inability of those same ancestors to speak; likewise, the child's initial forms of thought quite likely reflect the structures of consciousness of our early ancestors.

In *Up from Eden*,[67] Ken Wilber proposes a model for the development of consciousness. He breaks it down into several stages that follow an ascending path, which is not unlike the vertical path in the metaphor of man as human antenna that Tomatis used. In the first stage, the individual and his environment are still fused together. In other words, there is no sense of self, since a sense of self implies *separation and being distinct* from the environment. What prevails is sub-consciousness. The imagery of the Garden of Eden perfectly symbolizes that state of fusion between man and his environment, between the individual and the group, and between the ego and the unconscious, indissolubly bound together. From that perspective, the myth of the Fall then translates into the moment when the self separates and becomes distinct from Mother Nature in which it had been embedded. Still, "in the early stages of development, the self is centered on the body, and not so much on the mind — it is a body-ego, not a mental-ego." The latter stage, the mental ego, will appear later on, when it emerges and differentiates from the body. Wilber postulates that future development of consciousness will move man increasingly away from his original unconsciousness, each new level "recapitulating and integrating the lower ones."

Like our primitive ancestors, a newborn and his environment are fused, as stated by the world-renowned psychologist Jean Piaget when he wrote:[68] "During the early stages, the world and the self are one; neither term is distinguished from the other ... the self is material, so to speak." And the self is material because it identifies with a world that is neither mental nor of higher intelligence, symbols, concepts or higher emotions. This opinion, notes Wilber,[69] is "shared by the whole psychoanalytic movement, the entire Jungian tradition, the modern ego psychologists such as Malher, Loevinger and Kaplan, and the cognitive psychologists in general." In practical terms, the infant perceives the body of his mother as part of himself. At this stage, he is in a dream-like, autistic state.

The Fall—equivalent in this framework to the beginning of consciousness—occurs when the child cannot sustain the fantasy of oneness and starts to perceive his mother as a separate person (psychologists use the word "object" instead of person, referring to their conviction that infants cannot properly conceptualize a person at this early stage of thought). That separation from mother—and from mother Earth as the child attempts to rise to his feet—is experienced as a death in the primitive consciousness of the infant. He is figuratively expelled from Paradise and banished to Earth. Still, he will maintain some of the old magical fantasies by centering his attention on his body. In other words, as Freud, proclaimed:[70] "The ego is first and foremost a body ego." As Wilber points out:[71] "When the infant bites a blanket, it does not hurt; when he bites his thumb, it hurts. There is a difference, he learns, between the body and not-body ... Thus, out of the primitive material unity emerges the first real self-sense: the body-ego ... The infant *identifies* with a newly emergent body, with its sensations and emotions, and gradually learns to differentiate them from the physical cosmos at large."

This stage, when the child starts to differentiate himself from his environment, corresponds with the sensorimotor period, the same period during which the child makes relentless efforts to reach verticality, the prerequisite for language development. Moving away from the ground, the child is increasingly able to see the objects around him and to manipulate them. That requires increased motor control and muscular coordination. Increasing motor control gives the child the ability to grasp objects and manipulate them for extended periods of time, allowing the child to create memories not only of the object but also from his experience with it. Such an achievement would not be possible without increased verticality: it frees the hands and therefore allows manipulating objects in front of the eyes, chewing them, smelling them, pushing them away or pulling them closer, to the great pleasure of the child who gains a sense of physical mastery from these experiences. Although "the self's approach to the world is almost exclusively through *bodily categories*"[72] as we have just seen, body mastery enables the progressive emergence of mental categories that precipitate new developmental growth and the birth of the mental ego.

This happens, not so coincidently, when the vertical posture is finally reached or, to be more precise, when the vestibule and the cochlea start to reach the listening posture: a prerequisite for good reception and emission. At that point in time, as we already know, verticality positions the cochlea in the optimal position for sound analysis, making the development of language possible. The emergence and progressive mastery of language accelerates the development of the mental ego. Little by little, pre-verbal thinking gives way to abstractions as images are grouped in concepts. The object no longer needs to be present to be conjured up: a dog does not need to be in view of the child to exist, since the dog can now exist as a concept in the child's memory. Psychologists refer to this as object constancy. The capacity for abstraction is not limited to the world of material objects, but also applies to the self. The child starts to develop self-concepts that gradually forge a sense of ego.

Certainly the ego does not crystallize in a definitive and stable form but undergoes a series of further transformations as language increases and consciousness expands. The child will increasingly be able to manipulate symbols that transcend the physical world, as thought is no longer limited to actual physical objects. At this point, the child's mental world has reached a higher level of functioning, one dominated by concepts and symbols. This constitutes a jump from nature to culture, since the dominant mode of experience is now verbal communication. Relationships between people start to take precedence over relationships to the physical world. The mental-ego is now center-stage after integrating and transcending the previous stages of development.

The evolution of mankind as well as the growing up of a child can be seen as climbing a ladder. Each subsequent level of consciousness would then constitute the next rung of the ladder. They reflect the structures of consciousness that prevailed for thousands of years among our distant ancestors and that each of us re-enacts as we grow up. Climbing the ladder, or in other words, raising the "human antenna" is an ongoing process that is far from complete, as we shall see later. Reaching physical verticality has an offshoot: psychological verticality. While it is grafted on physical verticality, psychological verticality integrates it and transcends it. If that were not the case, we would stay bound to the earth and to the material world of objects.

This is not a purely academic debate, even if it may appear so at first glance, since it allows us to grasp some of the challenges that children face in growing up. The child is, in fact, facing a dilemma: to take a risk and practice skills that are still developing, and thus accept to grow up, or to be conservative and remain more dependent, until these skills are more solid. Notice that "growing up" implies verticality: to grow up is to become vertical, not only physically *but psychologically as well*. Even if a child does have the prerequisite physical skills, she may get stuck along the path due to lack of emotional maturity caused by changing family circumstances, a traumatic event, etc…

As he matures, a child has to give up the sense of being at the center of the universe — a feeling that otherwise fosters immaturity. This cosmos-centricity is reflected in "I am the sun; you are the (distant) stars" kind of thinking that can lead to "I do what I want and you follow me" behavior. This magical thinking that seems to have been the privileged mode of thinking of our distant ancestors is also part of the first years, when the infant and, then, the young child still perceives the outside world as an extension of herself, on which she can operate according to her wishes, fantasies and wants. In the same way that she did not feel initially separated from mom's body but at one with it, she feels for some variable length of time that there is no separation between the world and herself, and that she can act on it according to her desires. A bright five year old illustrated this point quite well by telling me that *he* had made the sun disappear behind a cloud when a more realistic and mature child would have observed that a cloud had just passed in front of the sun.

As magical thinking gradually gives way to a more realistic view of the world, the child starts to accept the constraints and laws governing the society in which she lives. That causes a great level of anxiety since it means accepting the "death" of the body-ego in order for the mental-ego to be born. Temper tantrums, cries and attention-seeking behavior are manifestations of the confusion, fear and even resistance to increasing responsibility and self-reliance. Since it takes less energy to maintain a horizontal course, children with developmental challenges may opt out of an ascent that strikes them as too difficult, remaining horizontal instead, resisting the psychological verticality inherent to growing up. In short, it is better to feel a sense of oneness with Mother Earth and to be fed by her, than to become a separate and lonely individual, fending for oneself. Nevertheless, growing children cannot cling to mother indefinitely nor can they retain the carefree sense of fusion associated during infancy with the mother's body, no matter how much they may wish to delay the inevitable march toward adulthood.

Proponents of attachment theory like John Bowlby, Mary Ainsworth, or more recently Dr. Bruce Perry emphasize that child development proceeds more smoothly if the child has developed a secure attachment to his or her primary caregiver — optimally, the mother. "Indeed," says Perry,[73] "many researchers and clinicians feel that the maternal-child attachment provides the working framework for all subsequent relationships that the child will develop." John Bowlby considers that the more confident children are the more their base is secure (that is, the attachment between them and their primary caregiver), and the more they can "venture steadily further from base and for increasing spans of time."[74] In short, the more secure they are, the more readily they accept the challenges of growing up, which are *symbolized* by the fact that they are able to move progressively further and further away from mom's reassuring presence.

For the most part, attachment theory has mainly focused on mothers. It is only more recently that it has started to look at the father's role. Early on in his research, Tomatis emphasized the pivotal role played by fathers in their child's development. He envisions the father as an intermediary between the safety represented by the proximity of the mother's body and the social world that captivates the child and yet inspires him with fear and anxiety. Tomatis believed that fathers could play an important role in helping their children to gain mastery of the social world. In doing so, they would contribute to further a well-adjusted development that would foster emotionally healthy relationships in the present and the future. In his mind, mothers and fathers came to represent two necessary and complementary polarities between nurture and socialization. He knew, of course, that it was a simplification—but one that could help us to visualize the difficult journey of the child as he matures, so we could more easily grasp the nature of the process. Yet, it might be good to keep in mind that things are not that simple as the focus now shifts from the mother's role to the father's role.

THE ROLE OF THE FATHER

The Voice of the Father

As was just noted, the role of the father in child development is too often underestimated and given short shrift in favor of the intensely studied relationship between mother and child. It is an obvious fact, though, that a child has a set of parents, each one playing a different but complementary role. Without the active presence of a father or someone playing that role, a child may not be able to reach a well-balanced psychological adjustment and find his place in the society in which he is born. As we will see later, the quality of that adjustment will also influence greatly the quality of the listening skills of the child.

A traditional view of fathers holds that they stay peripheral for a long time, at least as long as the infant needs bodily care. It goes along with a traditional work division between sexes in which women take care of children, especially when they are small, and men are out of the house making a living. That vision certainly still holds true in many traditional societies and still has a powerful hold, at least at an unconscious level, in more modern societies where a great number of women work outside the house.

The fact that some fathers play the role of the nurturer (in case, for instance, when he stays home and his wife goes to work) still does not totally erase differences. Studies[75] show that husbands sharing their infant's care with their wives can be very efficient and beneficial to the infant's development but in different ways. For instance, while mothers tend to slowly rock their babies and vocalize more than their husbands, fathers provide a different type of sensory experiences since they tend to be more aggressive and more active in their play. For example, fathers are more likely to hold the infant firmly and pretend to throw him up and down into the air, as if the baby was in some sort of elevator. That vestibular stimulation is a welcome addition to the less vigorous body stimulation received from mothers and usually delights babies. Overall, the presence of a "mothering father" is quite positive: five months old infants that were taken care of by their fathers vocalize more in presence of a stranger, explore more often the objects in their environment and are more willing to be held in the arms of unfamiliar people than infants of the same age mainly taken care of by their mother. Clearly, the father facilitates the infant's independence already at a very early age but, at this stage, the father is not perceived as such by the infant.

Reviewing a large body of research, Boris Cyrulnik, a French neurologist and psychiatrist, concludes that "up to the sixth month, all babies accept any foreign person as a maternal substitute"[76] but emphasizes that around that same age the nature of the child's attachment changes. From then on, even if the mother is frequently absent, the child's safety needs seems to be better met by the mother. Cyrulnik proposes an explanation to such a change. He notes that, around that time, the maturation of the visual pathways leading to the occipital lobe of the brain allows the organization of a full image. This makes it possible for the baby to hold in his mind the complete visual image of a face instead of perceiving it in the form of partial elements. That neuro-psychological development allows the infant to perceive a difference between a familiar visual image, such as the mother's image, and any other image. From that time on, when the infant is confronted with a new object or person, he looks first at his mother before making any move towards that new object or person. If during the first six months the movement of the nose and eyebrows were sufficient to trigger the infant's feeling of jubilation, after six months the recognition of the face triggers a similar feeling only if the face is familiar. If not, the baby will take refuge in his mother's arms to feel safe and reassured. Only then will he be able to reach for a foreign object or hold out his arms towards a stranger. And the more he has had a safe attachment with his mother, the more he will be attracted by new objects. The proof of this can be seen in the fact that infants who were prematurely separated from their mothers (if she was sick, for instance) during the first six months are much more frightened by any new objects or new persons than the infants who were not separated from mothers and had established a secure attachment.

It is at this point, when the infant's visual system is mature enough to form a complete image of a face and differentiate between competing images that Cyrulnik believes that the father's image coalesces more fully into the infant's mind and takes a new dimension. The fact that some fathers play a "motherly" role does not alter the overall picture. In fact, a Swedish study quoted by Cyrulnik[77] in which fathers stay at home while their spouses work outside, shows that infants attach themselves equally to both parents with no problem, regardless of the differences of style already mentioned. Still, around six months (that time frame is approximate, since some children mature faster than others), the infant starts to show a clear preference for his mother to have his safety needs met, even when she is absent part of the day because of work. Cyrulnik logically concludes by saying that the history of early interactions between mother-infant—which started in the womb—imbues the mother with a calming effect that becomes critical when the visual system matures and brings into focus the faces of people in the environment. Fathers who do not have such an intense history of early interactions are to some degree at a disadvantage, even when they are the most affectionate and involved fathers. Consequently, that disadvantage would tip the scales in favor of mothers as soon as the infant is able to discriminate faces. That infant's move toward mother at that moment in time, however, is certainly mitigated when fathers have shared the daily care of their baby. As we have seen, such care fosters an earlier desire for independence and exploration, and thus imbues the child with an additional sense of safety. In this regard, the interaction between husband-wife when it is a good and supportive one can only reinforce the conditions for a secure base from which the infant can strike out on his own.

The six months mark seems to open a window of opportunity for fathers to be finally promoted to the rank of fathers, since up till now babies accepted any stranger as a maternal substitute, even more so since faces were interchangeable. But what is the process that makes us call father our real father? There is obviously a time when the label "father" becomes attached to a particular man, when father becomes a concept in the child's mind. It is an end result, though, that does not take into account the period in which the child does not have yet access to language to verbalize the thought: "This is my daddy!" Still we are justified to imagine that there is a long period of gestation during which the father becomes progressively so in his child's eyes. It has certainly a lot to do with his presence around mother but, if there are other males figures in the family or in the close environment, how does the child pick up the one who is his father? The answer is somewhat paradoxical: it is the mother who gives birth to the father.

If the mother meets the infant's safety needs better than anyone else when the infant's visual system clearly differentiates faces, her way of being with others, the way she reassures her baby when a new person appears, greatly influences the baby toward that person. If she is relaxed, calm and tender, even during that encounter, she is likely to imbue her sense of safety to her baby and, thus, a desire to know that person. She is "transfusing" all the emotional content of her feelings for that person to her baby, who will partake in the same feelings and will recognize the face introduced by his mother as a familiar one. In fact, it is the relationship between the mother and that person that is "transfused" almost telepathically without the need for words.

Obviously, the relationship between wife and husband is the one that is going to weigh more than anything else in the balance and will be passed on to the child. The emotional dance that goes on between wife and husband echoes in the child's psyche. The mother's attachment to her husband gives the child permission to attach to father. It sends the message that such an attachment is safe and good, and, thus, promotes a blueprint for healthy relationships in the future. Other relationships cannot compare with the relationship between husband and wife. It has a special status, a depth of feelings and emotions attached to it, which singles it out. It can only anchor in the child's mind the importance of that man around mother, and create the conditions for a long-lasting attachment.

Even if later on the word "daddy" is attached to that man, by the mother certainly ("Go and get your daddy!" "Where is your daddy?" etc...) and by people around, the process of attachment predates language. If such words of introduction by mother or others have a more formal aspect, they come as a conclusion of a long sensory and emotional process. By her behavior, the mother is the one who really promotes the father to his status. And the more her relationship to her husband is secure and free from tensions, the more the relations between child and father are prone to be secure and trustful. Under those circumstances, the world itself becomes a safe place worth exploring for the child.

The mother's attitude is likely to stay pivotal between child and father for a long time. Her body language and tone of voice when she talks to the father are certainly indications of her attitude towards him. They condition the child's own behavior as he comes to acknowledge more and more the presence of the father in his world. Even when fathers are absent, mothers can successfully help the child to form a positive image of their fathers by talking positively about them while showing pictures or belongings of him. Under the best circumstances, the child will relinquish his exclusive attachment to mom and move on to attach to his father as well — and will do so more easily if mother has a strong emotional bond with her husband. The child's acceptance of his father as such, is in itself a psychological milestone. It is the first act of socialization of the child, an act that has long-lasting consequences, since it sets up a model for further relationships. Tomatis used to call that acceptance of the father as such "the meeting of the father." He gave it specific emphasis because it saw it as an implicit acceptance of growing up, of socializing, of projecting oneself into the future. Implicitly, the child accepts to learn and explore the world and to stretch out emotionally and intellectually from his safe base to face the challenges to come.

Not all children are able to "meet their father" and to accept the challenges of growing up. Traumas, diseases, circumstances of life may prevent the unfolding of that optimal scenario. More than anything else, marital problems or bitter, angry and demeaning parental relationships are likely to cause attachment failures and imperil perceptions of safety. If either parent inspires distrust or anxiety, the child either gravitates toward the parent who seems safer or withdraws altogether, deeming the world as untrustworthy. Distrust curtails a child's desire to explore his environment and dampens his intellectual curiosity, both crucial factors for growth and learning. He may also develop serious psychological problems, even pathological ones, often around attachment issues. Psychotherapists' offices are full of such cases.

It is important, though, to distinguish between cases related to a parenting failure and cases resulting, as it has been pointed out already, from a trauma or life circumstances that may break down the family system as a result of death, long-term diseases, poverty, etc … A special word is to be said about children who have not reached, for unknown reasons, a certain level of neuro-physiological maturation or are plagued by sensory problems. In that case, it is clear that one cannot apply the same criteria applying to a typically developing child. An autistic child, for instance, may treat both father and mother as objects, avoid eye contact, and suffer from multi-sensory problems that make socialization and acquiring language inordinately difficult. Clearly, the first priority in this event is to help that child overcome his sensory and processing difficulties so he can hopefully develop relationships, mature psychologically, and become a functioning member of his community. Blaming parents because their child does not "meet" the criteria for typical development (and, for instance, is unable to "meet" his father) is insensitive, reprehensible and borders on abuse of the family.

When the normally developing child has accepted his father — or has "met" his father to use Tomatis' terminology — the family structure is reorganized. Instead of having on one side the mother-child unit and the father on the other side, there is now a triangular structure. This increases complexity of the relationships within the family system. Raising a child becomes a balancing act in which both parents have to teach rules and impose consequences while trying to foster the autonomy and responsibility of the child. That balancing act is easier when both parents agree with each other, but one that inspires anxiety to the child when they don't. In the child's unconscious mind, mother is likely still tied to her role as nurturer and father to his role as agent of socialization. Of course, as the child matures, both parents have to play both roles, but the archetypal values that are attached to each one can act deeply, invisibly and unconsciously in the child's psyche and shape his behavior. A sickly child might push every single button of his mother as a nurturer in his desire to avoid the responsibilities that he feels he cannot take, rightly or wrongly so. The balance that the parents strike then will be essential to relieve the child from his anxieties, but also to relieve the mother, who does not want necessarily to be cornered in that position when she knows that it supports only the helplessness of the child and does not promote his emotional growth. Such an example still shows that the archetypal value of mother as the nurturer and father as the socialization agent are always lurking in the child's mind and needs to be dealt with by parents, even if they are not always aware of the different functions that the child unconsciously attributes to each one.

The triangular structure now put in place also teaches the child about gender differences. Mother is different from daddy, and that difference between genders regulates human relationships. That difference teaches the child about his own sexual identity, which allows him to differentiate even further and thus develop a representation of himself as a separate human being. That differentiation was already in the process long before it reached the child's awareness. As it has been said earlier, the differences of parenting style born out of gender differences introduce a dissonance in the daily routine. If the child were exclusively into the care of the mother, the stimulation received would be almost identical and would stop to have a stimulating effect because of its repetition. So the father introduces a difference[78]—a difference that arouses interest, forces to compare with prior information, and thus fosters thinking and a greater awareness of the surroundings.

The triangular family structure presents another aspect related to gender identification: it does teach implicitly about sexual conducts too. When a four-year old boy declares to his mother that he wants to marry her, the father gently reminds him that he cannot marry her because she belongs to daddy. Of course, mothers can give the same answer, although it is not sure if her words will have the same weight, since children tend to believe that mothers belong to them. Both answers, in any case, reaffirms the prohibitive role of the father as a deterrent to incest — ideally, of course, since that basic law of human relationships is regularly broken. The little boy knowing that he cannot live his sexuality within the family circle has no other choice than to find sexual partners outside the family, once he has become an adolescent. So, the father's presence pushes the child into the social world. It forces him to grow up, to face the demands of a world that does not necessarily abide by the laws of the "pleasure principle," but more often than not is subjected to the "reality principle."

The acceptance of father grows ideally as children mature. Imbued from the start with different values than mothers, they are able to manifest them through the care they give to their children. Being that intermediary between the safety symbolized by the mother's body and the external world, they can play a great role in assuaging their children's fear of being more autonomous by introducing them to the many facets of reality, explaining them, showings how things work and familiarizing the children with them. In this respect, a particular time frame seems favorable to actualize the father role. Psychologists call this period a phase of separation-individuation that takes place between age two and three (again, some children mature slower than others do, and, thus, the time frame is only indicative). Children of this age are not only able to move in their environment, providing that they have no motor problems, but their language development is progressing rapidly, making them able to express their wishes and to make themselves understood.

At first, the child might be able to take only a few steps away from mother to affirm her nascent autonomy, delighted to encounter new things in this expanded version of the universe. She is also prompt to trace back her steps at the first alert. Her world is not different from the world of the fairy tales: the child sets out on a path of discoveries, her senses taking in the brightness and the beauty of the new world, she talks to birds, dogs and trees, drifting slowly away toward a distant bridge. When a shadow crosses the sun or a monster appears—the monster being anything unknown that overpowers the senses of the child and her new but fragile sense of confidence, the child runs back to mother to take cover under her familiar shadow. This happy ending brings back the safety of the limited world enjoyed by the child. Still the boundless pleasure of exploring the world and taking hold of it pushes her again and again on the road of discovery. The boundaries of the inner and outer world expand slowly but surely.

Gentle encouragements from mothers prompting their children to continue their process of discovery can go a long way to reassure them. Fathers, if they wish, can be at the receiving end, taking along their children to further explore the world and instructing them gently about the rules, dangers and practices that govern that world. Although mothers certainly do the same, especially if they are single moms, some differences may apply in the way things are handled respectively by mother and father. While the child is linked to mother by a web of sensations and feelings that extend back to the womb, this is not as true for fathers who depend more on verbal communication to relate with the child. These differences in communication and perception explain why some fathers love their children at first from a distance until they are certain their involvement will not be seen as an intrusion. With the arrival of speech, many fathers feel they have a vehicle for bonding through language, much as the mother did with touch. That is probably why some more traditional views of fathers represent them as emissaries of the World and of the Word. In short, they are the ones who translate into words the social world in which the child is called to take an increasing role.

Fathers imbued with that mission can become over-zealous and somewhat inappropriate. My friend Suzan tells a very instructive and rather comical story that illustrates well some of those traditional functions of the father. One day she saw her husband with their two-year old on his lap, attempting to read her the *National Geographic*! His efforts to introduce his daughter to the world and to the words, was met with squeals and attempts to wriggle from her father's arms. She wanted the warm embrace of mommy (or daddy) and not the exotic world of Africa, with its lions, giraffes and elephants. She had no interest whatsoever in matching the pictures of those animals with the names her father was bellowing in hopes of imprinting them on her young brain. The little girl turned a deaf ear to the loud voice. This was inevitable since Suzan's daughter was not even three. Her father's wish to engage her might have succeeded had his lesson been couched in play rather than as a tutorial. At her age, she would have responded to animals presented through playful movements and sounds, given the freedom to retreat when things overwhelmed her. Her father's effort was not wrong but just poorly timed.

At least the father was willing to play his part and to engage his daughter at a critical moment when her sense of self was getting stronger as the result of increasing mastery of mobility and speech, and differentiation from her environment and caretakers. During that time of separation-individuation, the father's availability is critical and cannot be underestimated. If they exercise fully the different functions they are called upon to play, they will most likely be fully accepted as fathers. On the other hand, when they are not available, they are likely to be perceived with ambivalence by their children. Absence of the father may delay the separation-individuation process and the child may try to retain the original emotional fusion with the mother. That dynamics can reach pathological dimensions or generate psychological problems likely to be reverberating in relationships throughout life.

To summarize, there are three periods that contribute to the father's integration in the child's experience.

- During the first few months, the father is perceived as another mother, if at least the father is involved in the child's care.
- After the visual maturation has been established, the child starts to increasingly accept this peripheral figure as his father, as they interact more and more, under mother's watch. Attachment to the father is even stronger if the mother encourages actively the child to bond with his father.

- Between age two and three, when the child is finally able to talk and walk, the father can become an active agent of socialization, telling about the world and the rules that govern it and thus supporting the child in his efforts to gain mastery and independence.

At this last stage the father's role becomes pivotal: his presence helps strike a balance between dependence and autonomy, between a wish for unlimited nurturing and unlimited freedom. It prevents the dangers of emotional fusion between mother and child and helps her to increasingly distance herself from her child as this one matures. With appropriate help for difficulties cropping up along the way, the child grows in his ability to manage himself and his environment, enabling him to move into the future with confidence. Striking the right balance between love and limit setting frees the child to grow, ultimately leading to psychological balance. Indeed, the child must gradually move from material and psychological reliance on both mother and father to achieve autonomy. Acquiring material and emotional independence does not mean having to reject mother and father: on the contrary, the child's psychological freedom is the best guarantee for both parents that he will love them genuinely, without the sense of obligation often observed when relationships are or have been strained.

It is important here to assert that the development of that process from mother to father and beyond (beyond representing the emotional independence that the young adult has finally reached) has an influence on our ability to listen. Observing on one hand the Listening Test of children or adults coming to his consultation and hearing, on the other hand, the story of those children or adults, Tomatis started to realize the connections existing between both. As we have seen, the left ear came to represent *symbolically* the mother and the right ear the father — a discovery that sprang out of his clinical observations and that surprised him greatly at first. He did also observe that the quality of the relationship with each parent bore a relation with the aspect of the curves on the Listening Test. Some patterns observed over and again tended to have the same general meaning. For instance, later on we will see the impact of a bad relationship between father and child on the child's Listening Test. In general, Tomatis found out that changes on the listening curves appeared first on the left ear before moving to the right ear. In practice, it meant that the discrimination of sounds, the aspect of the curves improved first on the left ear before any significant change appeared on the right ear. There was, thus, a direction in the changes observed, from left to right, and, symbolically, from mother to father. In short, it followed the development stages and the process from mother to father and beyond as described above.

Yet, to fully understand the role of the father and his different functions in the child's development as well as their influence on listening, it is worth looking into what happens when fathers are absent or are frequently unavailable.

The Absent Father

I will never forget the day Dean walked into my office, holding his mother's hand. Dean was a frail but beautiful six year-old boy with curly blond hair and an apprehensive look on his face. He sat quietly and announced as a matter of introduction: "My mom and I live together. I don't have a father." His voice was sad. He slumped slightly in his chair as if the burden of not having a father weighed on him. Clearly, mom had heard this many times and matter-of-factly said: "Yes, we live together." She had come to the Center for information and not as a client. I felt, though, that she was thinking about how the Tomatis Method could help Dean, especially after she confided that he was sometimes depressed. I sent Dean into the playroom for a while to give her a chance to share her concerns more freely. Both mother and child were fairly isolated; mother worked from her home and was not involved in any relationship. They had a few friends but, except when he was in school, Dean was with her all the time. "What about his dad?" I asked. "I had an artificial insemination," she answered nervously. "I don't know anything about the donor. Dean is always asking me about his father. He wouldn't understand if I really explained to him how he was born. He is only six after all! I just tell him that his father is not here anymore and that I don't know how to find him!"

I spent some time with Dean afterwards playing a game. He told me again how much he would like to have a dad. He had an expectant look in his eyes as he said so, projecting on me all the longings and dreams for a father that he could only imagine and that I knew would never materialize. I have never forgotten the intensity of the desire burning in his eyes, nor the cloud of despair setting on his face when his mother came to announce that it was time to leave. It has been years now and occasionally I still think about Dean, wondering what has happened to him. The absence of a father will have no doubt weighed heavily on his future. I wish I could know and sometimes fear that things did not work out for the best. The literature on the topic is, after all, not a source of comfort but rather a cause for concern.

Fatherless America,[79] *Absent Father, Lost Sons*,[80] and *The Absent Father*[81] are some of the titles that can be found in bookshops throughout the country. In Europe, this list seems to lengthen every time I visit. They obviously reveal a serious social problem. If we look at the statistics, it becomes clear that fewer and fewer children live in families with a dad and mom. More and more, on the other hand, kids are raised by single moms who have to assume all parental roles. The patriarchal figure of the father has been abolished and looks irrelevant at the beginning of the twenty-first century.

In many households today, the father has become almost invisible and, when present, is so overburdened by the pressures of modern life that the time he can devote to his children has shrunk dramatically. Work has increasingly invaded personal time and the traditional division between home and the work place is getting blurred. Consequently, fathers are even less available. They always seem to be on the go. I know children who see their father only on weekends because he leaves home early in the morning before they wake up and comes back late at night when they are already asleep. The number of children who have no idea whatsoever of the kind of work their dad does always surprises me. "He works in an office." "*But what does he do?*" "Hum! I don't know." At best, I get: "he works with a computer" or "he sells things." Don't ask what dad does with computers or what things he sells because they really don't know. Fathers seem to live on some kind of a nebulous planet where children rarely set foot. On that planet father makes money, but that is about all they know. The role of the father as a breadwinner is clearly ingrained in the child's mind. They may sometimes form the idea that their dads are some kind of cash cow or ATM machine. In that case, he is not a father but a bank account. He is even more likely to appear as such if he is often absent and consequently does not exercise his role as a bridge to the social world or as interpreter of that world.

When parents are divorced, fathers have difficulty fulfilling their true functions, since most often they only see their children for weekends or short vacations. The rate of divorce is such today that more and more children are now living in single parent families and that parent is usually mom. The traditional scenario, which rests on the mother-father-child triangle to promote the child's psychological balance, is rapidly becoming difficult to sustain. The erosion of that classical triangular structure often means that the father's influence is limited, and that mothers do not get much emotional and even economical support in trying to raise children. Under those circumstances, children may have a much harder time to mature.

Among the many studies on absent fathers, let's look at a five-year longitudinal study conducted by P.S. Fry and Anat Sher.[82] The experimental group included 85 father-absent children; the control group 85 father-present children. Both groups were carefully selected and matched out of a pool of 400 white boys and girls, drawn from both urban and rural communities of Alberta, Canada. For the purpose of the study, father absence denoted permanent rather than brief recurrent absences. A screening procedure ensured that father absence had started before the child's 5th birthday and continued at least till the 8th birthday. Pre-tests took place when kids were 10 years old; post-tests were conducted five years later, when the kids were 15.

The results were telling. While there were no great differences in the test scores between the two groups when the kids were 10 years old, major differences appeared when retested at age 15, especially among boys. For example, father-absent boys scored significantly lower on the "Achievement Motivation and Educational Aspiration" scale than father-present boys. The difference was huge (16.44 versus 23.07) and highly significant. This scale includes competitiveness, desire for mastery, willingness to work hard and willingness to endure negative consequences. On this scale, girls didn't seem to suffer from the absence of a dad. Still, it would have been interesting to find out whether this finding was still true when girls reached the marrying stage, for instance.

However, on the "Ego-strength and Self-esteem" scale, both father-absent boys and girls alike scored significantly lower than father-present boys and girls. They scored lower on the following scales: Ability to share feelings, Feelings of adequacy, Sense of reality, Social self-confidence, and Social involvement. They scored higher on Social alienation and Self-centeredness. The authors concluded that "The present longitudinal results not only confirm earlier tentative findings ... concerning the detrimental effects of father absence on children's development, they also suggest that the adverse effects ...

are evident very early in the development of children *and are cumulative over time*" (italics are mine).

If you are not convinced, try to observe small gatherings of teenagers hanging around on street corners or in your local park. They don't walk, but drag their feet; they don't stand straight but are hunched over, face down, rarely making eye contact. They do not dress but disappear under extra-large clothes that obscure their sexual differences; they speak in a mumble or rasping voice that seems to come from deep down in their stomach; they do not listen but plug their ears with headphones broadcasting loud music. They often encounter life's challenges by resorting to drugs and other addictions, looking for some artificial paradise closely resembling the sense of oneness and timelessness they experienced in the womb or through the touch of mother's body. They are living proof of a weakened family structure that sometimes dissolves entirely. Grim, rebellious teenagers who may be observed around us are often dropouts of both school and family systems. In a way, they are the tip of the iceberg: symptoms of a more general malaise coming from debilitated families whose resources, often both emotional and financial, are insufficient for the challenge of raising children in our modern society.

Let's state it clearly: our society does not support a return to a traditional family organization. Even the most willing dad is often caught in a work organization that does not allow him to exercise his prerogatives as a dad. In many families, mothers are also forced to work to make ends meet. In both cases, parents are forced to curtail the time they can spend with their children. We can bemoan this situation to no avail. The wish to return to the traditional family structure will, however, stay just that: a wish. So, we'll have to look for alternative structures to replace the traditional triangular structure.

In exploring these alternatives, we first need to understand what expectations children harbor about mom and dad. Once we have these clearly defined, we can find ways to satisfy these needs in a new way. Kids still expect mom to be nurturing and dad to take them a few steps away from mom's world into a world that is different and, thus, exciting because it is new. If life were like fairy tales, we would say that mom plays the good fairy and dad is the good wizard who protects the child with the strength of his magic wand from the perils and monsters roaming the world. Those archetypal images are deeply ingrained in the unconscious, as we know from Depth Psychology. They represent the two poles of an innate program that needs to run its course for the child to reach psychological equilibrium.

So, how can a busy dad satisfy these needs? First of all, he may try to re-organize his busy schedule to spend more time with his children. After all, he knows how to set (business) priorities and once he's convinced that the future of his kids is at stake, he may be able to free up some time. It is not necessarily the *quantity* of time that matters but the *quality* of those moments, especially if they make the child feel unique and admired. That is why it is better not to talk about school during these precious moments, particularly if the child is struggling with reading and spelling. Those moments in a way must be magic: remember the father is a good wizard, not the terrible one who thunders and threatens because the grades are falling. If there are several children, it is best to have special moments with each one. A child does not feel unique in her father's eyes if she feels just a part of the pack of siblings. I remember years ago talking with a dad, a very successful businessman, who made it a point to send a postcard to his children on every one of his frequent travels abroad. He was clearly taking his duties as a father to heart. I pointed out to him that his children would be even happier if each of them received a postcard. It would reinforce the *personal* connection between father and child instead of the *collective* one that also exists within the family. He saw my point immediately and decided to apply it the next time he traveled. Each individualized postcard would make each child feel unique. With this simple act, this father fulfilled his children's wish to be reminded that he still loved them even when he was away.

I knew another father who took each of his children for a separate outing during the weekend. They of course did things together, but those one-on-one moments where an opportunity for both father and child to share some intimate moments in which both could share stories, laughs and dreams. This father also made it a point to take his children to his office to explain them what he did, so they could feel a connection with his world. There are many other ways for fathers to fulfill the role that children expect from them. These might be little things, even symbolic gestures, but they go a long way toward cementing the bond between father and child. As long as fathers have a clear idea of their role, they will act upon it and be creative in coming up with ideas and actions that will brighten their children's lives and reverberate into the future.

When there is no physical presence of fathers in the family, as in Dean's case, it falls to the mother to facilitate the child's identification with his gender as well as to deal with discipline. This identification is certainly easier for girls with single mothers than for boys. Daughter and mother have the same gender but a boy needs a male role model to clarify his own sexual identity. The only friends that Dean's mother saw regularly were also single moms. Male figures were generally absent from the family's environment. Under these circumstances, it is quite natural for Dean to seek attachment with any man who could help him validate his own masculine identity. This perfectly understandable longing for a father was also a sign that he unconsciously felt incomplete as a person. If I had had a chance to work with the mother, I would have worked through the fears that she seemed to experience being around men. I would have had to do quite a bit of education too to show her how it would be beneficial for Dean to have some men around him. Possibly a Big Brother, an uncle or a grandfatherly figure could have played the role of substitute dad for Dean.

We are now at a point in our society where the many new configurations of family systems force us to be creative. It is not a matter of being judgemental. It is more a matter of providing children with what is best for them and helping parents to cope in the best ways possible. Although the traditional triangular family structure is not always a viable option, it can be used as a general road map to create and invent ways that fit with what children expect: a (substitute) father who delivers the child from the always existing danger of emotional fusion with mother; a (substitute) father who, alongside mother, is a guide to the world and an interpreter of the rules that run the society in which children live. When they assume these functions, fathers or substitute fathers are likely to capture the unconditional love and friendship of children; on the other hand, when fathers want to be only friends to their children and not fulfill their role as fathers, they are likely to gain their disrespect and opposition.

Finally the mother plays an important role in shaping the child's image of his father. This is true for all families, but it is especially true for families where the father is often absent or completely out of the house. The child is likely to develop a positive image of his father if mother talks about him positively.[83] Her language, her voice intonations, her gestures, and her behavior shape the way the child sees his father. Talking about daddy when he is absent helps the child to develop a mental image of his father that softens the separation. Here again, the way mother describes the father is the primary factor: loving and caring words about dad go a long way to establish a positive image that contributes to the child's intellectual and mental growth. A negative appreciation of the father, on the other hand, deflates his importance and may stunt the child's desire for exploration and independence. In this latter case, he experiences dad as a fearful and untrustworthy figure, and is likely to transpose his fear of dad on the outside world.

It would, of course, be perfectly unfair to put all the responsibility of creating a positive image of the father, on mothers. There are enough dads in the world who have misbehaved so badly that they have completely destroyed their credibility as fathers, and leave no choice to the child but to take protection under mother's wing. Barred from "meeting" their father, children have no support for spreading their wings and developing a strong self-image. They are usually shy, fearful, anxious, and their sense of self is easily threatened. Their listening skills are weak and they are often unable to learn well. A good substitute dad could do wonders in such cases to repair some of the emotional damage that has been inflicted to the child's soul.

Listening to Father's Voice

The impact of the father on the child is rarely studied from the angle of listening. Working with tens of thousands of cases, Tomatis drew the conclusion that the father is instrumental in fostering the child's ability to listen well, provided that the relationship is one of mutual respect and understanding. Conversely, if the relationship is negative, the child's listening capacity is impaired. In this case, the listening curve of the child shows distortions in the language zone between 1,000 Hz and 2,000 Hz—the zone that Tomatis calls the language zone, thereby affecting the way that the child learns and communicates.

A student working towards his Master's Degree at La Verne University in Athens, Greece, tested that hypothesis.[84] He found a high correlation between problems in the father-son relation (as measured on the "Child's Attitude towards Father" scale, CAF in short, developed by Hudson), and a drop in zone 2 of the Listening Test (language zone). All boys who had problems with their dads also had distortions in the language-communication zone. Distortions in zone 2 can have various other reasons, as is evidenced by the fact that 40% of the boys without father-son problems also had a distorted curve. This study is at best a preliminary study as the sample is too small (20 boys, 5 of which had problems with their fathers) and did not study sufficient parameters. With all its limitations, this study confirms Tomatis' observation that a poor father-son relationship introduces distortions in the language zone.

Observing the deficit of listening skills among children who seemed to have difficulties in "meeting" their father, Tomatis had the idea of playing the voice of the father through the Electronic Ear following the sonic birth. At first glance, it appeared a sensible idea since he had already used the mother's voice in a previous stage. Remember here that while the child *unconsciously* never totally separates from his mother, the father is from day one a third party, the closest of the foreigners. "He is *the other*, said Tomatis, because he is different from mother." Thus, as the father symbolically represents the world at large, what better way than to guide the young child into the social world than to use the father's voice? That surely should increase the desire to dialogue with others, the hallmark of the humanization process.

It may have been an interesting idea but not a very good one, as Tomatis learned very quickly. Many of his young patients had furious reactions: they became angry, tearful and aggressive. Their earphones flew across the playroom more than once. Playing back the father's voice had to be stopped. Tomatis realized that it was quite difficult for kids to quickly switch from "baby talk" to logic-based language. Clearly, the father's voice evoked fear of giving up the well-trodden paths of the "baby world" to enter into a dialogue with a more adult world. "This intrusion by a third party (the father's voice) was felt like a true rape," explained Tomatis during an interview.[85] "It is not exaggerated to say that the introduction of the father's voice for some children is the equivalent of meeting the bear or the monster present in fairy tales." There can be only reactions of fight and aggression in response to that undesirable intrusion. "It is fascinating to observe how the introduction of the father's voice can bring about such an explosion. It is extraordinary instructive. It re-flects the image that the child entertains of his father. That image is quite significant, especially among left-ear dominant or ill-lateralized children who, by definition, refuse the right, the father, the Word (that is: the rules governing society that are first transmitted through the guidance of the parents and, later on, by the different social organizations that the child encounters). They are comfortably entrenched in their exclusive relationship with their mother and deliberately reject the father's voice, which symbolizes the link with society and is the springboard towards the external world that will free them, but that they refuse."

Tomatis realized that there was another way to guide the young child into the social world. Since language is the key element in social communication, he decided to replace the father's voice by simple vocal exercises in which the child would repeat pre-recorded words or sentences that would not trigger the negative feelings associated with a difficult father-child relationship. By doing so, the child could monitor the process and take an active part in it rather than being *forced* to enter into the social world symbolically represented by the father's voice. As we have seen earlier, language being processed faster through the right ear than the left ear, it was an appropriate moment to train the right ear to become the leading ear. Each word or sentence repeated by the child was thus fed back immediately to his right ear, inducing a process of self-listening that allows a progressive mastery and integration of the various components of language, and ultimately of social communication.

From a psychological standpoint, we could write this as an equation:

$$\text{FATHER} = \text{LANGUAGE} = \text{RIGHT EAR}$$

That equation underlies some of the traditional and symbolical functions of the father as representative of the world whose rules and ways are communicated through language. It also takes note of the fact that mastery of language itself is not solely rooted in good neurophysiological functioning — the right ear dominance — but also depends on psychological factors. The negative behavior observed by Tomatis when he used the father's voice directly, offers corroborative evidence of the validity of that equation. Even so, a more neutral context in which language is not tainted by negative associations, can still evoke the dread of that social world in which language channels emotions in more socially appropriate ways. Rules have to be followed and responsibility has to be taken for each word that is being spelled out. The journey to become an adult is a gradual process, characterized by leaps and bounds as well as regressions. As the equation above suggests, it can be made easier when fathers, alongside with mothers, are willing to involve themselves during that transition time, the time when the child is suspended between two worlds symbolized respectively by the world of mother and the world of father. The negotiation of that passage is likely to reverberate in the future, deciding the emotional balance of the child and the future adult.

REFUSING TO GROW UP

Telltale Signs for Parents to Watch for

Parents can observe this transition towards the world that the father represents symbolically, in the behavior of their children. The theoretical framework I discussed above may help to identify the important signs of that transition as well as the signs of a stubborn resistance to grow-up. I have chosen a case from my practice to illustrate some of the points described earlier, with the hope that it will help parents dealing with similar issues. The case obviously could be studied from various perspectives, but I have chosen to limit the discussion to a few points: the signs indicating a refusal to grow-up, that is to move from "a baby world" to a more adult world, and consequently from the use of "baby talk" to the use of a more logic-based language. Remember here that language is not limited to speech, but also includes body language, behavior and the associated feelings. Looking at it this way, we can also better understand the underlying dynamics involved: the push toward verticality and the opposite force: the push to stay on the horizontal level.

The little fellow who will guide us in this study was about 9 years old when he entered the stage. Thomas was an obese boy with a sullen baby face. He rarely smiled and more often than not was in a moody state. Those moods got even worse as soon as he did not get his way or was not the center of attention. Such an incident happened the first day in the waiting room, when Thomas got cross because his two brothers were winning a board game. That immediately started a temper tantrum: Thomas threw himself on the couch, swearing under his breath and trashing his arms and legs about, refusing the touch of his mother who wanted to calm him down.

The fact that he transmitted his disagreement through body language and not through verbal expression already indicated a language difficulty—in fact, his mother brought him for an evaluation because he had a terrible time learning to read. If he could or was willing to express his frustration *verbally*, chances were that he could delay its *physical* expression. In a nutshell it is a perfect illustration of the difference between "baby talk" and "adult talk." "Baby talk" uses physical behavior to express emotions while its counterpart, "adult talk," mainly uses verbal communication to translate the same emotions. In the first case, there is only reactivity to a present stimulus; in the second case, reaction is delayed and mastery achieved through the medium of language. Based on that first impression, I immediately had an idea where Thomas stood, emotionally and mentally. The fact that he threw himself on the couch—horizontally—, is symbolic of his desire to be treated like a baby in his crib under the constant care of mommy. That child was not going to stand vertically on his two feet to face the real world. He was totally entrenched in the world of his needs and desires, ready to lash out when they were not satisfied. He unconsciously wanted to stay the center of the cosmos with everyone gravitating around him to satisfy his needs. The whole picture pointed to a little tyrant with little tolerance for frustration.

Further evaluation revealed that Thomas was pretty clumsy and tended to avoid any demanding physical activity. In the playroom, he rarely stood but often laid on a mattress or sat on one of those huge beanbags that mold around the body in womb-like fashion. From there he tried to control his environment through moods and threats of temper tantrums, as if he were sitting on a king's throne. He obviously had a vestibular problem and his whole posture and attitude were also clearly symbolic of his refusal to listen to the call of growing up. It is as if the problem of physical balance is coupled with a problem of psychological balance: in short, neither physical nor psychological verticality had been reached since he didn't desire verticality. This is a child out of balance, because he has no standpoint — that is: no sense of self or, at best, only a tenuous one.

As the Dutch physician and anthroposophist Albert Soesman notes in a wonderful little book called *Our Twelve Senses,*[86] "the sense of balance is the direct expression of our actual being. This being is called "the **I**" in anthroposophy—"the **I**" of the human being. Indeed, this is the way we experience it. We experience that the human figure is the expression of "the **I**" for the very reason that we walk erect. *We experience the **I** as a straight line in human beings....* You can see this when an infant stands up for the first time. This is always a great triumph. It suddenly starts to experience its own being, and this is something tremendous. *Before, he was still a crawling baby. Now, all of sudden, he has become a real human being, now that he stands up. You experience yourself more intensely when you stand vertically. To stand straight up is to express one's being"* (my italics). If we apply this to Thomas, we can observe how his body language demonstrates that he was still a "crawling baby" that had no intention of expressing his being by straightening up and standing on his feet. As long as he continued to act in this way, his sense of self would stay weak.

Thomas' language was poor and hesitant as can be anticipated, since verticality and language go hand in hand. His language was shaped by his emotions and this was reflected by the constant use of exclamations, interjections, screams, swearwords and incomplete sentences. The body language that went with it showed no restraint: any frustration, real or imaginary, was expressed through a series of uncoordinated movements. It presented a perfect example of what I call "baby talk."

As expected, therapy went at a snail's pace. Thomas seemed to be a master at defeating any hope that he might change. One morning, his mother brought him to the Center, his two other brothers in tow since she could not get a baby-sitter. When he heard that she was about to leave to do some errands, Thomas immediately threw his earphones to the other side of the playroom. His arms folded on his chest, his face frowning and hostile, Thomas refused to obey his mother who asked him to put his headphones back on. In vain! He did not even bother to answer: his body language said it all, and it was a resolute No! He even avoided eye contact, his gaze fixed on his navel. He hated all of us, that was pretty clear, and especially mom who was now trying to gain his cooperation by swearing that she would bring him his favorite chocolate bar. Meanwhile she was trying to put the headphones back on his head, but he struggled, pushing his body away and fighting her with his fists. Once again, the headphones flew into the air. I had decided not to intervene at this point to see how far this new temper tantrum would go. The fight kept going, mom wondering after a while if, after all, the headphones were not bothering Thomas. "If they hurt you, we can ask Pierre for a new pair. Is that what you want?" No answer. "Your tummy is not hurting?" To me: "He did not want any breakfast this morning: he must be hungry. Are you hungry, Thomas? Just tell me and I will go out to get you a big muffin at that place we went the other day. Do you remember that place?" I observed that Thomas relaxed a little: now that mom took care of his *sensory* needs, now that she treated him as she would treat a baby, he felt strengthened in his position. He won. He had outshined his brothers in mom's attention. He consented to calm down, but not without a little bit of resistance to make sure that he kept mom on her toes. Finally, when she left, he had the headphones back on, but watch out if mom didn't bring back the promised big muffin!

Here we see again how "baby talk" is expressed through body language. There is something more worth observing: when mom temptingly offered to buy him a muffin in exchange for his cooperation, she unwittingly reinforced his fantasy of staying a baby. She was again the good fairy who used to feed him when he was still in the crib. The food came to him, he did not need to stand up and fetch it. This can only strengthen his sense that he can manipulate his environment according to his desires. He is quite powerful as long as he stays in that attitude of a "crying baby." By stubbornly refusing to listen to her discipline, he forces her to go down to the level of his needs. In this way, he refuses verticality and camps stubbornly on the "horizontal" field of his wants and desires.

The scene that followed mom's departure clearly shows another, quite characteristic aspect of this refusal to grow up, that is, the rejection of the rules that parents try to enforce to foster the psychological growth of their children and prepare their social integration. We were back in the playroom and, after fussing around for a short while, Thomas decided that he wanted us to play the board game called Sorry. The object of the game is to be the first player to get 4 pawns to their final destination. This is achieved by drawing cards that tell you how many spaces you need to move — forward or backward. If you draw the so-called Sorry card, then you can send back another player's pawn to the starting point. That's probably why the game is subtitled: the game of sweet revenge! Children usually love it, because it is easy and they can play those wonderful little tricks on others kids when they draw the Sorry card. Thomas knew the game very well and knew what each card meant. Not surprisingly, when I drew a four, he correctly told me that I should move my pawn *backward* four spaces. However, when immediately after that he drew a four, he insisted that he had the right to move his pawn four spaces *forward*. In other words, the rule applied only to me, not to him! When I underscored the inconsistency, he pretended not to have heard me and tried to move his pawn. I said to him quietly that he could not do so and that we had to follow the same rules. This time he got really angry, swore under his breath, and then got up: the game was over! He would not play with me! He even accused me of cheating. He went and sat on the big bean bag turning his back to me and continued to sulk.

If a child like Thomas cannot accept fair play and abide by the rules of such a simple game as Sorry, it is likely that any rule will be perceived as an encroachment upon his own rights — an encroachment even on his own personality. What the child was defending here was his perceived right to live in a state of magical thinking that continued to assert the primacy of his desires or wants. He was not listening to others — others are dangerous since they may impose rules. He only listened to himself. Kids like Thomas live in a sort of autistic-like state where others cannot intrude. They struggle bet-ween two worlds, symbolically represented by mother and father. By refusing the rules of Sorry, Thomas symbolically refused any regulation that could shape and structure his life and would help him to move more confidently and more responsibly into the surrounding world.

We may wonder at this point where Thomas' dad was since dad's symbolic and real role is to help their children negotiate the initial steps into the world. Well, Dad was around, but not much: he left home before the children got up and came back very late. They may have seen each other on weekends when Dad could manage a few hours away from his desk. Dad worked for one of those brand new Internet companies in the Silicone Valley that was going to go public in just a few weeks (the events took place near the end of 1999 at the peak of the Internet bubble economy). Dad had to work and work and work long hours, days and nights! The few times he brought Thomas to the Center, he immediately went into one of the small rooms we had, to work on his portable computer and get in touch with his office. He was really overworked, but was enjoying the challenge. He admitted that he had little time for the family but hoped to make up for the lost time later on. Do not get me wrong here: he was a very nice guy, loving his children and very concerned about their well-being, but social pressure kept him away from them. His wife was similarly overburdened with all the tasks of the household and the task of being the main provider of an education for the children. With all their heart and care, they did not fulfill though some of the conscious or unconscious expectations of their children, mainly about role expectations: Mom was still the nurturer but out of necessity she had taken on many of the attributes of dad's role since he was not around. Instead of blaming them, though, it is better to see them as victims of a social system that pays little attention to the needs of families and children in particular. Nothing is likely to change, if the system itself does not change to allow parents to be parents. At least, I hope that in reading Thomas' story, parents will be better able to catch some of the symptoms marking that time of transition, understand their meaning and intervene appropriately to help their children.

Adults Refusing to Grow up

The refusal to grow up is not limited to children. Some time ago, in a Mexican magazine,[87] I saw a picture of an enormous, almost naked man reclining on a couch, feet on a low table. He must have weighted at least 300 pounds and was totally hairless like a baby. A bowl of potato chips was precariously perched on his huge belly and he was eating them, one by one, while watching TV. He also had a bottle of beer to wash them down. He was the classic couch potato that we ridicule, maybe to escape the thought that we might be like him at times. His whole posture, his hairless body suggested also the image of a baby in constant need to be fed to be maintained alive. He was clearly too hypnotized by the images on the TV screen to pay attention to his hand going back and forth between the bowl and his mouth. It was a thoughtless and effortless gesture that we could imagine going on for ever and that prevented any frustration: something like sucking mom's breast for ever and ever, so we would not have to feel alone but one with her. The remote control on one of his thighs allowed him to change channels at will, so he could immediately zap out the annoying or boring image that could disturb his infantile fantasy of making the world appear according to his desires.

That this man was in an autistic-like state is clear, but if we look beyond this exaggerated image, we may get a glimpse of how we are now and then. In fact, this huge and hairless man, reclining like a little king on a couch could be a metaphor for all the moments when we do not feel like "rising to the occasion," "facing life" or "standing up." The choice of words is in itself already indicative of a dynamic between verticality and horizontality, between "standing up" or "lying down," or even "lying low." I do not think that we should necessarily blame ourselves because we do not always live up to our opportunities. However, at least we can become aware of the dynamic involved and realize the choice that is ours: the choice between an awakened life and a life that brings us back to that slumbering state. Writers like Jean Gebser or Ken Wilber eloquently compare this slumber to the original state out of which consciousness progressively arose.

The temptation to return to that original unconscious state is certainly always on our horizon like a big cloud that threatens to swallow us. Of course we want to be cuddled, loved and fed according to our unending list of wants and desires, as if we were still in mom's embrace. It is those feelings that advertising constantly plays to, trying to transform us into consumers of an unending list of material goods. We are led to believe that owning those goods will make us feel good. Our self-esteem, our well-being, says the social buzz, depends on the possession of those goods. In such a system, buying becomes a "peak experience", and "self-actualization" becomes a travesty of its original meaning: we "self-actualize" by being dedicated consumers and not by trying to be true to our selves. Narcissism and self-indulgence then become the key components of our behavior and of that prevalent immaturity denounced by social critics. Like Thomas who was holding on to his childish behavior, we would like to stay immersed in a universe that does not deny our desires but provides instant gratification. Growing up can be as difficult in adulthood as it is in childhood. Not surprisingly, the myth of an eternal (or at the least prolonged) youth permeates our society: getting old becomes a curse, not an opportunity of growing wiser (and more vertical), and finally being able to stand on our own.

If the self, though, is thought of as a point of gravity between the forces of verticality and horizontality, the balance is often lost under the social pressure of conforming to the prevalent social stereotypes. The self becomes alienated from itself, and often man turns into a stranger to himself. Instead of experiencing the "**I**" as a "straight line" and living more intensely as a result of verticality, to again quote Albert Soesman, we are more likely to experience our "**I**" as a broken or bent line, and thus live a less intense and often a depressed life. As we saw earlier, reaching physical verticality was the result of an unending series of trials and errors, spanning millions of years. In the same way that we progressively escaped the pull of gravity to finally stand erect, we are constantly challenged to escape a certain psychological inertia if we want to conquer psychological verticality, that is, maturity and independence. Then, and only then, can we listen to ourselves and to others in unadulterated ways. The journey, though, is not without ups and downs. It requires constant effort to escape the natural inertia in which our consciousness slumbers, as it did at the dawn of humanity when man had not emerged and separated from nature. As the great analytical psychologist Erich Neumann wrote,[88] "The ascent toward consciousness is the 'unnatural' thing in nature." It is thus up to each of us to do the "unnatural thing" and to try to rise time and again to fully realize our humanity.

RECAPITULATING THE JOURNEY

From birth onward, we are called upon to grow up to our full potential. Our guardian angels in this ongoing process are first our mother and then our father. Both have an essential and complimentary role to play in that humanizing process: mother as the nurturer, father as the agent of socialization. Both can provide what the psychologist D.W. Winnicott called a "good holding environment," that is, according to John Welwood, "a context of love and belonging that contributes to a basic sense of confidence and to overall psychological development."[89]

Growing up necessarily involves leaving mother's wing to confront the world, of which father is the symbolic representative. This step forward is for many children a scary one: they cannot let loose of being constantly nurtured — a quite natural comfort seeking attitude shared by all of us — since they want to preserve the magical thinking of infancy when mother is always there to gratify instantly their needs. In short, they want to forever stay babies who only need "baby talk" to express their emotions and desires. Giving up being nurtured like babies would mean the death of that privileged state that supports the fantasy that the child is the center of the universe (or the center of mother's attention, which is about the same since mom is *his* universe during infancy). It is only when the child feels secure that he can relinquish this fantasy and move on to the next step: the "meeting" with the father, which opens the doors of the world and leads to mastery and ultimately responsibility for oneself.

The Listening Therapy developed by Tomatis is based on the awareness of that universal process. It was by piecing together the observations of thousand of cases, that Tomatis realized that stimulating the ear with sound and music led patients to revisit and complete the process of growing up. It thus became standard practice to use the filtered mother's voice in the therapeutic process. Then, later on, after a "sonic birth," language exercises are introduced to recapitulate the steps taken initially by every child to master language and the socialization process. By moving through the different sonic phases, the child or adult has the possibility of completing, this time more thoroughly, the process that may originally have been marred by difficulties and obstacles.

Removing some of the obstacles that may have stunted our growth, releases the energy necessary to realize our full potential. Instead of fearing for ourselves, and constantly fighting to protect our ego against real or imaginary offenses, we feel an increased ease with ourselves and the world. Being able to listen to ourselves, we are able to better manage our emotions and take a step back to assess the situation at hand instead of being reactive. Anger is replaced by a calm assessment of the situation and a better appreciation of how to deal with it. As self-listening deepens, "emotional intelligence" grows accordingly. The capacity to know ourselves better in turn improves our ability to recognize emotions in others and to listen to them in an empathic way. We no longer project our fears or prejudices onto others, but can see their true nature and open our hearts in order to have a true dialogue, a dialogue of the minds, certainly, but more deeply a dialogue of the hearts. Then, the "human antenna" is able to operate fully as receiver and emitter without the filters usually imposed by the ego.

Listening is not only a state but also a direction: we are invited to listen more deeply, so that a deeper listening becomes the rule and not the exception. This path waits for us if we are willing to follow it. It is a difficult path, since it requires that we transcend our mental habits and the defenses of the ego, to stand erect and free, listening to the cosmos, as Tomatis put it, that is, to that transcendental dimension that takes us beyond our own personal boundaries. This is clearly the aim of many spiritual traditions or religions. As we will see in the next part, they all tend to emphasize a right posture and a right attitude as a condition to accessing the transpersonal realms. In other words, they emphasize physical and psychological verticality as condition to capturing the messages that come from that invisible and inaudible dimension — at least for those who cannot see or cannot hear them. Thus, after describing the "physical ear," "the learning ear" and "the psychological ear," we will turn now to the "spiritual ear" to discover the full meaning of Listening—and see the "human antenna" rising to its full potential.

PART V

THE SPIRITUAL EAR

"Man is called to become an antenna, which receives and transmits the music that gives life to the world, throughout its evolution."

"This process is not yet achieved and, for the moment, few are those who reach that goal."

Alfred A. Tomatis[90]

EVOLUTION AND CREATION

Tomatis' belief that evolution followed a purposeful path was the natural consequence of his study of the ear. The gradual development of the ear itself, the importance of an erect posture for language development, the adaptation and reshaping of the organs to make language possible, the lateralization process, the ensuing growth of the brain and the development of the symbolic function —all of those elements gradually combined in an ever-increasing complexity which seemed to imply an underlying blueprint unfolding slowly through evolution. In part because of his personal faith— Tomatis was an avowed Christian—and because of the findings of his research, Tomatis could not help but believe that evolution had a meaning rather than being the product of haphazard events. For this position he was much criticized but he was not a man to hide his personal views to increase the credibility of his scientific investigations. For him, the stringent requirements of scientific research did not need to suffer from his metaphysical views. On the contrary, science could enrich spiritual traditions by giving them a firm basis.

In fact, the ever-increasing complexity of the process of humanization suggested strongly that still more complexity might be expected. Evolution would continue, but at such a slow pace that it would be impossible for those now living to perceive it. From that perspective, man is just a transitional being called to evolve further. Like Sri Aurobindo, the Indian philosopher-sage, whose work he had read attentively, Tomatis could have written: "humanity is not the last rung of terrestrial creation."

The future face of man must be left to speculations, but the meaning of evolution is suggested by creation itself. Father Teilhard de Chardin, a French Jesuit and great paleontologist maintained in his monumental work, *The Phenomenon of Man*[91] that "at the heart of life, explaining its progression, is the impetus of a rise of consciousness." That ascent of consciousness to greater levels of richness is predicated on the capacity of the physical organism to achieve a greater complexity—an idea that Tomatis certainly would have concurred with, and which he had documented at great length in his research. The transformation of man into "a human antenna" appeared to Tomatis like a necessary and inescapable step already programmed into evolution itself. By transforming himself, man responds to "the impetus of a rise of consciousness" that moves evolution forward. That impetus towards increased consciousness originates from a Creator—or God—who has set in motion the creation itself. Being part of this creation means allowing the transformation to take place in oneself. Thus, we can perceive the hand of God throughout creation. It involves what Tomatis calls "True Listening," which is a form of attention that is not limited to the material world but reaches beyond the appearances to listen to the creation itself. Ultimately, such listening carries with it the hope for man to reunite and merge with the Creator, as is believed by many spiritual traditions.

The upward movement towards God, though, was preceded by a downward movement — which is described in a metaphoric way by the myth of the Fall. Evolution therefore appears as a progressive return to an original state, a oneness with God that has been lost. Without going into complex theological questions, we may simply say that such a vision of evolution is buttressed by the idea that God has created us to his image and, thus, that we participate in his essence. But He who is perfect has created us imperfect, so that He can bring us to a state of perfection under the conjoint influence of the Word and the Spirit. Still, man is free to collaborate with the work of God or to reject it and to strike out on his own, thinking that he can become God himself. That is the initial choice proposed to Adam. His decision to break away from God set in motion the human adventure, but resulted in a loss of connection with the spirit of God. And the further away the creation is from God, the more matter wins over spirit.

We can visualize that downward movement as a series of levels, stretching all the way from the absolute spiritual level to the lowest material level, like some sort of huge ladder whose rungs disappear in the absolute darkness of matter. In *Up From* Eden,[92] Wilber calls this downward movement "involution," noting that each level is a successive moving away from God. It is only "when involution is complete that evolution can begin" adds Wilber, noting that the spirit emerges again at the lowest level and passes through all the levels on its way up. Each step upward gets us closer to the original oneness with God, as our consciousness expands and we recover the memory of the spirit that lies dormant at each level. Such is the meaning of evolution; man finds meaning to his life by trying to climb up that immense ladder leading to God.

This image of ascension is in line with Tomatis' scientific research as well as his metaphysical speculations. It is again the idea of verticality, "the backbone of Tomatis' thinking," according to Tim Wilson who interviewed him in 1978 for a radio documentary.[93] In fact, using a biblical allusion, "Tomatis termed the human struggle towards uprightness, throughout eons of evolution, the "Jacob's struggle." This struggle to become erect is not limited to the body but embraces the three dimensions of our being: the body obviously, but also the mind and the spirit. It is an ongoing struggle that each man is free to join or not, but that, once embraced, changes the dynamics of life.

LISTENING TO "THE SOUND OF LIFE"

The struggle towards uprightness implies a vision of man quite different from a materialistic one in which he is reduced to its physical components, be they atoms, nerves or genes. If "God is dead," as Nietzsche proclaimed at the end of the 19th century, man is only matter. He is his own end. His life has no other meaning than to take care of his physical self, both body and soul being ultimately destined to decay and death. There is no afterlife, no transcendent principle: life is a dead end.

In his search for the spirit, Tomatis suggests, man needs to transform himself from a casual listener into what he calls in French an "*Écoutant*". We know what a "Seer" means in English: someone who is a clairvoyant, that is, who can see beyond material appearances. Likewise, the French word "*Écoutant*" describes someone who can hear and listen beyond the usual limitations imposed by our ears. Someone, in short, that can listen to the inaudible concert of the Cosmos and be in resonance with it. There is obviously a paradox here: How can we hear what is inaudible? That is possible, Tomatis asserts, since everything on earth is sound or vibration. Following a long evolutionary adaptation of our senses, our body has been tuned up so that our listening can fulfill its aim, which is to communicate *with the whole Cosmos*. Most of us are totally unaware of that capacity but it can be awakened as long as we desire it, and as long as we work on it. Although the capacity of being an "*Écoutant*" may be given spontaneously to a few, it is for most of us the end result of a long work on the self — a work that is quite similar in nature to that of a monk in the silence and solitude of a monastery. The consciousness of the "*Écoutant*" is fully awakened when he is in resonance with the rhythms of the cosmos. To accomplish that, he needs to be erect since "without verticality, affirms Tomatis, it is impossible to stimulate the brain to full consciousness."

But what does one really hear when the listening posture is taken and that the mind is in resonance with the vibrations of the cosmos? Here and there in his writings, Tomatis alludes to a sound that he calls "the sound of life." According to him, this sound is the echo of the original sound that sets in motion the creation. The Greek philosophers called it *Logos* and the Bible refers to it as the *Word* ("In the beginning was the Word"). That "sound" is perceived at a cellular level by the ear of a newborn. It resonates not only through man's body but also through the whole cosmos. In certain schools of meditation, it is called the "inaudible sound."

This "inaudible sound" — that Tomatis prefers to call 'the sound of life' — appears to be the result of the activities of the entire ear and particularly of the Corti cells hearing themselves live and vibrate. "The communication is so sharp between the Corti cells of the ear that the thousands of minuscule cilia (or hairs) that make them move perceive the slightest vibration ... including those that move the smallest parts of our body. That extraordinary perception lies in the higher range of frequencies that produce some type of sharp and crackling rustle," not very different from the filtered sounds created by the Electronic Ear. In that case, according to Tomatis, "the Corti cells function simultaneously as sender and receiver in a closed circulatory system."

In other words, the human antenna is not split into a receiver and an emitter, but both functions are fused into one, which, according to Tomatis represents "the summit in the hierarchy of achievements." The human antenna then sings in unison with the cosmos. In fact, claims Tomatis, "true dialogue" occurs when someone is in resonance with the Logos. "From the instant one is ready to hear, when one is in a posture of hearing, which is a posture of prayer, just as the monk tries to do, one comes near freedom. At that point, one can enter adoration and contemplation."

There is no reason to think that Tomatis is not talking from experience when he describes the "sound of life" itself. He may not have written much about it, but that is probably because it is difficult to express it in words. In fact, "it is difficult to conceive what can be "the sound of life" if it has not been "tasted," wrote Tomatis in "*La nuit utérine.*"[94] Those of us, who have known him well, know for sure that he had to experience things first so that he could try to give them a rationale. His search was not only a scientific one but also a personal one, and one that he pursued vigorously. From that perspective, he was not only a hearer but also a doer, and acquiring "the listening posture" was not just a concept but also an ongoing attempt to get closer to God. Those who came in contact with him were always surprised by the calm but radiating energy that came from him. The last time I saw him, he was already quite ill and knew that he was dying; still, his serenity and joy were unblemished. I left him with the feeling that I had encountered a truly "realized" being and that I may not see many more like him in the future. Certainly, his wife Léna can attest that till the end he continued that dialogue with the Logos by listening to the sound of life that permeates the cosmos.

Such a subtle quality of listening had to fight many obstacles to be achieved. In all his writings and interviews, Tomatis insisted on some prerequisites, but there was no guarantee that the student would become automatically an "*Écoutant.*" Since the search is exacting, we may feel discouraged at the thought of it, or take it up as a personal challenge. In fact we may learn something about ourselves just by the fact that we are searching.

LETTING GO

The work of listening described by Tomatis is primarily psychological work. In his book about Mozart,[100] he wrote: "the essential goal of my technique is to modify the psychological structure in order to free it from the chains that hinder listening." In another book, he talks about the personality as an envelope that obscures the perception of our true being. For him, the difference between essence and existence was fundamental. I have heard him remark occasionally: "*to exist is **not** to be*" or "*to be, one needs to forget about oneself.*" Existence was for him the domain of the ego, of the "small I", as the German psychologist and sage Karlfried Graf Dürckheim calls it. That "small I" prevents us from embracing our being, that is, that transcendental dimension existing beyond the limitations imposed by the ego. Being cannot be understood without reference to the Divine Essence or Oneness, out of which we originate. It is the experience of that dimension in our *present* life that constitutes the experience of Being. Tomatis describes it as "a life dynamic perceived at the cellular level." It allows us to access to consciousness, if we know how to listen. Still the tyranny of existence and of the ego deter most of us from "showing that original face, the one we had before birth," as a famous Zen koan puts it.

What is lost in the ego's fight for survival is the capacity to listen to the "sound of Life," and to transcend the level of consciousness that we have called the "consciousness" of the "small I." For Tomatis, "The sound of life is lost as soon as a person has to involve himself with the problems of existence. The concerns, the compulsions, the moods that arise from the difficult demands of everyday life destroy that extraordinary type of listening." More than our lifestyle, though, it is mainly the ego that is the obstacle. Amazed by its capacity to posture incessantly, Tomatis often referred to it jokingly as "the monkey in each of us." It is mainly a survivor, and all spiritual traditions — indeed, all schools of psychology — insist on the difficulty of letting go of the ego. It is the "small I" that imprisons us in the labyrinth of our mental life. It chatters non-stop, constantly tormented by an infinite list of desires, wants or moods. It is interested in *having* not in *being*. It measures its worth and power in terms of its wealth: experiences, money and things. The ego does not fight for change but for *status quo*. It is a creature of habits, a bundle of ready-to-wear ideas or prejudices. It calls up the image of a man progressively petrified, although his physical heart keeps ticking deep inside. It is a closed system that filters out new information and only cautiously admits what has been "pre-approved." It develops on a horizontal mode, not on a vertical one. Its motto could be the French proverb: *"Plus ça change, plus c'est la même chose,"* which can be translated as: "The more things change, the more they remain the same:" a not very optimistic view of human nature. Instead of the "transcendental I", we have the "small I." Man does not turn his face towards God anymore, but takes himself for god. Instead of listening to the concert of the cosmos, he listens to his own song: his ego song.

"Thus", writes Karlfried Graf Dürckheim in a passage of *The Way of Transformation,*[95] "we are torn between the two aspects of our human existence. And yet our lives in the world, as well as our participation in Transcendent Being, are but two poles of the *one self* that is ever striving within us towards realization. It is through the development of this self that oneness is realized in the human form. And given those conditions, *if we are upright within, it will inevitably mean that we are upright without* (my italics). For this reason, it is essential to discover in ourselves an attitude—even a physical posture—in which we can be open and submissive to the demands of our inner being while at the same time allowing the inner being to become visible and effective in the midst of our life in the world."

Karlfried Graf Dürckheim was one of the first Europeans to bring Zen to the western world and was quite versed in Jungian psychology. His teaching tied posture and inner work — a link that Tomatis often emphasized as well. Once again, it is worth citing Tomatis who says that if the posture is not perfect, it is very difficult to enter into real consciousness. Consequently, finding that posture is an important part of the inner work of letting go. It is not only a matter of physical verticality; in fact, the listening posture involves body, mind and spirit.

THE LISTENING POSTURE

When physical verticality is achieved, there is little energy needed to maintain the body in balance. While we are still struggling to reach that posture, a lot of irrelevant thoughts are still flooding us, and verticality itself is tentative. Each step toward the upright direction, though, decreases the constant agitation of the mental, that is, the resistance of the ego to letting go. One of the goals of the listening posture is certainly to reach that state of quietness in which "one can enter truly into real consciousness."

Tomatis was very specific about the details of the listening posture. When he had students practicing it, he always used the same, identical words, as if each one of them was of great importance. It is a fairly long list of instructions and I've put it into an annex rather than breaking the flow of this chapter. Those of you who want to introduce it in your daily practice will find it at the end of this book. Still, for the moment, I will synthesize its main aspects for the sake of clarity.

The goal of the listening posture is to be able to perceive the "sound of life:" this involves learning to play with the muscles of the middle ear in order to concentrate on the high frequency sounds among all the other sounds in the environment. This is done while sitting straight on a high, hard stool with the legs dangling and the head hanging slightly forward and the eyes closed. A great deal of the work consists in harmonizing the muscular tensions of the body but more especially in harmonizing the tensions of the muscles of the face. Those are pulled toward the back as if one wanted to make a tight, dense ponytail at the back of the head, near the vertex. As all the muscles of the face relax more deeply, the skin of the face becomes as smooth as velvet and wrinkle-free, and the breath reaches an unusual amplitude and rhythm. At a certain point, if things pro-

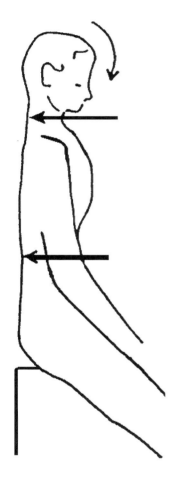

Figure 22: Correct posture

ceed undisturbed, "sounds become purer; they take on a clear, luminous timbre. The lows fade and change as they move toward the higher harmonics that they contain. The surroundings assume a radiant, live and vibrant color." Then, Tomatis says, "it seems as if the person were far away from herself with only one ear, the right, leading the left ear in its course to a point located just behind the vertex." It is as if that unique ear was resting on that point before moving away, first by a few inches, and further and further away to a distance of two or three hundred yards away. Then, it is possible after much practice, to "experience a sense of infinity" in which human boundaries dissolve. "The seat of listening rests in the infinite, it is no longer we who listen, as it is no longer we who sing when the song passes through us, just as it is no longer we who speak when we let words pass through us."

Although this listening ear wandering some 300 yards away from the head may appear strange to any "rational" person, Tomatis is not the first to emphasize this kind of auditory/listening training. In *The Future of the Body*,[96] Michael Murphy quotes the great contemplative treatise of Theravada Buddhism, the *Visuddhimagga* in which a very similar listening training is described. After a first phase in which the meditation student begins to identify the gross sounds, then the more and more subtle sounds, he tries to delimit a listening area, saying to himself:

"I will hear sounds within this area, then two finger-breadths, four finger-breadths, eight finger-breadths, a span, a *ratana* (24 finger-breadths), the interior of the room, the verandah, the building, the surrounding walks, the park belonging to the community, the alms-resort village, the district, and so on. This is how he should extend it by delimited stages."

One can almost visualize the ear of that meditation student moving away through space, in the same fashion that Tomatis describes it in a more scientific way. We may also assume that listening to sounds within one finger-breadth, two finger-breadths, etc ... requires stretching the vertebral column upward as in the listening posture in order to position the different components of the ear for optimal perception. In this sense, Tomatis often noted, people of antiquity had developed a keen knowledge of sounds based on a careful study of the body and its possibilities. This is usually lost to our contemporaries.

In that passage of the *Visuddhimagga*, the goal of the exercise is described, but not the posture; however, it is very likely that this is very close to the Zazen posture described by Shunryu Suzuki in *Zen Mind, Beginner's Mind*:[97]

"The most important thing in the zazen posture is to keep your spine straight. Your ears and shoulders should be on line. Relax your shoulders, and push up towards the ceiling with the back of your head. And you should pull your chin in. When your chin is tilted up, you have no strength in your posture; you are probably dreaming. Also to gain in your posture, press your diaphragm down towards your *hara*, or lower abdomen. This will help you maintain your physical and mental balance…"

"You should be sitting straight as if you were supporting the sky with your head… To take this posture itself is the purpose of your practice. When you have this posture, you have the right state of mind, so there is no need to attain some special state."

One cannot help noticing all the characteristics shared between the Listening Posture and the Zazen posture. Although they originate from different sources, they both share the ideal of verticality as a necessary condition. In an article published in 1991 in the French Review of Yoga,[98] Tomatis points out that the lotus posture, like the listening posture, expresses the same type of dynamic between the forces that pull us down to earth and the energies that pull up us toward the sky. The apparent physical differences cannot mask their commonalities. Spiritual traditions from both East and West do in fact emphasize the search for the good posture as a preliminary to spiritual work. The body is used as an instrument to perceive the original oneness of our being; more than just being a body weighted down by matter, it is an erect body, a body of sounds, a crystal ready to vibrate and produce sounds that echo the original sound, that "sound of life" that, according to Tomatis, is more easily heard in the depths of the night, when all is silent.

MAKING SOUNDS

As the son of a famous opera singer, Tomatis became familiar with singing technique at a very early age. Later on, as a medical doctor, he treated many great singers who had damaged their voice by lack of a good singing technique. It was clear to him that their voice problems were often the result of a lack of auto-control due to poor listening. To repair their voice, they had first to listen better, and that involves working on posture — on the listening posture, to be precise — since production of good quality sounds depends upon it. Tomatis, over the years, developed an audio-vocal training in which he emphasized the conditions required to produce beautiful sounds. It is only when the posture is perfect that the larynx makes contact with the vertebral column and, thus, transmits vibrations to the skull and then to the entire skeleton. "The sound produced is not in the mouth, nor in the body, but in fact in the bones. It is all the bones of the body which are singing ... The voice excites bone conduction, giving the impression that the sound originates from "outside," from beyond the body." This technique, according to Tomatis, was well known from the ancients "who knew that once it reaches perfect auditory posture, the body reaches out and literally incorporates all the sound that comes from outside and from within. This assumes a vertical posture. It is impossible to stimulate the brain to full consciousness without verticality."

I still remember the first time I heard Tomatis demonstrating how to produce that bony sound. He filled the large room with a magnificent AUM that was everywhere and seemed to come from nowhere. Had I not known that he was making that sound, I would have been unable to identify its source. To this day, I still think that in making that sound, he gave us an opportunity to hear and taste the sound of life, and resonate in harmony with the unending resonance that fills the cosmos.

The Spiritual Ear

I have put in a separate appendix the instructions needed to try to produce that magnificent sound. As a rule of thumb, they should not be attempted without first achieving the listening posture.

Producing sounds, however beautiful they are, is not an end in itself in Tomatis' mind. Of course, the professional singer will benefit greatly by practicing the exercise devised by Tomatis, but any one who is on a spiritual quest might benefit from it too. The reason is that singing or making sounds is an important way to produce energy to charge the brain, and that praying or immersing oneself in contemplation requires a lot of energy.

There is an oft-repeated story to demonstrate this assertion. In 1967, Tomatis was called to a French monastery to try to explain some strange epidemic of fatigue that had reduced most of the monks to a near vegetative state. "They were slumping in their cells like wet dishrags," says Tomatis. Many medical specialists had been called in without any result. Lately, a famous medical doctor had changed their diet, telling them that they were dying from starvation on their almost vegetarian diet — forgetting of course, that the monks had followed that diet since the 12th century without falling ill. They started to eat meat and potatoes, and their health got worse. When Tomatis arrived, he realized that recently the monks had changed a perennial rule that had characterized the life of the monastery since Saint Benedict. A new and young abbot, who thought of himself as a revolutionary, had convinced the monks to eliminate chanting from the daily schedule. According to him, chant served no useful purpose, and they would be better off using the time for other things. They became more and more tired, and soon decided to abolish their night vigil and to go to bed early and rest till they were no longer tired. The more they slept the more tired and depressed they became. They were obviously unaware that their chanting up till now had served to "charge" them. It was vital to restore that tradition, since with the vow of silence, they could benefit neither from the sounds of their own voice nor from the voices of their fellow monks. They lacked the stimulation that would keep them energized. Tomatis installed Electronic Ears in the monastery and re-introduced their chanting immediately. Six months later, "all of them had gone back to their normal activities, that is, their prayer, their few hours of sleep, and the legendary Benedictine work schedule."

Such an example demonstrates beyond a doubt that "sounds are as good as two cups of coffee," as Tomatis liked to say. It also demonstrates that "to meditate, to reach the plane of prayer, demands an extraordinary cortical activity." If that were not the case, parasitic thoughts would assail the mind and flood it preventing to reach a fully awakened consciousness. In fact, without an enormous cortical charge, it is impossible to dominate the subconscious and to meditate, pray or even focus deeply."

That seems to be the conclusion reached by other spiritual traditions that also emphasize the role of chanting. Commenting on those traditions, Tomatis notes: "in India there is a whole yoga of sound, Mantra yoga. In Mantra yoga, the posture has to be perfect, which explains why some people have destroyed themselves in doing the mantra without knowing the key to proper listening. A mantra can damage a person much faster that it can restore him. So there is definitively a danger. In order to do a mantra well one should know well both practice and theory, and especially the way to listen." This way is obviously the listening posture.

Throughout his career, Tomatis gave countless audio-vocal seminars, often to clients who had first benefited from a listening reeducation with the Electronic Ear. He felt that people should not have to depend on a machine every time that their life circumstances would impair their listening abilities. Mastering the exercise was for him the key that would set people free from the dependence on the machine. Producing sounds as he taught would put them quickly on the way to recovery. The practice itself has another advantage rarely noticed: producing the sounds correctly requires letting go of the ego. It is in fact a spiritual practice. "You are not making anything, Tomatis would say, it is the sound that passes through you." He would then add with a mischievous smile: "Of course, doing nothing is difficult," knowing quite well that the ego feels like dying if it is not "doing something."

I remember Tomatis working with a German woman singer during the last seminar he ever gave. She had taken the seminar already several times but with little benefit. However, she kept coming back, deciding to "have" the sound right this time. She looked very rigid and sat like a Diva that everyone should admire. She had certainly learned many professional tricks on the opera stage, but not the virtue of simplicity and humility, and you could almost feel her persona walking ahead of her body as a visible aura. She started her exercise, with the careful coaching of Tomatis, but none of his comments could convince her to drop her mask. It did not go very well for her, and in the end she was still a mile away from understanding that she needed to "do nothing" to produce the sound correctly. Afterwards, Tomatis told me that she would probably end up des-troying her voice because she could not let go of her ego while singing. She wanted to *have* the sound but she was not prepared to *be* her real self as a pre-requisite. There was nothing to be done if she was not ready for that sacrifice.

Working on the listening posture and producing the humming sound with the right attitude can energize the brain and the entire nervous system. The whole body experiences a sense of well-being, the emotions are stable and an expansion of consciousness occurs. Through the sound that passes and vibrates through it, the body becomes a vibrant antenna, which resonates in harmony with the environment that the sound has set in resonance. The difference between inside and outside disappear and there is only one field of resonance through which the Word or the sound of life passes warmly, beautifully, giving us the taste of the original oneness.

SACRED MUSIC, SACRED CHANTS

Many sacred chants have the power to energize the brain and facilitate its opening to the transcendental dimension. According to Tomatis, whatever their tradition of origin, they all require the listening posture to be sung properly. When they are sung correctly, the listener is caught up in the dynamics of the chant and adopts this posture automatically, as if he were propped up by the sounds emitted. That, Tomatis often explained, is because the body is literally "sculpted" by sounds. The monk who enters a Benedictine monastery has to sing Gregorian chant for six to eight hours a day, but obviously he is unable to sing well at first. He has not yet found the listening posture and, consequently, is not in the optimal condition to produce sounds correctly. That is why he is placed in the center of the choir, so that the sounds produced by other monks around him gradually "sculpt" his body. This leads him to adopt the right posture for listening and, thus, for producing sound.

Many people who took the seminars that Tomatis taught on audio-vocal technique often noticed bodily changes. I still remember noticing changes in my posture and in my breath, and a feeling of unusual warmth in my whole body. Living for six or eight hours immersed in this very particular bath of sounds, I felt so energized that I could barely sleep. Yet, I was not tired the next morning and awoke with a joy in life that I wish I could always feel. There was a heightened perception of my surroundings and of other people, without the sense of separation that we often feel. In fact, I felt more *present* than ever to the phenomenon of life.

Sacred songs "charge" the brain to lead people into a state of prayer. Tomatis asserted: "it is impossible to arrive at a state of permanent consciousness without having the opportunity of always being charged." Singing sacred song, such as Gregorian chant, requires having the ideal listening curve. When we do have it, not only can we recharge ourselves optimally by using our voice, but also we can charge others in the same way. Monks singing Gregorian chant are using it as "a unique and fantastic energy food" that brings about the right spiritual posture. Another characteristic inherent in chant is that it also leads the singer and the listener into a state of serenity. Tomatis attributes this to the fact that "Gregorian has no tempo but has only rhythm. If you listen closely to the Gregorian inflection, you have the impression that the singer never breathes. This slow breathing is a sort of respiratory yoga. The singer must be in a state of absolute tranquility in order to be able to do it. And by inducing the listener to enter in the same deep breathing, he leads him little by little to share the same state of tranquility."

"A chant of such quality is certainly an expression of the physiological rhythms that sustain life," Tomatis says. Those rhythms are often disturbed by emotional factors, but Gregorian chant has the capacity to bring us back to a state of balance in which the rhythms of the body are in harmony with the fundamental rhythms of the cosmos. "Gregorian chant allows us to perceive the vibration of the soul when it reaches the register of serenity. Then, man is involved in a timeless communication and regains his natural breathing, that is, unstressed and without gasping. Through the Gregorian modulations, he encounters reality, which is the true path towards realization … To tell the truth, Gregorian chant gives a glimpse of paradise to those who wish it … Man is reintegrated into the creation and sings the glory of the Creator."

It is not difficult to understand why Tomatis used so much Gregorian chant for therapeutic purposes: it "charges" the brain of the client and induces a state of serenity (through its influence on breathing) leading to an expansion of consciousness. Then, "the soul recovers immediately its essential vibration, its essential rhythms, which belong to an original state that existed prior to the learning requirements imposed by culture and society."

Many of his remarks on Gregorian Chant may apply to other sacred songs too. Studying the Vedic, Buddhist and Tibetan psalmody, or analyzing the song of the dervishes, or the Jewish chant, Tomatis concluded: "There are no sacred songs per se but tones that, thanks to the quality of their emission, generate enough energy so that the brain can sustain a metaphysical dynamic."

The "quality of emission," though, is an essential factor that is not always respected. In this case, the sound has no charging effect and can even be detrimental to the health of the person making them. As an example, Tomatis pointed out the defective way the Tibetan AUM was produced by westerners, fascinated by Eastern spiritual traditions. Not only is the sound not sacred anymore, but poor emission can damage the larynx, alter the voice and upset the psychological balance of the singer. "It is a real charging sound, but it can only be transmitted from Master to disciple when the latter is ready." "When most of us in the West make an AUM we make a flat sound that is without timbre, empty. It is a sound in the throat that does not lead to anything, but on the contrary tires the subject."

We find here again Tomatis' belief that geography and culture shape our perception and production of sounds. Sacred songs do not escape that rule. The Tibetan AUM is produced in very specific conditions. "The Tibetan lamas, because of the high altitude where they live, are forced to emit bass tones, since the higher the altitude, the more difficult high frequencies sounds are to produce. This phenomenon is related to atmospheric pressure and the pressure in high altitude makes it very hard to maintain a high-pitched fundamental tone, rich in harmonics, without slipping into falsetto. Contrary to what we perceive with our western ears, Tibetan psalmody is very rich in high frequencies but the singer must add low frequencies at the same time. He does this "by changing the position of the larynx to sound the lower-pitched fundamental. It is on the consistency and control of this fundamental that the quality of the overtones depends on." In short, advised Tomatis, we might be better off trying to practice Gregorian chant, which is made to be sung at lower altitude, than trying to produce Tibetan mantras, except of course, if we are Tibetans.

The technical aspect of sacred song should not make us lose sight of the goal of sacred song itself, that is, a transformation of the inner being. "The effect of cortical charge is specially needed when one wishes to bury oneself in prayer. In fact, few activities require so much energy. Every monk knows how difficult it is to pray without being distracted by some idea or by some recollection ... that erases memory: I mean by this that essential, profound, ontological memory that reveals the presence of the divine in any vibration of our being. But we have to be freed from the usual attitudes to be led into those secret and far-away regions where only the heart listens." As Tomatis reminds us, at the end of the exercise of the listening posture: "Only those who are deeply dedicated to opening themselves up to the dimension of True Listening may reach that stage in which the Word passes through the voice of the heart."

"OUR HEART BREATHES THROUGH THE EAR"

These are the words of the French mystic Saint François de Salle. They describe the mysterious link between the ear and the heart, that only makes sense to those whose heart is open and have the essential experience of Being. "Listen" is an injunction that is often heard in the scriptures of religious and spirituals traditions. The Bible itself, pointed out Tomatis, uses the word more than one thousand times in the Old Testament and 425 in the New Testament. It is clearly one of the key words of the Scriptures. In each case, God calls man to listen and to open his heart, since "hardening our heart," as the psalmist reminds us in psalm 95, is in fact closing our ear. In fact, if we do not love, we do not listen. Our ears and hearts are then "circumcised" as the prophet Jeremiah puts it in his strong language.

Opening the ear is thus the first step, if we want to hear God. God speaks to man, repeats the Bible, but man needs to listen to Him. "But if from there you seek the Lord your God, you will find him if you look for him with all your heart and all your soul,"[99] that is with all your intelligence and will, with all the fervor of your feelings and desires. The "heart" here is considered as the seat of any conscious, intellectual, affective or moral activity. Strangely enough, that definition seems to echo new research on the heart, that concludes that the heart has indeed an intelligence and wisdom — a fact well antici-pated by those who had opened their ears and hearts to the trans-cendental dimension of Being.

Listening with the heart is thus what Tomatis calls True Listening. It is also the message of all spiritual traditions. Through True Listening God or the Divine Presence can be perceived, but this cannot be accomplish without obedience — a word whose Latin root is *ob audire* which means to obey and to listen at the same time. In fact, it is the ego that needs to be sacrificed so that the Word of God can fill man and transform him to His image. "Unfortunately," comments Tomatis in his 1978 interview with Tim Wilson, "to obey is seen as a constraint: man does not want to. To obey is to let oneself go completely in listening. Who is it that speaks? It is the Logos that speaks. It is the Universe—or God—that speaks, and we are here to translate the universe. But in order to do that, we must realize that we depend neither on our own creativity nor on our own thoughts, but on the universe itself ... The work of man is to do what God asks of us and what God wants most is for His own to obey Him. So there is a whole internal dynamic which is basically the psychology of breaking down our "me," which is colossal ... And so everything begins with obedience. That is perfect listening."

Then, in this position "where man lets himself go to listen to the universe," he is able to perceive the fundamental rhythms of the universe which are echoed by his own, and so to transcribe all that the universe has to say. Few are in this situation, since few of us can yet reach that level, but we have the testimony of some who may be precursors of what man can eventually become as evolution continues and consciousness rises to higher levels. Among them, Tomatis included people like Plato, Socrates, Pythagoras, the Buddha, Lao-tze, Jesus, but also, closer to our time, the great figure of Albert Einstein. They were all *Écoutants,*" people who were able to transcribe what the universe was telling them. One of Tomatis' favorites, though, was Mozart whose music he compared to "a celestial message." In the book he wrote on Mozart[100]—one of his last books and certainly a spiritual testament—Tomatis sums up all his philosophy of life and explains why the music of Mozart can bring us closer to that state of Being that is waiting to be revealed in each of us.

THE DIVINE MOZART

Since Mozart's time, musicologists and listeners have used the adjective "divine" to describe his music. They obviously refer to a quality in his music that they do not find in others composers, even of those counted as Great. Although Tomatis greatly admired musicians such as Haydn, Beethoven or Wagner, Mozart was the only one for him who "leads us to a place where we start to *be*," a place where we can find our essence instead of feeling fragmented by the vagaries of the ego. That place where Mozart leads us is "our place of birth, a place where only beauty, transcendence and joy of living exist … Thanks to him, we vibrate, we discover ourselves; we are put in musical resonance with the universe. This is the Mozart miracle: to put human beings in unison with universal harmony." This harmony helps us to recover the memory of who we are. Retrieving that memory, though, is mostly "out of reach of our adult mentalities, because we are far removed from our origins and are buried under the pile of memories that need to be forgotten. These are just the sediments of our education and tend to make our soul more opaque."

"In the deepest recesses of our ontological consciousness," Tomatis continues, "an echo resonates that reminds us of our desire to integrate the universe in its totality, without erroneous judgments, without distortions …It is that echo that Mozart's music evokes to free us and awaken us to the consciousness of our Being. If we listen, it brings about a rebirth to our transcendental dimension that makes us fully humans."

But why Mozart? He is for Tomatis an *initiate* (from the Latin *initium* = beginning), someone who has access to a level not commonly reached by others, as result of a revelation. The Latin word carries also the idea of origin, of what is at the beginning, that is, that state of Being, the memory of which is lost as the result of existing. Mozart was an *Initiate* because of his capacity to live at that level, especially when he was composing. In fact, he was known to write entire pieces of music as if they were dictated to him by some divine inspiration. That is why Tomatis remarks: "Intuition flows through Mozart (it is not *his* intuition)." For this, he was a realized "*Écoutant*" listening to the cosmos and to God, and transcribing what Plato called the music of the spheres. "There is no other expression than God's praise in everything he composed," writes Tomatis who adds that Mozart's attitude like Socrates' "is not egoistic" because "he knew how to differentiate between essence and existence."

Not only does Mozart forget himself when he composes, because he is capturing the rhythms of the universe under the influence of the Divine, but he also invites us to vibrate at the same level and, like him, "to stand on a culminating point, from which everything is seen, everything is unveiled." Mozart is thus an initiator to the transcendental world whose rhythms he transposes in his music. Better, his music "reveals the musician in each of us as if we were the authors of what he writes. It seems that the musical phrases flow in ourselves in a way that could be no different." They do so because we, as human beings, are resonating and "the musician in ourselves" is awakened every time we are in harmony with the music.

As a physician, Tomatis couldn't help but notice that the cause of our attraction to, or rejection of, a certain piece of music has to do with our personal sensibility or our temperament. "Music springs from one nervous system to another nervous system. The first one is the emitter; the second one is the receptor." Still, "some musical rhythms are felt as if they are blocking the rhythms of the body, preventing them from finding their own beat." That is why we must find a rhythm that echoes our natural rhythm. In fact, "everything is music for those who can perceive the cadences, distinguish their combinations, discover the vital rhythms in their multiplicity and transcribe them so that they become accessible." Only the one who is awakened to those rhythms, like Mozart, "can awaken those fundamental rhythms existing in each of us." Then, the rhythm of the music and the rhythms of the body coincide, and music is not felt as imposed upon body or mind. Moreover, cardiac and respiratory rhythms are freed, and movements are in harmony with the totality of our deeper self. When these conditions are fulfilled "everyone vibrates in unison with his own fundamental vibrations, the ones around which every individual develops, in search of his own future." The power to touch anyone, regardless of time or place, explains for Tomatis the universality of Mozart's music. "Mozart is the only one I know who reaches that level or, more exactly, who never leaves it. Listening to Mozart, every man finds again the deep resonance of his soul." And in that moment, man, the human antenna, vibrates to the rhythm of creation and perceives, at least temporarily, the true nature of his being that has been in him since the beginning.

Some will certainly say that Tomatis idealizes the music of Mozart. To those he would probably answer as he wrote in his book on Mozart: "Mozart's universe cannot be understood by those who cannot suspect what *being* is, and who cannot envision such reality." Such an answer may not satisfy the skeptics, but it may prompt us to become a "listening ear," which for Tomatis, "is the outcome of human development." The music of Mozart invites us to experience a foretaste of the person we may *be*, namely to become an "*Écoutant*," finally living in the vertical dimension of our transcendental nature.

And so it is a call to *be* that resonates in the music of Mozart, a call to *be* that echoes through the entire work of Tomatis, and aspires to be recognized by each of us. It is this call which is at the core of all spiritual traditions. To hear this call, we must develop a Listening Ear. The entire work of Tomatis points in that direction.

Conclusion

Conclusion

Dr. and Mrs. Tomatis

Tomatis' work highlights the crucial role of the ear in our lives. While emphasizing some of the well-known functions of the ear, such as balance, coordination and hearing, he also underlines other functions that are not so well-known and, thus, are surprising to many. The idea that the ear acts as a dynamo that "charges" the brain through the high frequencies sounds may at first appear just a fancy idea till the moment when that charging effect is really experienced. The vital role of the right ear in language processing is another important discovery made by Tomatis to understand the learning difficulties of children and adults. His Listening Test is a new and fascinating tool to diagnose a vast array of problems and to design treatment interventions. And last but not least, he demonstrated that our desire to listen — or not listen — conditions the way we perceive sounds, impacting many facets of our lives.

One of the main themes Tomatis continuously emphasized was that there is a profound difference between hearing and listening. While hearing is a passive activity, listening requires desire, commitment and attention. Listening does indeed involve our whole being: both our body and our mind. Tomatis showed that many problems arise when we do not listen well. Those problems, however, disappear when we are trained to listen more efficiently.

The value of Tomatis' ideas rests in last resort in their ability to heal. The examples of recovery throughout this book illustrate some of the areas where it has shown the greatest results. In children, the Method is particularly beneficial in the treatment of vestibular problems, sensory integration issues, speech and learning problems as well as behavioral problems. Adults suffering from low energy level, procrastination, lack of direction or listening problems may also benefit from Tomatis' inventions. Finally, people eager to learn a foreign language, boost their creativity, improve their musical skills, or actors and singers who want to improve their diction or their voice will greatly benefit from the Tomatis Method. In fact, when listening improves as the result of the treatment designed by Tomatis, life takes on a different color, and what was felt impossible may all of a sudden become possible. Overall, in many children and adults, the treatment often leads to a new openness, a higher self-esteem and a more optimistic outlook on life that transcends the difficulties of the past and allows a new start.

From the start, Tomatis' research was oriented by the need to find practical solutions that would relieve the suffering of his clients. His theory about listening emerged as the result of a constant exchange between research and thousands of clinical observations.

To explain the many and often surprising changes in his clients, Tomatis had to integrate in his theory the recent discoveries in a variety of disciplines: neurology, cognitive sciences, education, linguistics and psychology. Early on in his research, he discovered that hearing and speech are linked. In a nutshell, our voice can only produce the frequencies that we hear well. Tomatis concluded that "man is an ear" and that the whole body is built as an antenna to receive and emit sounds. Still good quality of emission and reception depends on verticality — a fact clearly demonstrated by the fact that the children he treated improved their verbal performance as soon as they became more erect. Considering the respective role of the vestibule and the cochlea, both part of the inner ear, Tomatis emphasized that verticality positions the cochlea to function optimally, to analyze sounds accurately. In order to be able to listen in increasingly subtle ways, the body first needs to be tuned to become a perfect antenna. To achieve that goal, Tomatis developed an electronic device that modifies music in such a way that it can train both the vestibule and the cochlea to perform optimally. That device he called an Electronic Ear.

Observing how his clients reacted to sound stimulation, also led him to closely study the links between listening and psychology. One of the things he observed was that there was an obvious correlation between the way people listen and certain moods and behaviors. Little by little Tomatis started to realize that our listening could easily be distorted by traumas, circumstances of life or education. Those distortions often prevented his clients from listening well: some lost the ability to accurately perceive certain frequencies, other no longer could discriminate well the different tonalities, etc. This affected not only how they listened to others, but it also distorted the way they listened to themselves, and so potentially shaped their psychological lives in very dysfunctional ways. The Listening Test was the tool to diagnose the problem. The unique method of sound stimulation using the Electronic Ear was the tool to treat the problem, by erasing the obstacles to poor listening, and so restoring our psychological wellbeing.

Tomatis observed that many of the listening difficulties of his clients started in childhood, for example, as a result of birth traumas, health problems, inadequate parenting or abandonment. Those life circumstances often led to an unconscious refusal to listen. To reawaken the desire to listen, he developed a treatment modality that tried to replicate the different sonic phases a child goes through when growing up. This led him to use a recording of the mother's filtered voice to emulate what the fetus might have heard in the womb, in the initial phase of the treatment. That phase was followed by a "sonic birth" and concluded by a series of vocal exercises, whose level of difficulty matches the progression of language acquisition in children. In short, the therapeutic modality designed by Tomatis creates the conditions for providing a good holding environment to impart the client a solid sense of security and to strengthen his or her desire to listen in a more optimal way.

Auditory stimulation first affects the body, specifically verticality, balance and coordination. Then, it gradually impacts other areas of functioning, leading to a sense of general well-being and inner freedom that improves both the reception and emission of information. It is as if a sense of psychological verticality developes while listening improved, each progress leading to a subtler form of attention. In Tomatis' view, the struggle towards uprightness is indeed not limited to the physical dimension but embraces other dimensions. He knew too well that psychological verticality would not be reached as long as his clients would resist changing and would refuse to open their ears — that is, to let go of the ego. True listening could not be achieved without this sacrifice.

That conclusion coincides with the one reached by many religious and spiritual traditions, which Tomatis explored throughout his life. A man of faith, deeply rooted in the Catholic religion, Tomatis was nevertheless open to the suggestions and ideas of other faiths and spiritual traditions. For him, all religions look for ways of developing that True Listening to which he devoted his research and his life. And like them, he emphasized the vital role of the right posture and the right attitude as the necessary conditions to embrace the divine. He was convinced that we have to fully become an ear to finally find our true essence and become an *Écoutant*—that is, that perfect Listener, able to perceive God through the music of the cosmos.

It is this vision of "man as an ear" that gives cohesion to Tomatis' work. He was himself well aware that not everyone would share it. Still, it is not necessary to share his philosophy to benefit from the different applications that he developed as the result of his scientific investigations. He used to say that the Tomatis Method was like a "spark" that would induce changes and encourage people to use more their innate potential. Ultimately, it is up to them to decide how much they want to listen, to "spark" and to awaken their lives, and where it should lead them.

Appendixes

Appendix 1

RESEARCH RESULTS

The Tomatis Method has been tested rigorously and has been found to be very effective in the treatment of learning difficulties and behavior problems.

● **In 1999, Tim Gilmor published a meta analysis based on five studies involving 231 children.** The study was published in the International Journal of Listening, a peer reviewed journal.[101] A Meta Analysis is a very powerful statistical tool, extensively used in medical research. It allows the researcher to combine the data from several studies, and arrive at more definite conclusions than the original studies. **The study showed that the Tomatis Method significantly improves:**

- Linguistic skills
- Psychomotor skills
- Personal and social adjustment skills
- Cognitive skills and
- Auditory skills

The meta analysis was based on the following publications:

- **Dr. Tim Gilmor**, who studied 102 children at the Tomatis Center in Toronto.[102, 103]
- **Dr. Byron Rourke** of the University of Windsor, Ontario, who studied 25 learning disabled children from nine to fourteen years of age, following them over a period of one year.[104]

- **Dr. Barbara Wilson** of the North Shore University Hospital in Ontario, who studied 26 language-impaired preschool children over a period of nine months.[105]
- **Dr. John Kershner** of the Ontario Institute for Studies in Education, who followed the progress of 32 underachieving children, ages eight to twelve years.[106, 107]
- **Peter Mould**, Chief Remedial Teacher of Brickwall House, East Sussex, who followed the progress of two groups of 46 severely dyslexic boys, ages ten to fifteen, over a two year period.[108]

● **The Tomatis Center in Toronto, Canada, also studied the results of the Listening Therapy on over 400 children and adolescents.**[109] They all had well-documented histories of learning problems, as well as a pattern of under achievement on psycho-educational tests. The results of the treatment were graded by the parents. In this test, 95% of the parents responded that the program had helped their children. **The parents saw improvements in the following areas:**

Skill or Ability	Percent of Improvement
Greater Communication Abilities	89%
Better Attention Span	86%
Frustration Level Decreased	80%
Reading Comprehension Increased	85%
Quality of Speech Improved	74%
Memory Improved	73%
Better Spelling Aptitude	69%
Showed more maturity	84%

In a follow-up six months after the program, 83% of those children in the study had maintained the improvements and/or had continued to make even further gains. An additional 14% of the children had maintained some of the gains. Only 3% had maintained none of the improvements.

- **A Canadian researcher, H.A. Stutt[110] concluded that the Tomatis Listening Program produces benefits beyond what could be expected by maturation or remedial education alone.** The benefits mentioned by Stutt include:

  - A significant increase in I.Q.
  - Better reading skills
  - More perceptual processing
  - Increased academic skills
  - A general sense of adjustment
  - More developed communication skills
  - A greater ability to verbally express thoughts and feelings

- **Dr. Joan Neysmith-Roy from the Department of Psychology in Regina has conducted a careful study with six severely autistic boys.**[111] This study confirms the clinical evidence that autistic children benefit from the Tomatis Method. "Three (50%) of the boys demonstrated positive behavior changes by the end of the treatment. One boy was no longer considered autistic; two boys showed mild symptoms of autism and three boys remained within the severely autistic range. Of particular interest were the changes that occurred in the pre-linguistic areas of five of the six boys. These included Adaptation to Change, Listening Response, Non verbal Communication, Emotional Response and Activity Level. …. The author suggests that the Tomatis method may be helpful in making pre-linguistic behaviors manageable and thus help prepare the child to learn basic skills necessary for the development of language and learning." Dr. Joan Neysmith-Roy also wrote a doctoral dissertation on the impact of the Tomatis Method on dyslexic boys.[112]

- **In 1983, De Bruto[113] conducted a carefully controlled study to investigate the efficacy of the Tomatis Method on severely developmentally delayed people.** Thirty inmates of the Witrand Care and Rehabilitation Center (South Africa), aged 4 to 14 years and previously diagnosed as severely developmentally delayed, but with the ability to sit and walk, were randomly assigned to three groups which received:

    Group A: auditory stimulation (Tomatis) and a sensory motor stimulation program.
    Group B: music stimulation (without the Tomatis effect) plus the same sensory stimulation program.
    Group C: no treatment.

    Psychological tests included the Bailey Scales of Infant Development and a measure of responsiveness. The results indicated that both experimental groups manifested an increase in mental age, but the increase in the Tomatis stimulation group (group A) was significantly higher than in group B. No change was found in group C. Whereas no significant differences in terms of responsiveness in group A and B were observed prior to the stimulation program, a statistically significant reduction of self-directed responses, together with a significant increase in object-directed responses occurred after the Tomatis stimulation program.

- **Alexandra Economou and Tony Evangelopoulou studies the impact of the Tomatis Method on people with mild-moderate noise-in-duced hearing loss.**[114] They concluded that "sound training constitutes a promising approach in reducing noise-induced hearing loss. ...

Training sessions with the Electronic Ear resulted in 12 dB and 30 dB shifts on average in the most affected ears, with threshold reductions of up to 45 dB in the most affected frequencies."

- **Research done by D. Deborah Swain showed that the Tomatis Method significantly improves auditory processing skills.** This retrospective study evaluated the results of Tomatis auditory stimulation on 41 randomly selected clients that had auditory processing problems. The effect of the treatment was measured using TAPS (Test of Auditory Perceptual Skills) and TCC (Token test for Children). The study showed highly significant improvements in immediate auditory memory, auditory sequencing, interpretation and following directions, auditory discrimination and auditory cohesion. Reductions in auditory latency were also noted. The study has been submitted for publication.

- **During the 1980's, the Tomatis Listening Program began being used in several French schools with funds allocated by The Ministry of Education.**[115] The participants were chosen on the basis of the severity of their school difficulties. While conducting the Tomatis Listening Program in these environments, away from the clinics, has been far from ideal, the results were good enough for the program to be conducted year after year at the insistent requests of parents. The parents saw positive and lasting changes in their children's lives and took a stand to keep the program in place.

- **Studies also have been conducted on stuttering,**[116] **laterality,**[117, 118] **anxiety and depression**[119] **showing that positive effects were being obtained by the Tomatis treatment.**

Appendix 2

THE LISTENING POSTURE

Instructions given by Dr. Tomatis. To lear more, see: *THE EAR AND THE VOICE*, by Alfred Tomatis, Scarecrow Press, 2004. Translated and adopted by Roberta Prada Pierre Sollier and Francis Keeping.

"How does one do the Listening Posture? It is all a question of training."

"The ideal is to sit comfortably on a hard, high stool, dangling the legs if possible. The edge of a table will also do perfectly. Close your eyes and allow the head to seek the position of balance. It will hang slightly forward because the vestibule searches for the horizontal plane of the head that runs through the lower surface of the utricle. This parallels an imaginary line following the lower border of your closed upper eyelid and connecting with the opening of the right auditory canal. In that position, the top of the head is situated at the point that is its true vertex."

"The work consists in trying to pick out the high frequency sounds among all other sounds in the environment. This is not as easy as it sounds because you first have to learn how to play with the muscles of the middle ear. How do you do that? Begin by imagining that the whole scalp pulls back as if you wanted to make a tight, dense ponytail at the back of your head, near the vertex. While doing so, the horizontal lines on the forehead tend to disappear."

"Better still if it succeeds, you feel a very clear sensation at the scalp line on the forehead. You will feel as if the forehead is as smooth as velvet. You will also feel a cool sensation spreading across this area. It only takes a few moments to acquire and maintain this position."

"Now you are ready to try to widen the skin of the forehead to the maximum as though you wanted it to touch the walls of the room. Continue to feel this for several moments. Now, feel as if you were pulling the skin of the forehead back to become part of that little ponytail behind the vertex. Pull strongly so the skin is well stretched. Be careful when you pull to not raise the head. It must remain immobile at the angle described above. Now, if you have any vertical creases in the forehead, especially in the middle, they will disappear. The forehead becomes full and stretched, giving it a silky feeling."

"You will know when you have mastered this second step because there will be some vasomotor changes. The face flushes, heats up and then pales. At the same time, breath becomes more ample, profound, quiet and regular. The breath reaches an unusual amplitude and rhythm. It becomes free and natural, as it should be."

"When the skin is pulled back this way, you will notice that the upper lids close naturally, as the result of their weight, instead of being intentionally held closed. You may feel a slight trembling of the eyelids at the side of the orbits. Then try to stretch the skin under the eyes until it touches the sides of the orbits. The face relaxes; wrinkles in the face partially fade. The facial muscles move as if they were under a thin layer of rubber or plastic."

"When this is done, pull it back into the little ponytail. This is, in reality, 'a physiological face lift' that involves all the muscles of the face. I have seen many faces that looked flabby, aged, lined and expressionless, transfigured by repeating that exercise."

"Now that the only effort consists in pulling all the muscles of the face toward the back, let the upper lip rest on the lower lip, as a capital on a column, so that a tranquil half-smile discreetly appears on the face. There is a balance between the orbicular muscles, which circle the mouth, and the muscles at the corner of the mouth. As a result of this balance, the lower jaw is in contact with the upper jaw without any tension. These efforts give the face an unusually relaxed and rested appearance. This is, in fact, the way it should always look: without lines, wrinkles and hollows, without the deep marks of concern that come from the anxieties and worries of everyday life."

"This stage is so pleasant that one may wish to remain suspended there, but training must go on. Still, it is important to keep this peaceful face and relaxed mouth while continuing to perceive the environment. Then everything changes. Sounds become purer; they take on a clear luminous timbre. The lows fade and change as if they move toward the higher harmonics that they contain. The surroundings assume a radiant, live and vibrant color."

"After you have gone through this stage, which can happen quickly, you have to try to find out your real voice in the same way, by seeking out higher harmonics. This is neither easy nor obvious because when you begin to perceive the voice that way you will have a strong sensation of listening to your voice for the first time. It seems as though you were far away from yourself with only one ear, the right, which leads the left ear in its course to a point located just behind the vertex in the same place as your little ponytail."

"From a physiological point of view, this place is called the point of fusion. There, the ear rests temporarily, because it feels as if it wants to be freed from its attachment to the skull. Just imagine the ear gliding along an axis that runs from the nostrils to the point of fusion. It seems to get further away from this point at the same time that it appears to get larger. It will quickly move a distance of several fractions of an inch, then some inches, and then several yards to finally settle easily two or three hundred yards away. This is, of course, an impression, but an impression deeply felt for a flash as though it were real. A few lucky individuals, after they have done this for a long time, will one day spontaneously experience a sensation of infinity. But they are the exception."

"Let me point out that you must not disconnect from your body at any time as you do this exercise. You have to stay in your body while you are listening, as if your ear had gone far away to a specific place, a far away refuge where the concerns of life cannot interfere and where life is experienced as it should be. The ideal would be to perceive your own voice as if it were anchored in that far away place, on that summit that seems to be the seat of consciousness, the reference point from which we can objectify our understanding of ourselves and others."

"The further away this point is, the nearer we are listening to the other, beyond the confusions of human condition. The seat of listening rests in the infinite, it is no longer we who listen, as it is no longer we who sing when the song passes through us, just as it is no longer we who speak when we let words pass through us."

"If it is true that some seek this kind of listening, it is also true that they may move through life with such weightiness that they remain stuck in the material world. Only those who are deeply dedicated to opening themselves up to the dimension of True Listening may reach that state in which the Word passes through the voice of the heart. Saint Benedict expresses this well when he says; "Hear, O my son, the words of the Lord, and incline the heart's ear.""

Appendix 3

HUMMING SOUNDS

Excerpt from *How to practice humming sounds.* From *L'oreille et le voix* by Alfred Tomatis, Robert Laffret, 1987.

"Several means are used to achieve bone conduction. First and foremost, we need to awaken this sensation through sounds produced with a closed mouth, that is, by humming. Subjects must be in the listening posture, with the spinal cord as straight as possible and the head inclined slightly forward. Then we ask that they hum. Generally the first attempts end up with a sound that is produced in the mouth because subjects close their lips while the lower jaw is allowed to drop. At the same time the tongue is lowered and rests on the floor of the mouth. This creates a cavity behind the lips, giving rise to a dead, difficult to modulate sound without much quality."

"This is not what we are looking for. We need to make clear that by closing the mouth we also mean that the teeth touch but without any contraction of the muscles in the lower jaw. It is, rather, a simple contact of the teeth. Under those conditions, the tongue occupies the whole mouth. The point of the tongue rises up to the hard palate, also without strong pressure being exerted."

"It is rare for a subject under these conditions to resist the desire to project the sound in front of him as if he needed to feel it come out at the level of the face in the direction of the eventual listener. This way of thinking is so habitual that it may seem difficult to think about it or do it in another way. Yet, doing it in the accustomed way means you can no longer use the mouth as a channel, leaving the hum to rise in the nose as the only alternative. The resulting sound is hardly better than in the first case; it is so nasal that it is unattractive."

"These two ways are identified by a neuro-sensory analysis. Either the mouth resonates with a dead sound, heavy, devoid of "ping," guttural, lacking quality and without the possibility of adding harmonics, or the voice is nasal. Though easier to produce, this is hardly more acceptable since it is remarkable only in sounding extremely nasal."

"Where, then, does the sound come from, if not from the mouth or nose? It arises from the entire body through the excitation of the spinal column due to the contact between the larynx and the cervical vertebrae. To achieve such an emission, it is sufficient to imagine an attentive ear listening at the level of the neck. Sound produced in this way gives the impression of coming towards listeners from behind a singer whose back is turned toward the audience."

"Sound produced in this way takes a special timber, very dense, colorful and lofty. It has good quality, is luminous, vibrant, light and full of space. It has an ethereal quality and seems to be outside the body. This sound is at the very least surprising. It literally awakens the environment with a velvet and dense sonority. It carries with ease. The listener will have a hard time locating it. He has the impression that the entire chamber resonates with the sound produced in it. What is more, this sound can be quickly modulated over two or three octaves without costing the singer any effort. This is bone conduction."

"To make progress, you must exercise this faculty as much as possible. After training this hum for some time, the student will be able to enlarge the sound, not in making it bigger but by making it denser. Then it will extend his range both upwards and downwards."

"This is the basic exercise and must be carried out with great attention and perseverance. It will surely take hours over the course of several weeks. This is the first step for everyone who wants to achieve a good quality emission. It is an essential phase and cannot be skipped."

REFERENCES

1. A. A. Tomatis, The Conscious Ear, Station Hill Press. 1991.
2. Sigmund Freud, Civilization and its Discontents, The standard edition of the complete psychological works of Sigmund Freud, vol. 20.
3. A. A. Tomatis, La Nuit Uterine, Stock, 1981.
4. Saint-Exupéry, The Little Prince, Harcourt Brace Jovanovich, 1943.
5. A, Moch, La sourde oreille. Grandir dans le bruit, Privat, 1985.
6. Bernard Auriol, La Clef des Sons, Érès, 1991, page 20.
7. Borg and Counter, The Middle-Ear Muscles, Erik Borg and S. Al-len Counter, Scientific American, August 1989.
8. A. A. Tomatis, Vers l'écoute humaine, tome 1, Les Editions ESF, 1979, page 143.
9. A. A. Tomatis, The Electronic Ear and New Theories on Auditory Physiology, 1st Congress of Audio-Psycho-Phonology, Paris (1972), page 10.
10. Jean Ayres, Sensory Integration and the Child, Western Psychological Services, 1979, p. 37.
11. A. A. Tomatis, La Nuit Uterine, Stock, 1981, page 93.
12. Wever at all, 1948, quoted in Bernard Auriol, La Clef des Sons, Érès, 1991.
13. E. Leipp, La Machine à écouter—Essai de psycho-acoustique, Masson, 1977.
14. A. A. Tomatis, Vertiges, Ergo-Press, 1989.
15. A. A. Tomatis, The Ear and the Voice, Scarecrow Press, translated by Roberta Prada, Pierre Sollier and Francis Keeping, p. 51-52.
16. A.A. Tomatis, Vers l'écoute Humaine, ESF, 1983, volume 2, p.134.
17. A.A. Tomatis, La Nuit Uterine, Stock, 1981, p. 86.
18. Seely, Stephens and Tate, Anatomy & Physiology, 3rd edition, Mosby, 1995, page 506.
19. A. A. Tomatis, 2nd International Congress on Audio-Psycho-Phonology, 1972.
20. A. A. Tomatis, Vers l'Ecoute Humaine II, Les editions ESF, 1983, page 68.
21. Joel Davis, The Mother Tongue, Carol Publishing Group, 1994
22. Emily Shotter, Sound Localization in VR Systems: A Literature Review, www.essex.ac.uk

[23] William M Hartmann, Signals, Sound and Sensation, AIP Press, 1997. Also: How We Localize Sound, www.aip.org
[24] Gardner M.B. and Gardner R. S. (1973) Problem of localization in the medium plane: effect of pinnae occlusion. *Journal of the Acoustical Society of America*, 53 (2), 400 - 408
[25] Bernard Auriol, La Clef des Sons, Érès, 1991, quoting Moreau, p.156.
[26] A. A. Tomatis, The Ear and the Voice, translated and adapted by Roberta Prada, Pierre Sollier and Francis Keeping.
[27] A. A. Tomatis, La Nuit Uterine, Stock, 1981, page 93
[28] A. A. Tomatis, La Nuit Uterine, Stock, 1981, page 93 & 94
[29] M.C. Diamond, A.B. Scheibel and L.M. Elson, The Human Brain (1985), chapter 6-23.
[30] Stanley Coren, The Left-hander Syndrome, First Vintage Books Edition, 1993.
[31] C. Porac, L. Rees and T. Buller, Left-handedness: Behavioral Applications and Anomalities, Elsevier, 1990.
[32] A. A. Tomatis, L'Oreille at la Voix, page 177, simplified rendering.
[33] Guy Baleydier, private communication.
[34] A. A. Tomatis, The Ear and the Language, Moulin Publishing, 1996.
[35] A. A. Tomatis, *Écouter l'Univers* (Listening to the Universe), Ro-bert Laffont, 1996, not translated into English.
[36] *Diagnostic and Statistical Manual of Mental Disorders*, published by The American Psychiatric Association.
[37] See Gerard Coles, The Learning Mystique, a critical look at "lear-ning disabilities", Pantheon Books, New York, 1987; Peter R. Breggin, Toxic Psychiatry (1994); Talking back to Ritalin: What Doctors Aren't telling you about stimulants for children (1998).
[38] Edward Hallowell and John J. Ratey, Driven to Distraction.
[39] Elliot S. Valenstein, *Blaming the Brain*, The Free Press, 1998.
[40] Judith Rapoport from the National Institute for Mental Health, quoted by Elliot S. Valenstein in Blaming the Brain, p.133.
[41] John Carman, San Francisco Chronicle, 4-10-2001.
[42] Jean Ayres, Sensory Integration and the Child, Western Psycho-logical Services, 1979, page 74.

43	While the audiometer used by Tomatis is identical to those used by audiologists, it has been calibrated differently. One of the diffe-rences is that the bone conduction curve has been shifted downward.
44	Science, reported by the New York Times on April 4, 2001.
45	A. A. Tomatis, The Conscious Ear, p 70-71.
46	Internal Report of the Athénée Royal, 7780 Comines, Belgium
47	A.A. Tomatis, Introduction to the Listening Test, remarks made during the Third International Congress of Audio-psycho-phono-logy (1973).
48	A.A. Tomatis, The Conscious Ear, p. 39.
49	A. A. Tomatis, Introduction to the Listening Test, Observations made-during the 3rd International Congress of Audio-Psycho-Phonology (Antwerp, 1973).
50	A. A. Tomatis, Introduction to the Listening Test, Observations made during the 3rd International Congress of Audio-Psycho-Phonology (Antwerp, 1973).
51	B. Auriol, La Clef des sons, Érès. 1991.
52	E. Deneys, Étude des effets de la musique sur la personnalité à travers l'audio-psycho-phonologie, Maîtrise de psychologie, Toulouse, Juin 1986, unpublished, quoted by B. Auriol.
53	Rachel A. Luxon, The Harmonious, Healing Voice, unpublished
54	David Chamberlain, Prenatal Intelligence in T. Blum(ed) Prenatal Perception, Learning and Bonding, Leonardo Publishers, Berlin, 1993.
55	David B. Chamberlain, Prenatal Intelligence, in "Prenatal Percep-tion, Learning and Bonding," by Thomas Blum, Leonardo Publishers, 1993, page 10.
56	Blum and al, "Prenatal Interventions and Human Proto – Deve-lop-ment" in "Prenatal Perception, Learning and Bonding", by Thomas Blum, Leonardo Publishers, 1993, p. 111.
57	V. E. Negus, The Mechanisms of the Larynx, W. M. Heinemann, Medical Books Ltd, 1929.
58	A.A. Tomatis, Neuf Mois au Paradis, Ergo-Press, 1989, p 163, 174.

59 A.A. Tomatis, Neuf Mois au Paradis, Ergo-Press, 1989, p 142.
60 Don Campbell, The Mozart Effect, Avon Books, New York, 1997.
61 D. Klopfenstein, Préparation des accouchées sous oreille électronique, 2e Symposium International sur l'éducation prénatale, Saint-Raphaël, 1988.
62 A.A. Tomatis, Neuf Mois au Paradis, Ergo-Press, 1989, p. 144.
63 Caroline d'Ortho et Brigitte Monnet, La Méthode Tomatis, Préparation phonique à l'accouchement à Foch, Travail de fin d'études, 1991.
64 A.A. Tomatis, Neuf Mois au Paradis, Ergo-Press, 1989, p. 136.
65 T. Berry Brazelton, Bertrand G. Cramer, The Earliest Relation-ship, Addison-Wesley Publishing Company, Inc. 1990, p. 53.
66 William S. Condon and Louis W. Sanders, Synchrony demonstrated between movements of the neonate and adult speech. Child Development 45(1975): 456–462.
67 Ken Wilber, Up From Eden, A Transpersonal View of Human Evolution, Anchor press/Doubleday, 1981.
68 Gruber, H and Vonecke, J, The Essential Piaget, Basic Books, New York, 1977.
67 Ken Wilber, Up from Eden, a Transpersonal View of Human Development, p. 179, Quest Books, 1981.
70 S. Freud, The Ego and the Id, Standard Edition, vol. 19.
71 K. Wiber, The Atman Project, Quest Books, 1980.
72 K. Wiber, The Atman Project, Quest Books, 1980.
73 Dr. Bruce Perry, Bonding and Attachment in maltreated children: Consequences of Emotional Neglect in Childhood, http://teacher.scholastic.com/professional/bruceperry/bonding.htm
74 John Bowlby, A Secure Base, p.11, Basic Books, 1988.
75 Lamb M.E and al. (1982) Mother and Father Infant Interaction Involving Play and Holding in Traditional and Non Traditional Swedish Families, Developmental Psychology, 18, pp. 215-221, Quoted in Boris Cyrulnik, Sous le Signed du Lien, Hachette Littératures, 1989.
76 Boris Cyrulnik, Sous le Signe du Lien, p. 109, Hachette Littéra-tures, 1989.

REFERENCES

77 See Lamb M. E. and al. Reference 4.
78 Boris Cyrulnik, Sous le Signed du Lien, pp. 122-123, Hachette Littératures, 1989.
79 Fatherless America, David Blankenhorn, Basic Books, Harper Collins Publisher, 1996.
80 Absent father, Lost sons, Guy Corneau, Shambala, 1991.
81 The absent Father, Alix Pirani, Routledge, 1988.
82 P. S. Fry and Anat Sher, the *British Journal of Developmental Psy-chology* (1984, 2, 167-178)
83 Boris Cyrulnik, Sous le Signe du Lien, p 122, Hachette, 1989.
84 Agapi Dendaki, The father-Son Relationship and the Son's Acoustic Curve Distortions, Master Thesis, La Verne University, Athens (Greece), 1995.
85 Interview with Tomatis.
86 Albert Soesman, Our Twelve Senses, Hawthorn Press, 1990.
87 Muy Interesante, año 19, número 08.
88 Erich Neumann, The Origins and History of Consciousness, Princetown University Press, Bollingen Series, 1954.
89 The psychology of Awakening, John Welwood, Shambala Publi-cations, 2000.
90 A.A. Tomatis, Écouter l'Univers, Robert Laffont, 1996.
91 Teilhard de Chardin, The Phenomenon of Man, New York: Har-per, 1964.
92 Wilber, Up From Eden, Quest Books, 1981.
93 Tim Wilson who interviewed Tomatis in 1978 for a radio documen-tary. Many quotes of this chapter come from that interview.
94 A.A. Tomatis, La nuit utérine, Stock, 1981.
95 Karlfried Graf Dürckheim, The Way of Transformation, Unwin Hyman Limited, 1980.
96 Michael Murphy, The Future of the Body, Jeremy P. Tarcher, Inc, 1992.
97 Shunryu Suzuki, Zen Mind, Beginner's Mind.
98 A.A. Tomatis, in the French Review of Yoga, 1991.
99 Deuteronomy 4, 29.
100 A.A. Tomatis, Pourquoi Mozart?, Fixot, 1991, not translated

[101] Gilmor, T.M. (1999), The Efficacy of the Tomatis method for Children with Learning and Communication Disorders, International Journal of Listening, 13, 12.

[102] Gilmor, T.M. (1982), A pre-test and post-test survey of children and adolescents' performance before and after completing the To-matis Program. Research Report, MDS Inc., Toronto, Ontario.

[103] Gilmor, T.M. (1984), A pre-test and post-test survey of children and adolescents' performance before and after completing the To-matis Program. Final Report, MDS Inc., Toronto, Ontario.

[104] Rourke, B.P. & Russel, D.L. (1982), The Tomatis Method applied to older learning disabled children: An evaluation. Paper presented at the Opening Communication Conference, Toronto, November 1982.

[105] Wilson, Iavociello, Metlay, Risucci, Rosati & Palmaccio (1982) The Tomatis Project / Final Report, Department of Neurology, North Shore University Hospital and Hofstra University, Depart-ment of psychology. Paper presented at the Opening Commu-nication Conference, Toronto, Ontario.

[106] Kershner, J., Cummings, R., Clarke, K., Hadfield, A., & Kershner, B. (1986). Evaluation of the Tomatis Listening Training Program with learning disabled children. Canadian Journal of Special Edu-cation, 2, 1-32.

[107] Kershner, J., Cummings, R., Clarke, K., Hadfield, A., & Kershner, B. (1986). Two year evaluation of the Tomatis Listening Program with learning disabled children. Learning Disability Quarterly, 13, 43-53.

[108] Mould, P. (1985), An evaluation of dyslexic boy's response to the Tomatis Listening Training Programme: Interim Report. Brickwall House, Northiam, East Sussex, England.

[109] Private Communication.

[110] Stutt, H.A. (1983), The Tomatis method: A review of current research. Montreal: Mc Gill University

[111] Joan M. Neysmith-Roy, The Tomatis Method with severely autistic boys: Individual case studies of behavioral changes, S. Afr. J. Psychology. 2001, 31 (1).

[112] Roy, J. (1982), Cognitive control functioning and spontaneous speech: Intensive case studies of Audio-Psycho-Phonological re-medial training with five dyslexic boys. Doctoral Dissertation, University of Ottawa.

[113] De Bruto, C.M.E. (1983), Audio-psycho-phonology and the mentally retarded child: An empirical investigation Paper presented at the First Congress on Audio-Psycho-phonology. Potchefstroom.

[114] Alexandra Economou and Tony Evangelopoulou, The use of sound training technology in mild-moderate hearing loss, Proceedings of the 4th European Conference on Noise Control, EURONOISE 2001.

[115] Private Communication.

[116] Van Jaarsveld, 1973, 1974, quoted by Pieter E. van Jaarsveld and Wynand F. du Plessis, in S. Afr. Tydskr. Sielk. 1988, 18 (4).

[117] Van Wyck (1974), idem

[118] Badenhorst (1975) n'Rorschachstudie van regssydiges en linksluiteraars met gemengde laterale voorkeure. Ongepubliseerde M-graadskripsie, Potchefstroom, Universiteit vir CHO: Potchefstroom

[119] Du Plessis, (1982). Beangste en nie-beangste eerstejaardamestudente:' Klinies-psigologiese verkenning. Ongepubliseerde doktorale proefskrif, Potchefstroom Universiteit vir CHO: Potchefstroom.

To find the address of the nearest Tomatis Center, please check:

www. tomatis.com
or
www.tomatis-group.com

Neither the author of this book nor the publisher assumes any responsibility for the work done at the centers listed on these websites.